Things as They Are

Things as They Are

Things as They Are
Nafs al-Amr and the Metaphysical Foundations of Objective Truth

HASAN SPIKER

TABAH RESEARCH

CLASSIFICATION OF THE SCIENCES PROJECT TABAH PAPERS SERIES | NUMBER 2 | 2021

Things as They Are: *Nafs al-Amr* and the Metaphysical Foundations of Objective Truth
ISBN: 978-9948-8607-4-7

Cover image © by Matt Gibson

All praise is to Allah alone, the Lord of the Worlds
And may He send His benedictions upon
our master Muḥammad, his Kin
and his Companions
and grant them
peace

Summary

In a philosophical idiom that attempts to be intelligible to the reader who is not traditionally trained, this study outlines various dimensions of traditional Islamic 'correspondence' theories of truth. It particularly argues that purely intelligible, 'abstract' concepts, universal natures, and general principles objectively apply to the world, against schools of thought that contend that they are subjectively imposed. It is only by discerning the congruity or discordance of these fundamental instruments of general metaphysics with forms of extramental reality, that we are able to avoid the implication that their lack of sensible referents implies our knowledge of the world – which is contingent upon the employment of these instruments – must be ultimately subjective. These intelligible entities, universal natures, and general principles can thus only be validated by situating them within an all-encompassing theory of objective reality and truth, in the Islamic tradition *nafs al-amr* or 'things as they are'. Transcending individual minds and sensible reality, such a theory must be sufficiently broad to account for the ultimate ontological and henological status of such universal and abstract principles and forms. This study demonstrates that a synthetical approach to the nature of objective reality and truth, drawing on the Avicennan and *kalām*, and especially Platonic and Akbarian traditions, is capable of effectively responding to subjectivist, anti-metaphysical views on the nature of the world and our knowledge of it. It purports to do this in a manner that strengthens the deepest foundations underlying traditional natural theology, illustrating that the physical world of particulars is 'intelligible' (in the sense of 'objectively knowable') exactly because it is a branch of an 'intelligible' (as the contrary of 'sensible'), non-physically instantiated world.

About the Author

HASAN SPIKER is a researcher at Tabah Foundation, and spent his formative years in Cambridge, England. He then moved to the Middle East, where for twelve years he studied the Islamic intellectual sciences, and also completed his memorization of the Qur'an. Spiker subsequently completed a philosophy degree at the University of London, and an MPhil in philosophical theology at the University of Cambridge, where he is also presently completing his doctoral studies, and carrying out research at the Cambridge Centre for the Study of Platonism.

اللَّهُمَّ أَرِنَا الْأَشْيَاءَ كَمَا هِيَ

O God, show us things as they are!

— Supplication of the Forefathers (*al-salaf*)

Contents

CONTENTS   ix

PREFACE TO THE SERIES   xi

FOREWORD   xv

Chapter 1. *Nafs al-Amr* and the Possibility of Objective Truth: An Introduction to the Problem   1

    1.1 Nafs al-Amr and the Meaning of 'Objectivity'   1

    1.2 Difficulties for Nafs al-Amr in the Context of Various Sciences   5

    1.3 Nafs al-Amr in Logic, Epistemology, and Metaphysics   13

Chapter 2. The Study of Things as They Are in Themselves: History and Method   27

    2.1 Nafs al-Amr and the Proposition   27

    2.2 Truth and Things as They Are: Historical Sketches   30

    2.3 Logical, Epistemological, and Metaphysical Propaedeutics   61

       2.3.1 The Predicative Scope of Nafs al-Amr   61

       2.3.2 Real and Relational Composite Quiddities   67

Chapter 3. Abstract Objects and Metaphysical Necessity   82

    3.1 Taftāzānī on Nafs al-Amr Known and Unknowable   82

    3.2 The Road to Taşköprüzade's Synthesis: Qūshjī, 'Alā'uddīn, and Dawānī   89

    3.3 'Where Then Are They?' Ibn Bahā'uddīn on Intelligible Entities   97

Chapter 4. *Nafs al-Amr* and the Exemplary Forms of Cognition   100

    4.1 Qayṣarī and Nafs al-Amr as the Immutable Archetypes   100

4.2 Transcending the Transcendental: 'Metaprinciples' and the Henological Ascent — 118

4.2.1 A Short Excursus on Unity and Being — 120

4.2.2 Metaprinciples and Transcendentals in Nafs al-Amr — 128

4.3 Taşköprüzade's Solution and Synthesis — 142

4.4 Later Developments and Notes on the Subalternation of the Sciences — 147

Conclusion — 154

NOTES — 165

BIBLIOGRAPHY — 219

Preface to the Series

THE PAPERS INAUGURATED in this new series are essentially an exercise in conceptual disambiguation relating to the central problem of what could be termed cognitive hierarchy, and the role and implication of principled thought to the *turāth*. The intent was not so much to present an academic exercise in erudite prose but rather to engage ideas around the consequences of presuming a classification of the sciences in order to catalyse a persuasive discourse on pedagogical protocols, on the framing of a modernist refurbishment of the religious sciences, and the centrality and need for the rooting of all intellectual adventures in first principles. There is nothing new essentially in these essays, in as far as one could say that the bricks and mortar of a building are nothing new, but what is presented represents perhaps a new architectural resolution as to how those same bricks and mortar may be utilized more effectively.

The Classification of the Sciences Project was initiated in late 2015 at Tabah Research, a division of Tabah Foundation. Having expended ten years since its inauguration in disseminating lectures and studies, researchers at the Foundation came to have a clearer idea of the state of contemporary intellectual discourse in the Islamic world predominantly in relation to the religious sciences. What effectively came to notice was that much of the confusion surrounding adherence to traditional models of education revolved around a correct understanding of traditional hierarchies that necessitated certain pedagogical methodologies. The commissioning of this project arose due to several reasons. The foremost of those was the spread of modernist secularist viewpoints in relation to education and traditional knowledge. Despite the many advantages and benefits of the universal model of university education of the last century, one can scarcely avoid its connection with an increase in latitudinarian attitudes to knowledge, or, one can say, the democratization of knowledge. It is safe to say that access to university or school education is not the same as access to knowledge. Furthermore, the accumulation and learning of facts can never be synonymous with, nor amount to, scientific knowledge.[1] In contrast, knowledge in the traditional model is attained through principles that govern the relationship of things, the order of things. Moreover, the underlying structure of metaphysics that imbues all theoretical knowledge ensures that the fetidness of reason can never strangulate transcendent aspirations, as metaphysics ensures that the framework of knowledge belongs to *theoria*, ensuring the necessity of vision for the completion or perfection of the cognitive process.

On a more foundational note, the animating principles of the project stem unashamedly from the complete metaphysical acceptance of the Ash'ari creed, despite the unconventional manner in which it might be presented, and an unqualified adherence to the school of Imam Junayd in *Ihsān*. The contemporary waning of the Ash'ari creed in many intellectual circles due to the general and modernist recoil from such central and critical ideas has largely not been ameliorated. The recent attempt to stem such a credal desuetude by way of a reactionary and muscular neo-Ash'arism has led to a dangerous rationalization of *'aqīda* more befitting the ambience of a wrestling pit and its corresponding etiquette, rather than the sober scholarly forum demanded by the subject matter.

The authority of pedagogical methodologies in the transmission of the Islamic sciences is another point in question that has led to much pondering. Once again, much ink has been spilt on whether traditional methodologies should 'keep up with the times', or adhere to more critical and historicist positions, or even be abolished. The question that could be distilled from such abundant objections is the one that asks whether traditional methodologies of transmission were necessarily part and parcel of the discipline being inculcated, and thus sacrosanct at their core, or whether they were merely incidental and of practical significance alone. That is to say, whether one can separate transmission procedure from substantive knowledge. The answer to this question and the manner in which it is answered necessarily determines the future of the Islamic intellectual sciences.

We contend that any discourse on these aforesaid matters must be based on, understand, and commit to metaphysical coherence. By this we mean that sound discourse must be in line with metaphysical principles, being themselves reflections of the order of Reality. The first paper in the series explores one of those first principles of metaphysics, the principle of identity in its logical form, namely, the principle of non-contradiction, and the relationship between its metaphysical and logical dimensions.

The second paper explores the nature of definition and whether the latter is effective in advancing conceptual knowledge that may be deemed essential or objective. The third paper examines the notion of objectivity by setting out the various understandings of the theory of *nafs al-amr*, or things in themselves. If reason is relational, then how do we situate and come to know the object of our thought in itself shorn of that subjective relationality?

The truth and how we arrive at it in the Islamic intellectual tradition provide the main focus of the first three papers. The centrality of the role of the sciences in treating the various levels of reality is purported to be key to understanding the necessity for hierarchy, and if hierarchy, then order of knowledge. Every intellectual perception is subject to a science, that is to say, it pertains to a science in the order of knowledge. Just as reality is multilateral in its aspects, so is knowledge, in that one may speak of a direct correlation between levels of existence or reality and levels of knowledge. This is a cosmological truth as well as a metaphysical truth, as the world can never be known simply as one-dimensional in the traditional perspective. The symbolic frame of mind, necessary to any serious metaphysical work, arises from a vision of the universe as wheels within wheels, intertwined and interrelated dimensions revealing a synthetic unity that ensures continuity of theological meaning. It is to see things in reality in their unitive rather than in their separative aspects. This viewpoint sees the world as metaphysically transparent, a place that may be sifted for the understanding of the qualities and attributes of God, and thus allowing us to put everything in its place, and more importantly, to see everything in its rightful place.

The realm of reason is essential to understanding and situating the realm of the *'aqliyyāt*, wherein the three foundational papers in the series can be situated. Just as the truths of reason can never be incompatible with the Qur'ān and Sunna, we can safely say that the truths of the Qur'ān and Sunna can never be unreasonable. Having said that, reason naturally plays a mediating role for truths but up to a point, since it is the passivity of the intellect that ensures the higher echelons of cognitive capacity. The use of logic is determinant of sound discourse and essential for the determination of sound judgements. Logic, however, is largely a methodology, a tool, rather than knowledge per se, one that validates the process of thought but cannot create the content of thought. One must first therefore have something on which logic can work, a premise from which one might proceed. Its basis thus lies in metaphysics, and because there is no break in reality, the rational is premised on Reality, not only extramental reality as generally understood.

The logical thus can never contradict the metaphysical, and the metaphysical can never in turn be illogical. This seamlessness between the two orders is critical to the safeguarding of a sound intellectual discourse representing no less than a principial underpinning of logic by metaphysics. Although invariably the truths of metaphysics are imposed upon us, much as Reality is imposed upon us, the intellectual realm is there to allow us to expose those truths, uncovering and discovering them by principial deliberation or insight. It is in this way that every age must call for a return to principle, if it is to safeguard the ability for the human soul to understand its existential condition, a condition that remains the same regardless of time and place.

Karim Lahham (series editor)
Oxford
19 January 2021

Foreword

THE SEARCH FOR TRUTH is of all pursuits the most essential to being human; and it proclaims the deepest of longings. For truth is the finite perspective coming face to face, at long last, with things as they are. The search for truth amounts precisely, and irrespective of any theoretical entanglement, to the life's journey of every person, confronting the state of separation, the 'falsehood' to which existence as an individual knowing subject cannot but amount, for as long as we remain unable to perceive *what* we are.

> ... sick with desire
> And fastened to a dying animal
> It knows not what it is

As long as the knowing subject is unable to recognize *itself* in the mirror of unity and being – that is, as continuous therewith, and with all of the distinct realities that spring forth from it – and as long as we cannot see ourselves, qua knowing subjects, as emerging from, and returning to, a distinct reality that is *beyond* ourselves, we must remain the atomized individuals for whom all reality but the subjective is ultimately unintelligible. From the separation of falsehood, then, the escape to the integration of truth becomes possible only when the finite *perspective* comes to the (initially paradoxical) realization that it is part of the fabric of being *as it is in itself*. It is because we *are* reality, then, a part of reality, that we can indeed know reality.

Yet the situation of modernity, or postmodernity, has been engendered by thinkers who have believed that it is precisely *our being human* that rules out the possibility of our achieving truth, and of our ever being able to come face to face with things as they really are. Now, in our age of 'post-truth', we are continually made vividly aware that while we may speak of '*my* truth' and '*your* truth', '*the* truth' is strictly proscribed. That is, the excesses of the philosophers of later modernity have finally trickled down to contort the common sense of the majority.

It is no exaggeration to say that the most direct philosophical progenitor of the strange state of metaphysical and epistemological affairs in which we generally find ourselves today, is the view that the human perspective is necessarily cut off from extramental reality, precisely because its specifically human modes of 'knowing', its logical, mathematical, and 'metaphysical' principles, do not truly arise from anything extramental; they are ultimately purely mental, and thus subjective. The clear consequence of this is that they are only capable of *imposing* themselves upon reality, thus *veiling* reality, and rendering 'objective' knowledge completely impossible of access.

Our logic, for example, with its universal concepts, its formal structures, and its assumptions of objective entailment and necessity, arises from nothing in extramental reality. When Nietzsche – whose radical thought represents the culmination of this tendency – affirmed that 'Logic depends on presuppositions with which nothing in the real world corresponds' (*Human, All Too Human*),[1] he had defined the emerging spirit of a brave new world. For Nietzsche, the inescapability of perspective directly entails the impossibility of *objective* perspective:

> How far the perspectival character of existence extends or whether it has any other character at all ... cannot be determined even by the most assiduous and painfully conscientious analysis and self-examination of the intellect: since in the course of this analysis the human intellect cannot avoid viewing itself in its perspectival forms and only in them. We cannot see round our own corner: it is a hopeless piece of curiosity to want to know what could exist for other species of intellect and perspective (*The Gay Science*).[2]

Yet does the claim to have *knowledge* that one certainly *cannot* see round one's own corner, not exactly entail a claim that one is indeed capable of seeing round one's corner after all? Those who would definitively deny the possibility of knowledge cannot help but do so from a human perspective bringing to bear the very cognitive apparatuses putatively rooted in nothing in reality; yet how, then, has that merely human perspective been able to yield 'facts' about reality, so metaphysical and so grand, such as reality's unknowability? In this study, it is starting from precisely this type of argument that we evaluate the emergence of modern metaphysical subjectivism in some of Nietzsche's intellectual forebears, particularly in 'the sage of Königsberg', since he is, for so many subsequent thinkers, the father of philosophical modernity.

One of the facts that will be uncovered early in the course of the investigations of this work (an auspicious sign, it is to be hoped, of the fitness of our traditions to treat and remedy the misperceptions that have motivated the now startlingly widespread errors of ultimate subjectivism) is that the question of *nafs al-amr* was historically framed precisely as the question of how it is that the intrinsic apparatuses of our human 'perspective', that is, our abstract concepts and principles and structures, might 'correspond' to reality, and thus be rendered true. Our knowledge of reality can after all only be 'objective' if the cognitive apparatuses by which we purport to know reality are truly rooted therein. Yet how can such 'correspondence' be possible, if we are faced with a world composed of nothing more than empirical particulars?

In the course of our argument, we will encounter many treatments of the multifarious issues that arise from and attend the apparent aporias of *nafs al-amr,* and find that the dogmatically assumed Peripateticism (*al-mashshā'iyya*) of many strands of the *falsafa* and *kalām* traditions does not often render them great service in solving them. In the course of our investigations, we will discover a rich tradition of criticism of these immanentist assumptions, some of which unexpectedly emanates from the *kalām* tradition (Rāzī), and the greater part, from the school of the followers of Ibn 'Arabī. As we will find, such approaches would also go on to influence some of the most significant thinkers in the later *kalām* tradition.

In this study, we will provide a demonstration that immanentism about intelligible reality must be transcended if the reality of objective truth is to be established again for our time. In doing so, we draw deeply on the work of our great predecessors. Yet ours is fundamentally a *philosophical* argument, not an exercise in historiography or codicology. At times, I have come up against difficulties that our intellectual forebears, despite their immeasurably greater stature, simply did not have to face; my solutions, accordingly, sometimes demand the uncovering of principles and conceptual distinctions that I have not found in their works. Ours is not an exercise in glorified stamp-collecting or fossil classification, and if I ever fall short in these areas, I can only beg the reader's indulgence.

Naturally, I have made historical and exegetical statements that I have reason to believe to be true, and if I am ever successful in providing an accurate account of the views of others, or a nuanced historical narrative, well and good. But again, it is not our main purpose; because our main purpose, in the course of determining what *nafs al-amr is*, is to correspond to *nafs al-amr* itself.

This study is one of the fruits of Tabah Foundation's 'Classification of the Sciences' (*tartīb al-ʿulūm*) project, led by Dr Karim Lahham. I thank Tabah Foundation for its generous and multifarious support, and for its steadfastness in standing by this unique project, through thick and thin. And I would like to thank all of my teachers and masters, past and present, intellectual and spiritual, without whom I was and would be very lost, and who have given me everything I have.

> The pleasure of life is only in the company of the *fuqarāʾ* – they
> are the sultans, the masters, and the princes

Chapter 1

Nafs al-Amr and the Possibility of Objective Truth: An Introduction to the Problem

1.1 Nafs al-Amr and the Meaning of 'Objectivity'

What is it that justifies belief in the objectivity of putative truths, expressed by means of metaphysical terms that do not possess sensible or extramental particular truthmakers? Following the intimations of Plato and Aristotle, the notion that the truth of a proposition is its correspondence to forms of independent reality transcending the knowing subject is central to the most historically predominant schools of philosophy, and the main forms of Islamic philosophy and theology are no exception. Yet in an age in which methodological scepticism and relativism are ubiquitous, can compelling grounds be given for retaining the traditional objectivist view, especially in so far as these sceptical attitudes pertain to the statuses of abstract predicates and universal propositions? If the sensible particulars that make up the physical world are unable to account for numerous types of abstract truths, what is the objective reality to which these latter correspond? How, indeed, can we know that they truly apply to sensible particulars, and that the metaphysical conclusions yielded by a combination of their application to sensible particulars and the demonstrative method of deduction from first principles are in fact objective? Faced with relentlessly and routinely applied leitmotifs of doubt in so much of modern philosophical discourse, questions pertaining to this and other foundational challenges have arisen in the minds of many Muslims; do our diverse Islamic philosophical and theological traditions truly possess sufficient intellectual resources to take on the contemporary challenges of subjectivism, relativism, nominalism, deflationism, and the multifarious incarnations of scepticism threatening to shake the foundations of our revealed view of the world?

In this study, we will provide strong substantiation for the widely held postulate that the later Avicennan, late *kalām*, and Akbarian schools of Islamic thought are endowed with original and largely unexplored epistemological and metaphysical riches. We will contend that such powerful resources render these schools eminently capable of dealing with all manner of philosophical challenges, including providing real warrant for objectivist, correspondence views of both physical and metaphysical truth. Although we will argue that a synthetical approach drawing on each of the three schools is alone capable of providing a total justification of objectivism in its most compelling and nuanced form, each approach taken on its own nonetheless safeguards traditional metaphysics and theology from the scepticism of subjectivist criticism.

Chief amongst these resources is a metaphysical concept employed across the three traditions, *nafs al-amr*, or 'the thing itself', which in the Islamic and Arabic philosophical tradition underlies a correspondence theory of the objectivity of truth of an exceptional and indeed unparalleled clarity, versatility, and scope.

Part of a basic definition of *nafs al-amr*, appearing in Tahānawī's *Kashshāf* (completed in 1150/1754), a classic example of a later dictionary of the developed Islamic sciences, tells us that

> [*nafs al-amr*] means a thing itself, in itself (*ma'nāhu nafs al-shay' fī ḥaddi dhātihi*) and so were you to say that a thing 'exists in things as they are in themselves' (*mawjūd fī nafs al-amr*), this would mean that its existence is not contingent on the perspective of a subject (*i'tibār mu'tabir*) or someone's supposition (*farḍi fāriḍ*).[1]

Although for its own purposes this definition is fundamentally sound, it appears not to tell us anything about what it *means* for a thing to exist 'in itself', except in terms of a negative qualification, namely, that its existence must *not* be contingent on a perspective or supposition. Yet what is the positive meaning of *nafs al-amr*, 'the thing itself' or 'things as they are'? Is this simply a general term, used to describe our vague intuitions of a thing's identity, or a proposition's truth? Or does it refer to an actual ontological domain or level of being in which these 'things as they are' inhere – whether it is the physical world, the human mind, or something beyond these two – a level of being that propositions are rendered true by 'corresponding' to?

Diverse identifications of the nature of *nafs al-amr* were made across the various forms of later Islamic theology and philosophy. As we will see in this study, some identified *nafs al-amr* with metaphysical entities, like the Avicennan Agent Intellect (*al-ʿaql al-faʿʿāl*), or the Akbarian 'Immutable Archetypes' (*al-aʿyān al-thābita*).[2] These types of theories, though highly divergent in many important ways, shared in emphasizing that human minds are fundamentally *receptacles* of a truth that originates in an intelligible realm even more fully real than the world of sense experience. It is only through the mind's conjunction with that truth, by means of the effusion of those higher realms into the sublunar world, that knowledge can be attained, for truth is in essence a metaphysical phenomenon.

Other thinkers adopted what can seem to be a reductively epistemological approach to *nafs al-amr*, by suggesting that it simply refers to the truth-judgement that arises from the intuition of both self-evident and speculative necessity.[3] Yet others made the more prosaic but nonetheless ontological identification of *nafs al-amr* with a combination of the individuated extramental world and the mind.[4] We will argue that this latter approach tends to beg the question (in the traditional sense of assuming something that ought to be proved first), namely, that the mere obtainment of true propositions in minds can validly *account* for their truth.

Whence the importance of the question of the identity of *nafs al-amr*, particularly in the times in which we are living? The requirements of genuine logical rigour entail the insufficiency of the mere provision of putative proofs for the tenets of Islamic creed. This is because even more fundamentally, our *method* of providing proof must be demonstrated to be sound. As we indicated at the beginning of this chapter, our contemporary circumstances dictate that justification must be newly provided for the metaphysical principles presupposed by our natural theology. How can we be certain that these principles and concepts, which do not seem to have referents in the physical world, actually possess an objective extramental basis? This is an aspect of the question of the ontological status of 'intelligible' entities[5] (namely, those that are not the objects of the senses, but are directly known by the mind), and of the question of if, and if so, how, they apply to sensible particulars so as to render the world truly intelligible (in the other sense of 'intelligible', which means 'objectively knowable'). These are two of the most fundamental questions in all of philosophy. If the human mind itself is the wellspring and original, *ultimate* locus of certain types of intelligible entities fundamental to the operation of the sciences, it seems impossible to escape from the implication of subjectivism, which calls the validity of the whole edifice of traditional natural theology into serious question.

It is the determination of the nature of *nafs al-amr* – the 'domain of reference' that makes true propositions true, and in which the objects or states of affairs to which they refer ultimately subsist – that constitutes the key to guaranteeing that objective extramental basis. If 'abstract objects', alongside a broader range of intelligible concepts and principles, can be shown to be rooted in *nafs al-amr* conceived as an ontological reality, and can be shown, in *nafs al-amr*, to genuinely apply to the world of sensible experience, the soundness of the metaphysics-based natural theology upon which the traditional Islamic worldview depends will have been borne out at the most fundamental of levels.[6] It will have been demonstrated that they are truly objective principles of sciences worthy of the name. Moreover, the traditional claim that the other sciences are subordinated to metaphysics and derive their first principles therefrom will find substantiation. For if the metaphysical first principles and 'abstract' universal concepts underpinning the sciences can be shown to rest on firm foundations, indeed, to inhere in a level of existence *beyond* that of immediate individual experience, we will possess an ontological justification for our sense of their supra-subjective truth, instead of being forced to find 'warrant' for those principles 'phenomenologically' in the sheer fact of subjective perception. This would in turn serve to forestall the sceptical attempt (which has in the main arisen from certain streams and rivulets of post-seventeenth-century Western philosophy) to undermine the traditional metaphysics presupposed by natural theology.[7] It might also contribute to the prevention of an equally perilous phenomenon – modern practitioners of *kalām* coming to be intimidated by the sceptical challenge of modern philosophy and the apparently overwhelming success of modern science, such that *kalām* as traditionally understood is undermined, in finding itself compelled to make certain foundational concessions to the prevailing intellectual Weltanschauungen of the modern age. Inevitably, this would lead to a subversion of their own discipline, enabling it to operate from these often Pyrrhonist starting points. The aim underlying such a move might be to capacitate *kalām* in a new role as a mere validator, a 'handmaiden', of an inductive modern science that aspires to the realization of merely probable 'models', but not to 'truth' as traditionally understood. One major stream of contemporary anti-metaphysical analytic philosophy has already, self-proclaimedly, met this very fate.[8] Already, signs of the gathering popularity of such approaches amongst certain contemporary practitioners of *kalām* are sadly all too conspicuous.

For the vast majority of Western philosophical history, and for many up until the present day, objective metaphysical knowledge has been understood to be within the reach of humankind. Indeed, it was philosophy that served to validate the truth claims of all of the other sciences. As in the Islamic tradition, this view found some of its roots in theories of truth ultimately traceable to Plato and Aristotle, and the 'Neoplatonic' tradition that succeeded them. These shared origins developed in the writings of Avicenna into a distinctive logical, epistemological, and metaphysical system, of an almost unparalleled comprehensiveness and maturity, whose influence was uniquely central to both Islamic philosophy and medieval European scholasticism.

Thereafter, of course, the two traditions largely parted ways. This study chiefly concerns theories of the ultimate metaphysical guarantors of truth claims within Islamic philosophical traditions, the most valuable developments of which came in the period after the Western and Islamic traditions diverged. However, in Chapter 2, we provide a short exposition of the most fundamental features of the development, in the Western tradition, of theories of the grounds of metaphysical truth. This is both in order to bring theories from our own tradition into sharper relief, as well as to implicitly frame the question of how these theories might be applicable to the dominant contemporary philosophical context. After all, this context amounts to the degeneration of a Western philosophical heritage whose roots extend back to a time when Western and Islamic philosophy shared much in common.

1.2 *Difficulties for Nafs al-Amr in the Context of Various Sciences*

In this study, we will attempt to detail some of the most important Islamic schools of thought on the nature of *nafs al-amr*: those of Avicennan philosophers (these are the group really intended when the vague term *'al-ḥukamā'* is used, in most of the usage of *kalām* theologians) and later *kalām* theologians (*muta'akhkhirī al-mutakallimīn*), as well as of Sufi metaphysicians of the school of Ibn 'Arabī (*ahl al-taḥqīq*).[9] At first sight, turning the discovery of this objective foundation in the Islamic tradition to our complete advantage is complicated by the rather anodyne treatment the majority of works that employ *nafs al-amr* to refer to 'reality' or 'the actual fact' can seem to confer upon it. Although in its origins a metaphysical term,[10] it is employed throughout the Islamic sciences – especially in law (*fiqh*), principles of law (*uṣūl al-fiqh*), Qur'anic exegesis (*tafsīr*), and, of course, logic (*manṭiq*), *kalām* theology, and metaphysical Sufism ('*ilm al-ḥaqā'iq*/'*ilm al-taḥqīq*).[11] However, when *nafs al-amr* is defined at all (and not merely utilized as a logical convenience),[12] questions of ontological status tend to be left aside. That is, although a broadly realist, correspondence theory of truth is employed throughout works of the Islamic sciences, it is often one which the authors in question do not seem to attempt to justify on any foundational level.

An example found in the exegesis of Burhān al-Dīn Abū al-Ḥasan al-Biqā'ī (d. 884/1480) would seem to fit this description (although it should be acknowledged that his attempt to demonstrate the link between the epistemology implicit in the Qur'an and *nafs al-amr* is commendable). Commenting on Q53:28, 'They follow but conjecture, and conjecture avails naught against truth (*al-ḥaqq*)', he tells us that *nafs al-amr* is 'the reality of a thing and its essence' (*ḥaqīqat al-shay' wa-dhātuhu*).[13] He then tells us that 'conjecture' (*ẓann*) is censured in the verse because it can never lead to certain knowledge of a thing as it is in *nafs al-amr*. However, without further explanation, and given Biqā'ī's own definition of *nafs al-amr*, this would seem to translate into '[conjecture] can never lead to having certain knowledge of a thing as [that thing] *is*, in the reality of the thing and its essence', a quasi-tautological definition (given that 'as that thing is' and 'the reality of the thing and its essence' are almost indistinguishable) that simply begs the question. Biqā'ī's treatment has failed to do justice to the profound vision of *nafs al-amr* that other exegetes have discerned in the Qur'an.[14]

On a metaphysically naïve but ubiquitous account of *nafs al-amr*, on the level of assents, a *true* proposition or theory is simply defined as one that corresponds to the real state of affairs that is the referent of the expression; a false proposition or theory is one that does not. With respect to essences, a thing exists in *nafs al-amr* if it is 'a thing that exists in the reality of that thing and its essence' – not, perhaps, an entirely satisfying definition of 'objective existence'. Thus, if *nafs al-amr* as 'the reality of a thing and its essence' (*ḥaqīqat al-shay' wa-dhātuhu*) is not further qualified and elucidated, then to define a true proposition as one that corresponds to *nafs al-amr* simply amounts to stating that such a true proposition corresponds to how things really are – to 'reality' – yet without the identity of this 'reality' being specified, nor any criterion for its identification being offered, which is inconvenient to say the least. To say that a proposition or theory corresponds to *nafs al-amr* becomes an effective synonym for the *assertion* of its truth, that is, '*truth* is correspondence to things in their *true* nature.' Yet what is a 'true' nature, what is a thing as it is in itself, and what is the touchstone of a real and objective nature, principle, or state of affairs?

In fact, *nafs al-amr* as 'the reality of a thing and its essence' (*ḥaqīqat al-shay' wa-dhātuhu*) is a definition that is perfectly valid on its own terms, and widely cited. However, it cannot serve as an ultimate, fully explanatory definition. This is because it presupposes, rather than provides, the ontology that would explain what type of existence 'the reality of a thing and its essence' actually refers to. If it is read as itself constituting that ontology, we are left without an explanation; our 'correspondence' theory thus rests on shaky foundations.

Yet the inadequacy of many accounts of *nafs al-amr* should not perhaps come as a surprise, given the inherent difficulties involved in attempting to resolve all of the very numerous logical and philosophical problems that the question of *nafs al-amr* entails. Numerous *'ulamā'* who have used the term *nafs al-amr* have specialized in sciences representing concerns very distant from those of metaphysics. Perhaps this explains the words of the great Ottoman mystical theologian Ibn Bahā'uddīn (d. 958/1551) in his *al-Qawl al-faṣl*, namely, that everyone writing in the sciences without exception uses the term *nafs al-amr*, yet very few of those who use it understand what it means.[15]

There is a deeper tradition of Islamic thought, however, in which highly nuanced debates are to be encountered regarding the exact ontological grounds underlying claims for the possibility that our knowledge genuinely corresponds to this mysterious 'objective realm'. These deeper debates extend to the real identity of *nafs al-amr*, an identification that must be attempted because of the tensions created by the existence of propositions that clearly do not have referents in extramental particulars (*fī al-khārij*) but which are true and therefore 'correspond to *nafs al-amr*' – truths about intelligible principles, and abstract and non-existent objects,[16] for example. The notion that simple correspondence to referents in the ordinary sensible world of extramental particulars can account for all truths is thus discounted, and 'extramental particulars' is consequently ruled out as a candidate for *nafs al-amr*. Attempts to identify *nafs al-amr* with the mind (*al-dhihn*), in any absolute sense, are similarly shown to be ill-fated; ironically for theories of objectivity, they ultimately necessitate absolute subjectivism.

Al-khārij, 'extramental particulars' (literally 'the outside' but meaning 'outside the mind' or 'extramental'), completes the three-fold *kalām* and *ḥikma* division of the most general and often overlapping modes of subsistence[17] within which objects obtain, the other two being *al-dhihn*, the mind, and *nafs al-amr*. A recurrent theme in this study is that, on some more expansive ontologies, *nafs al-amr* can constitute a mode of subsistence in which entities can inhere completely independently of both minds and extramental particulars as usually understood. But what precisely are *al-khārij* and *al-dhihn*? In what sense can they be identified with *nafs al-amr*, and in what sense can they not?

To illustrate the meaning of *al-khārij*, let us look at why the restriction 'particulars' has had to be added to its English translation (and why, we would argue, translations that simply render the term 'extramental reality' or similar are misleading). In the sense that their existence is not mind dependent, existents in *nafs al-amr* exist 'extramentally' just as much as *khārijī* entities do. The fundamental difference between *al-khārij* and the broader *nafs al-amr* is that a '*khārijī*' entity refers only to an individual and therefore 'individuated' (*mutaʿayyin*) entity; put in the simplest terms, an entity that is a particularized instantiation of a universal essence, and therefore capable in principle of being pointed at (or otherwise singled out as an individual thing), like the actual individual person called Zayd, a particular instantiation of 'human being'. This is because 'extramental existents are necessarily accompanied by individuation',[18] and 'cannot thus [exist in] uninstantiated [form]'[19] according to the broadly Peripatetic, Avicennan, and *kalām* views. As we will see as the argument of this study unfolds, bias towards the particular and the individual (and, in the inevitably vast majority of cases, this means the *empirical* particular) as the primary unit of extramental reality (such that 'existence' becomes a consequence of individuation) does not represent a self-evident conclusion, nor even a demonstrable one. It in fact arises from Aristotle's explicitly anti-Platonic redefinition of primary being or 'substance' (*ousia*) in his developed account in *Metaphysics* Z. For Plato and the Platonic tradition, only the Forms can qualify as *ousia*, in that they are the 'intelligible substrata', in themselves neither 'universal' nor 'particular',[20] that bestow both being and knowability upon their participating individuals, and that necessarily exist *prior* to their individuals. For Aristotle, substance is form, in so far as form is the cause of the being of a 'compound material substance',[21] but form can only *exist* immanently, in a particularized hylomorphic fusion. Avicenna's general anti-Platonic discourse, and specific polemic against the Forms, is largely derived directly from Aristotle,[22] and informs his own immanentist teaching. In the post-Rāzian *kalām* reception of Avicenna subsequent to his substantial integration into the *kalām* curriculum, Avicenna's teaching goes on to intermingle with previous broadly immanentist *kalām* doctrines, to produce decisive formulations stating the putative necessity that existence must depend upon individuation as a particular, which were in turn made subject to Akbarian critiques such as that of Ibn Bahā'uddīn, which refers to 'those whose purview is restricted to outward appearances', and who

> have restricted being to that lowest of its degrees, which they call extramental existence (*al-wujūd al-khārijī*); they thus say that if a quiddity is not individuated, it does not exist, making existence into a subsidiary of individuation. The truth of the matter is that the degree of Being is prior to all other of the degrees, that is, the degrees of genera and species, to say nothing of [the degree of] individual particulars.[23]

Al-khārij can be used in different contexts; in most cases it is synonymous with 'particularized essences' (*al-aʿyān*);[24] *al-khārij* is also used as a synonym for *nafs al-amr*,[25] although this is uncommon. When it is taken to mean particularized essences, which is how it will be used in this study in accordance with its dominant usage across the broad sweep of later Islamic thought, it refers to individuals which instantiate a nature – Zayd, ʿAmr, William, or John, for example, who embody or instantiate the nature 'man'. Moreover, 'this' person, 'this' tree, and 'this' mountain (that is, the person, tree, or mountain that one can physically point out), and so on. Without the restriction 'particulars', then, *al-khārij* would be indistinguishable from *nafs al-amr*. As we will see throughout this study, defining *al-khārij* as 'extramental *particulars*' correctly ensures that it is of an immeasurably more limited scope than *nafs al-amr* properly construed in its Platonic-Akbarian *taḥqīq*, for *nafs al-amr* includes but is not bound by particularization.

It must be granted that in the context of certain sciences the simple identification of *nafs al-amr* with, for example, extramental particulars (*al-khārij*) gives the impression of being a matter of simple common sense. One amongst innumerable similar examples can be found in Ibrāhīm al-Bājūrī's (d. 1276/1860) work of Islamic law, *Ḥāshiya ʿalā Ibn Qāsim*, where in the course of a discussion of 'admission of rights' (*iqrār*), he says

> the impermissibility [of making a false 'admission' of a debt] when the intention is to deprive heirs [of their rights] is undoubted, and it is impermissible for the person for whom the admission was made (*al-muqarr lahu*) to take [the payment] if [he knows that] the [person making the admission] is not telling the truth in *nafs al-amr*.[26]

Here, *nafs al-amr* is simply the context of social relations, the actual state of affairs regarding which one could *not* truthfully say that a hypothetical individual had owed an alleged lender money. In this context, *nafs al-amr* conceived as extramental particulars (*al-khārij*) seems, at least at first sight, to adequately account for the situation's possible truth-value. If the man is telling the truth about the debt, it is because, in an event in the past, money had actually been received from 'the person for whom the legal admission of a debt was made' – his words would thus correspond to *nafs al-amr*. On the surface, then, it would be plausible for *nafs al-amr* in this context to simply constitute '*al-khārij*' – in this case, the 'physical' substances and properties of the lender and the debtor and the 'physical' form of the money they exchange. Yet when we subject this situation to philosophical scrutiny, even in this commonplace situation there is a problem with stopping at *al-khārij*. What of the intelligible concept of a 'debt', which has no extramental individuated subsistence? Must 'the mind' now be brought to bear, to supplement *al-khārij*?

Of course, the identity of *nafs al-amr* is not the subject matter of Islamic jurisprudence, any more than the nature of abstract concepts is. Thus, the jurist must (quite correctly) assume an apparently 'common sense' notion of *nafs al-amr*, or else, if he is more philosophically inclined, turn to the discipline that actually has the determination of the real identity of *nafs al-amr* as part of its subject matter, namely metaphysics. Money 'physically' changing hands is a phenomenon pertaining purely to the spatial motion of substances; conversely, the notions of 'ownership', and 'borrowing' –

the obligation to submit to a time-conditional agreement regarding the return of wealth – are purely intelligible entities, which have no form of strictly physical instantiation. Again, non-acknowledgement of this fact poses no problem to the discipline of Islamic law, which rightly does not enquire into ontological statuses – rightly that is, if we presuppose the traditional adherence to a subordinated model of strictly demarcated sciences, in which the special subject matter of the specific sciences is respected, yet in which the full coherence and intelligibility of even the specific sciences depends upon knowledge of the 'universal' science of metaphysics (and in other contexts, of revelation). That is, a 'common sense' notion of *nafs al-amr* is sufficient for *fiqh*'s native purposes, but only someone with a knowledge of metaphysics will be able to place the domain, ontologically speaking, in which *fiqh* truly operates.

One example of a different type of difficulty for interpreting *nafs al-amr* is presented by Ibn Kathīr's (700–74/1300–73) use of *nafs al-amr* in his exegesis of Qur'an 2:188, *Consume not your goods between you in vanity; neither proffer it to the judges, that you may sinfully consume a portion of other men's goods, and that wittingly*[27],

> The ruling of a judge does not change anything in *nafs al-amr*
> – it does not make permissible, in *nafs al-amr*, something
> which is [really] impermissible, nor does it make impermis-
> sible something that is [really] permissible. It is only that [the
> judge's ruling] is *outwardly* binding; if it corresponds to *nafs
> al-amr*, then well and good.[28]

The clear implication here is that there are objective moral and legal truths. Something does not become right because a judge has said that it is so; rather, it is only truly right, if it 'corresponds to *nafs al-amr*'. Clearly here, the 'mind and extramental particulars' are both irrelevant as guarantors of this objectivity. Moral and legal truths cannot become individuated in particulars, which precludes *al-khārij* serving as this guarantor; moreover, although objective moral and legal truths *obtain* in minds, they are not *derived* from minds, which is exactly the point of Ibn Kathīr's words above. Rather, in discerning moral and legal truths, minds correspond to something necessarily extramental; otherwise, these 'truths' would indeed come into existence at the very moment the judge makes his ruling, and be entirely contingent upon the judge's ruling, and would thus count as utterly subjective. Yet 'where' are these moral and legal truths? Ibn Kathīr is clearly referring to God's true law, as opposed to the jurist's possibly inaccurate conception of it; but 'where' is God's law, which is true in '*nafs al-amr*'?

Yet another illustrative example of one of the types of question raised by the use of the *nafs al-amr* correspondence theory in diverse scholastic contexts comes from a very different type of book, 'Abd al-Razzāq al-Kāshānī's (d. 730/1330) mystical exegesis of the Qur'an (often mistakenly attributed to Ibn 'Arabī himself).

> *O my father, I saw eleven planets, and the sun and the moon, I saw them prostrating to me.* This is an example of a dream vision. In [our exegesis of] Sūrat Hūd, we noted that [these dream visions] require an interpretation. [In this case, such an interpretation would explain why], from the lofty souls [of Yūsuf's family] – whose prostration to him was, from the Unseen, shown to [his] soul– Yūsuf's imaginative faculty (*al-mutakhayyila*) moved to the planets, the sun and the moon which were, in *nafs al-amr*, none other than his parents and brothers.[29]

In the context of Kāshānī's Akbarian ontology, the planets, sun and moon in the verse are manifestations, in the world of imaginal representations (*'ālam al-mithāl*),[30] of Yūsuf's parents and brothers, peace be upon him, and this is a fact that is true 'in *nafs al-amr*.'

According to this ontology, all essences are simultaneously manifest in numerous degrees of being, one of which is the world of imaginal representations, in which essences appear in numerous subtle bodily forms.

This manifestation in the world of imaginal representations is itself only a more limited 'locus of manifestation' (*maẓhar*) of their existences in the world of spirits (*'ālam al-arwāḥ*), and of their ultimate subsistence in the Immutable Archetypes of God's knowledge. Their existence in the 'sensible' world of extramental particulars is simply the final level of the manifestation of their essences.[31]

Thus, the proposition 'the planets, sun and moon in the world of imaginal representations signified, in a particular context, Yūsuf's family members' cannot derive its truth from 'corresponding' to extramental particulars, the mind, or indeed to *'ālam al-mithāl*. On this Akbarian ontology, our familiar world, that we experience with the help of our five senses (for our purposes here, the world of extramental particulars)[32] is subordinate to *ʿālam al-mithāl*, so it would be absurd to say that a proposition involving *ʿālam al-mithāl* could derive its truth from corresponding to a level of manifestation more limited than itself.[33] Neither can *ʿālam al-mithāl* be the *ultimate* guarantor of the truth relation, because since, like 'extramental particulars', it also constitutes a subordinate level of being, it cannot *ultimately* have determined what sort of relation should obtain between itself and other levels of being. On this account, then, *nafs al-amr* must be something beyond both extramental particulars and *ʿālam al-mithāl*, and must constitute a degree of being in which the type of relation that should obtain between them is determined.

Scholastic contexts which naturally adopt some form of 'common sense', or even 'neutral' attitude towards ontology, as in the example cited from Bājūrī, require only very minimalistic accounts of the nature of *nafs al-amr* in order to be justified on their own terms. The example from Ibn Kathīr is clearly more perplexing; and Kāshānī's use of *nafs al-amr* exists at the other end of the spectrum of its use in, say, *fiqh*; presupposing a complex and explicitly affirmed ontology, it also demands a sophisticated concept of *nafs al-amr* wide enough to account for how relationships between different 'degrees' of existence could have ever been determined. Indeed, exactly because of the Akbarian account's subtlety and scope, a central argument in this study will be that the identification of *nafs al-amr* directly entailed by the Akbarian ontology is the sole broad theory able to truly and fully account for the existence of objective truths, and indeed, the very phenomenon of truth – regardless of whether or not that Akbarian ontology is accepted in all its details.

1.3 Nafs al-Amr in Logic, Epistemology, and Metaphysics

Each of the foregoing examples, regardless of the particular difficulties they present for the task of identifying the nature of *nafs al-amr*, share in a recognition of some sense of supra-subjective truth. This sense was, in the various schools of the Arabic and Islamic philosophical tradition, explored and validated through three main sets of specific questions pertaining to '*nafs al-amr*', or 'the thing as it is in itself', which we might conveniently characterize as logical, epistemological and metaphysical. In the logical sphere, this was chiefly the question of predicative scope.

Has *nafs al-amr* a wider predicative scope than the individuated world of extramental particulars (*al-khārij*), or the mind (*al-dhihn*)? Can the same proposition be true with regard to all of these loci (*al-khārij, al-dhihn* and *nafs al-amr*), or are the first two mutually exclusive, in cases in which they correspond to *nafs al-amr*? These questions will be treated in our discussion below of al-Sayyid al-Sharīf al-Jurjānī's famous treatise on *nafs al-amr*.

On a more properly metaphysical level of discourse, numerous questions arise. Can all types of existent quiddities and essences be said to be confined to extramental particulars and the mind, or is it impossible for certain of them to be limited to these categories, such that the invocation of a third 'location' becomes necessary, namely *nafs al-amr* thus conceived? This is a question we will examine during our consideration of Saʿd al-Dīn al-Taftāzānī and al-Jurjānī's respective discussions of 'real' and 'relational' composite quiddities (*al-māhiyyāt al-murakkaba al-ḥaqīqiyya wa al-iḍāfiyya*).

These two topics will be taken up in section 2.3 *Logical, epistemological and metaphysical propaedeutics*, one of the most technical sections in this study. The purpose of that section is to provide some of the most helpful conceptual apparatuses aiding an understanding of the broader philosophical issues at stake in the question of *nafs al-amr*. However, at need, that section might be bypassed without harming the general argument of the paper.

The metaphysical topic most central to this study, however, is the serious challenge posed by intelligible, 'abstract' entities and truths, and indeed, the very concept of 'truth', to the notion that, broadly put, the truth of a proposition is merely its correspondence to sensible and mental phenomena. The tension becomes particularly acute when we consider the possible subjectivist implication of positing that 'the mind' is the original locus of these intelligible objects and truths. We will meet with formulations of and solutions to this and related problems by Fakhr al-Dīn al-Rāzī, Ibn Bahāʾuddīn, Taşköprüzade (900–68/1495–1561), Ismail Gelenbevi (1143–1204/1730–90) and others. On the ontological level, we are faced with the problem of the positive identification of *nafs al-amr*. Is it an actual level or degree of being, a world in and of itself? In answering this question, Naṣīr al-Dīn al-Ṭūsī, and especially Dāwūd al-Qayṣarī have put forward influential theories. One of the most comprehensive of all answers to the question was that offered by the Ottoman sage Taşköprüzade, who synthesized aspects of Avicennan and Akbarian thought to provide a theory that accounts for numerous related philosophical issues, such as the question of how the concept of *nafs al-amr* relates to the notion of exemplary forms, as well as to abstraction theory.

There can be little doubt that we live today in a world in which traditional metaphysics – as the 'universal science' that critically specifies the general principles of all other sciences, and guarantees their coherence and objectivity,[34] has been almost entirely relegated to the status of a historical curiosity, if not forgotten altogether.[35] The consequent absence of universally acknowledged first principles, required to assure of the fundamental intelligibility and indeed objectivity of debate in matters philosophical, is (although this is rarely explicitly acknowledged), certainly very sorely felt by those aspiring to have philosophy be taken seriously as 'science' once more.[36] For the academic mainstream in the European Middle Ages, and in the Islamic world for long after that period, (broadly Avicennan) metaphysics or 'first philosophy' was supreme, indeed the most 'scientific' of the sciences, its principles serving as the theoretical underpinnings for all of the other sciences.[37] This predominance continued in the West until the decline of scholasticism and the rise of the corpuscularian natural philosophy in the seventeenth century; and in the Islamic world, before the destruction, in the late 19th and early 20th centuries, of the traditional curricula in the great centres of learning, such as al-Azhar in Egypt, Farangi Mahall in India, and the madrasas of Ottoman Turkey and Iraq.[38]

The basic insight that makes the concept of *nafs al-amr* so critical, and that most of the developed theories of *nafs al-amr* we will be considering share in, is that although truth claims of whatever kind are doubtless mind-dependent in terms of their mental formulation and subsistence, their truth or otherwise is something that cannot be accounted for by 'the mind' in isolation. This is because the mind is not the ultimate source of the abstract and universal concepts and first principles that inform each instance of human knowing. Likewise, the mind possesses no faculty whereby it can self-verify the modes of cognition with which it is naturally equipped; without intuiting its true ontological status as the limiting locus of truths which emanate from an extramental, intelligible domain, a human mind imprisoned within itself must give in to subjectivity. It is only by discerning the congruity or discordance of the mental phenomena responsible for the formulation of these truth-claims with manifestly extramental phenomena that this implication of subjectivism can be avoided - and it is then that the question of the scope of the 'extramental' arises.[39]

This point notwithstanding, it is also important, in order to bring the question of *nafs al-amr* into sharper relief, that it be distinguished from another form of truth-justification. The question of the *ontological* justification of the sciences, *nafs al-amr*, (here, broadly speaking, a 'correspondence' theory) is distinct from that of the *internal* justification of the sciences (in modern parlance i.e., the 'foundationalist' theory).[40] Although intimately intertwined and both centrally important to a full account of truth, these are distinct metaphysical themes.

The classic 'foundationalist' theory in Islamic philosophy grounds inferential, speculative, theoretical (*naẓarī*) propositions – which are not analytically self-evident, but require syllogistic or other forms of proof – firmly in necessary (*ḍarūrī*), and self-evident (*badīhī*) propositions, the epistemic 'roots of the mountain' to which the build-up of propositions can be traced, and which guarantee their self-coherent truth. Yet even this is not enough for a full account of truth. The brute phenomenological fact of this form of foundationalist justification – the fact that we encounter it experientially[41] – does not account for its *being*, nor provide it with more than self-referential truth-validity; that is, it cannot assure us beyond a shadow of a doubt that first principles correspond to *nafs al-amr*. The proximate locus of self-evident propositions and innate concepts is the mind of the individual subject. But as we will hear from a number of prominent Islamic philosophers in the course of this paper, the fact of dwelling in a mind is no guarantee of truth – for otherwise, obviously false propositions, like 'every animal is a man' or '1 + 2 = 2' would have to be true just because we can 'think' them. For example, the principles 'nothing comes from nothing' and 'it is impossible that a thing both be and not be in exactly the same manner and conditions' seem true to us; indeed, the bases of many other truths. Yet if the only evidence we have for this is the fact that we encounter such principles in our internal landscape and *cannot help* but assent to them, we are in no wise justified in claiming that there is a strictly *ontological* justification – something about the nature of being and the world – for believing them to be true – *unless* we are also to acknowledge that they must correspond to something beyond themselves, which can account for that appearance and that encounter. That is, for anything – even something as fundamental as the logical principle of non-contradiction – to be ontologically and not merely 'phenomenologically' valid, it must correspond to something beyond its appearances, something rooted in the nature of being itself, that can account for and validate its truth within the particular 'logical' contexts in which it appears.

Since these fundamental principles are 'intelligible' entities, which do not have individual referents in extramental particulars, the next question that must be asked is, 'what is the ultimate ontological status of intelligible entities?'[42] In some sense (whether entirely consciously or not), we certainly experience such 'intelligible entities', the principle of non-contradiction, the figures of the syllogism, the pure concepts of identity, necessity, possibility, unity, multiplicity, abstract mathematical entities and so on. Ordinary rational cognition cannot operate without them. Moreover, we all bear witness to their utility, and indeed indispensability, throughout the diverse branches of human knowledge. But do their particularized instances in the loci of the mind and the physical world external to the mind, constitute the ultimate guarantors of their supra-subjective reality? If not, whence do they come, and in what form do they ultimately subsist? That is, what independent, extramental feature, mode or realm of existence does our knowledge *itself* correspond *to*, including all the cognitive and representational apparatuses from which it is inseparable? Knowledge after all, is knowledge *of* something existing *in* reality. If 'reality' *is* no more than the very phenomenon of perception itself, in itself, whence our distinction between true and false propositions? If the contents of our minds are 'reality itself', we have once again awoken in the nightmare of solipsistic idealism; we have no control over the intelligible features of our objects of knowledge, and yet no way to see past our modes of knowing them, to any extramental realm that might have given rise to them.

There are a few truths which promptly rescue us from these sceptical thoughts. One is that our knowledge in its particular modality is obviously contingent with respect to its particular modus, because the specifically human mode of knowing did not have to be the way it is.[43] This very possibility provides strong evidence that knowledge *itself*, as it is in its specifically 'human' form, arises from an extramental, intelligible reality that contains more possibilities of *knowing and known* than those manifest in the particular structure of the human mind. Moreover, and closely related, human knowledge is contingent, which is to say that we are obviously not the efficient causes of our own knowledge. This is shown by the fact that our experience of knowledge is evidently primarily affective (*infi'ālī*) rather than active (*fi'lī*), that is, one of being acted-upon, rather than of doing. As human beings we are, as it were, 'forced' to *know*, in the broadest sense of 'know' – we are unable to choose not to do so. Consequently, no single human being, in the sheer brute fact of the rational nature of his identity or individual nature, could possibly ever account for the universal phenomenon of knowledge itself; along with his very being, it has been caused by something outside of himself, and made to become individuated in each member of his species (including presently non-existent, possible future members of the species), in a unique manner in each case. Our knowledge, then, if it is 'true', must plainly proceed from a realm or reality outside of itself, in other words, one that is extra-mental, one capable of causing the universal phenomenon of knowledge to become manifest in each individual member of the human species.

In this study, within the context of the indigenous resources of Islamic philosophy, we will try to ascertain whether it is possible, justifiably, to attempt to identify the nature of this 'realm', *nafs al-amr*, or 'things as they are in themselves'. The mere exploration of this most fundamental of questions will, we contend, be instrumental in suggesting the outlines of any future theological system able to serve the genuine and faithful continuation of a higher Sunni *kalām*, a type of *kalām* that is today seriously and literally at risk of extinction. As we have said, there exist a number of approaches to dealing with *nafs al-amr*. Perhaps the most distinctive aspect of this study is that it hopes to be open to the full scope of the sources of knowledge that the *'ulamā'* drew upon in their formulations of various theories of *nafs al-amr*, even though some of these sources may feel unfamiliar or seem incredible to many who have grown up surrounded by the general epistemological assumptions that character-ize contemporary fashion.[44] That is, we hope to be open to the results of the scholar-sages who acknowledged that underlying and informing the discursive intellect (*al-'aql min ḥaythu huwa mutafakkir*), there is always the receptive intellect (*al-'aql min ḥaythu huwa qābil*).

> Intellects have a limit, at which they must come to a halt in so far as they are discursive, not in so far as they are receptive.[45]

This magisterial Akbarian distinction is one of the most fruitful in all of what, for the sake of convenience, we might call 'philosophy', although clearly the purpose of the distinction is partly to demonstrate how philosophy as commonly understood might be transcended, and indeed, that strictly speaking there can really be no such thing as 'pure' reason. Briefly, the receptive intellect is the human intellect as the affective (*infi'ālī*) receptacle of knowledge. In general terms, this encompasses its receptivity to all possible types of knowledge, whether, for example, sense knowledge, or that provided by the revelation of sacred texts; perhaps the most important dimension of this distinction, in the context of widening the scope of knowledge of *nafs al-amr*, is the receptivity of this aspect of intellect to the gnosis of mystical unveiling (*kashf*). The important point is that this is knowledge that man is 'taught'. He cannot not experience the particular corner of the sensible world that has been destined to be all he knows of that sensible world; he cannot not encounter the holy effusion of the Qur'anic revelation, if it has been determined that this should be his lot. He is receptive to all manner of insights, intuitions, dreams and premonitions, and indeed to true *kashf*, in which discursive thinking plays no essential part. What is more, it is this 'experience', sense experience, the experience of the one over the many, and perhaps revelational and mystical as well, if he is given them, which the discursive intellect tries to make sense of, and cannot escape being wholly informed by.

The discursive intellect is 'reason': the intellect that employs necessary first principles and innate concepts, organizes premises, constructs syllogisms and discerns necessary entailment: the rational mind of speculative philosophy. While *al-Shaykh al-Akbar* Ibn 'Arabī (560–637/1165–1240) ('the Greatest Master') does acknowledge that it is within the proper competence of the 'discursive intellect' to demonstrate fundamental articles of faith like God's existence and unity, and the reality of Divine messengers and revelation,[46] it often has difficulty understanding truths provided by the very revelation it has proven to be real, about the actual nature of God and His spiritual world, sometimes even denying these truths altogether on the basis of 'proofs' of their apparent logical impossibility (the Mu'tazilī rejection of the beatific vision and the 'philosophers'' rejection of the bodily resurrection spring to mind). Of course, these particular rational 'proofs' are not, says Ibn 'Arabī, true proofs in *nafs al-amr*.[47] The essences of such matters cannot be arrived at through the exercise of mere reason; reason must thus be aided by direct experience. This is because the discursive intellect requires 'matter' to work on – on its own, it can provide little more than empty logical form.

In his *Futūḥāt*, the Greatest Master goes on to give a full account of this internal contingency of the discursive intellect.

> When the cogitative faculty (*al-quwwa al-mufakkira*) proceeds to the imagery (*al-khayāl*), it is dependent on the form-bearing faculty (*al-quwwa al-muṣawwira*), in order to construct by means of it, out of the matters that have been apprehended by the imagery, the form of evidence regarding a particular thing, and a conclusive proof wherein it can be grounded in sensible knowledge or necessary principles – which are [both] set within [man's] natural disposition. Now, when thought (*al-fikr*) conceives of that proof, the intellect (*al-ʿaql*) then takes it from it and passes judgement upon the object of proof. There is no faculty but that it has impediments and errors that need to be differentiated from that which is established and accurate. Look then, my brother, how impoverished the intellect is, in that it knows nothing we have mentioned except through these faculties, that themselves have such defects ... we have come to know that the intellect has nothing of itself, and that all of the knowledge it acquires only obtains because [the intellect] is characterized by the attribute of *receptivity* (*qabūl*) ... its receiving from its Lord that which He Most High says about Himself, then, is superior to its receiving from its thought.[48]

The imagery can in the first instance only work on what it receives from the senses. If the memory does not then retain what has obtained in the imagery, it will be lost. This deprives the imagery of numerous aspects of the proper representation of the full range of sensible particulars. The faculty of memory will then stand in need of the faculty that can remind it (*al-quwwa al-mudhakkira*). The point is, underlying reason, there are numerous faculties quite susceptible to deficiency or error, which reason itself has no control over. Thought (*al-fikr*) is a 'blind follower' (*muqallid*) of the imagery, and the imagery is a blind follower of the senses, and over and beyond thought's blind following, it is not even able to keep hold of its thoughts without help from the memory, and the faculty that reminds the memory. In itself, reason possesses no knowledge at all, except its innate necessary principles (*al-ḍarūriyyāt al-latī fuṭira ʿalayhā*);

how strange, then, that despite knowing reason's radical contingency upon these faculties, people continue to find it far-fetched that underlying reason there exists a more fundamental faculty which, with spiritual exercises and the transcendence of mere thought can, as quasi-necessary but not sufficient conditions, give different and more trustworthy results than those yielded by unaided reason.

Reason is the human, universalizing intellectual faculty reflecting, and able to discern, the hierarchical order of intelligible relations, like those of identity and difference, priority and posteriority, subordinacy and superordinacy, participation and subsumption, causal relations, and so on, that are constitutive of the 'intelligible structure' governing both sensible-particular and universal being, as well as being which transcends both the sensible-particular and the universal. By combining these elements in accordance with the rules of logic, rules that themselves reflect this ontological, and even more fundamentally, henological backdrop of hierarchy and priority, reason can achieve its goal, which is to arrive, guided by the principle of non-contradiction, at natures and essences in their full distinctnesses.

Yet reason is almost totally at the mercy of even more fundamental human faculties, which provide the actual *content* (the 'matter') of intellection. For example, when reason utilizes the term 'horse' in a proposition, it is not because reason has been able to conjure real individual animals into existence by some sort of syllogistic process, and this is because the syllogistic process *presupposes*, rather than provides, the matter that it works upon. Instead, the particular individual animals that one meets (whence the term 'animal' is abstracted, as the 'matter' for some instance of speculative reasoning), are *given* to one's cognition. If circumstances have not enabled one to have ever seen or heard of a horse, one will not be able to reason about them at all. Reason itself, then, is quite helpless. It does nothing more than to impose *the form* (for example, a particular figure and mood of the syllogism), onto matter that it cannot strictly speaking choose, but that is rather *given* to it.

To assist us in absorbing this quite radical distinction, the implications of which are foundational to our treatment of theories of *nafs al-amr*, let us briefly indicate how it is able to show up the limitations of purely logical or even 'metaphysical' treatments.[49] The purely logical might simply determine the referents and predicative scope of the different types of propositions that it utilizes. It is a requirement of the intelligibility and coherence of the logical system that logic must assume, for example, that mental propositions are of wider predicative scope than propositions that correspond to extramental particulars, since one can at least *conceive* of all manner of entities that do not correspond to extramental particulars.

Logic can impart to us the fact that some abstract propositions, which derive their truth-value neither from minds nor extramental particulars, must instead 'correspond to *nafs al-amr*', just as do all real extramental entities, and some, but not all, mental propositions. It might even be within logic's scope to define a thing in *nafs al-amr* as 'a thing as it is, in itself.' However, logic can do no more than this. It cannot uncover an ontology. It is not its function to affirm or negate the existence of 'the mind', 'extramental particulars' or *nafs al-amr*, or to determine what they are in themselves. After all, logic studies conceptions and assents, in so far as they lead to the discovery of new, previously unknown conceptions and assents. On the other hand, it does not investigate conceptions and assents 'with respect to their existing or not existing in the mind, or with respect to [whether they] subsist in *nafs al-amr*, irrespective of the perspective of a subject, or constitute [the object of a] pure perspective, like the fangs of a ghoul, and like mental propositions. Logic does not investigate them from these viewpoints, because they are not relevant to its aim.'[50] In fact, logic cannot act independently to prove anything, because

> proof only takes place by means of a demonstration that has a [particular] form that obtains via logic, and particular matter that cannot be known from it (logic) ... the particularities of [the] *matter* [of propositions] cannot be known through logic. The only thing one derives from [the science of logic] is knowledge of the general suitability of principles, which are known through other sciences, to all [possible] results (*natā'ij*). Even though all of the principles of logic are necessary, it is certainly the case that mistakes can be made pertaining to the aspect that constitutes [the] matter [of propositions].[51]

Consequently, logic cannot even tell us whether *nafs al-amr* itself actually exists at all. Paradoxically, although it is the science that we utilize to try to guarantee our arrival at truth, it is unable to tell us whether there is even such a thing as truth.

Instead, it is philosophy that has this task. According to a widespread descriptive definition, it is 'the science of the states of the essences of existent things, as they are, to the extent of man's capacity, in *nafs al-amr*.'[52] One branch of philosophy studies entities that 'do not depend on matter, neither in extramental particulars nor in intellection, and this is the highest science, and is known as the Divine Science, and as "first philosophy", and "universal science", and "metaphysics" ...'[53] The science of metaphysics discerns that truth cannot be reducible to correspondence to extramental particulars, because extramental particulars cannot themselves account for abstract truths or the reality of first principles, nor even for the accurate correspondence of the mind to the world of extramental particulars. Nor can truth be reducible to correspondence to the mind, for false, nonsensical and impossible propositions obtain in minds. Truth, thus, must be correspondence to a third realm, *nafs al-amr*, which transcends the mind.

Metaphysics then acknowledges that if *nafs al-amr* did not actually *exist*, truth, which is correspondence to it, would be an empty fantasy. Thus, it must next seek to determine the actual nature of the entity or realm that is '*nafs al-amr*.' Yet it is here that things break down. By reflecting on extramental facts, mental entities, propositions, and the phenomenon of truth as a universal, Peripatetic metaphysics has enabled us to deduce that *nafs al-amr* is an *existent* guarantor of truth beyond both the mind and extramental particulars. Yet it can do little more than speculate about *what* it in fact *is*. It does not enable us to meet *nafs al-amr*. The discursive intellect can go no further than this, unless the receptive intellect provides it with more 'matter', that is, more experiential content to apply itself to.

The theories of Ibn Bahā'uddīn (see Section 3.3) and Qayṣarī (Chapter 4), both writers in the broadly Platonizing school of Ibn 'Arabī, each employ or presuppose some degree of rational demonstration, but perfect the results of rational demonstration with intuitive and spiritual results and the data of revelation, providing a path to integrative and universalizing theories of truth, which are demonstrably more explanative, and less susceptible to contradiction and sceptical challenges, than theories that preclude those latter sources of knowledge. Indeed, their master Ṣadr al-Dīn al-Qūnawī had made clear in his writings that representatives of that school share a vocabulary with more conventional philosophy for a very good reason. It is because the mystical vision of reality fully encompasses the vision of reality that can be achieved via philosophy, and can thus anticipate the degree of reality that philosophical methods will be able to comprehend, in the event that the mystical vision be expressed in these philosophical terms, which is often the best language for this purpose. Due to the 'plenitude of the Divine largesse', such a 'discourse becomes two distinct discourses', such that the speculative philosopher may achieve, in reading such works, a high degree of truth that illuminates his intellectual journey, even if he is as yet unable to join the ranks of the mystical reader, who perceives the full denotation of its meanings via mystical unveiling.[54] In occupying various intelligible 'positions' of priority and posteriority, in the hierarchical scheme of order uncovered by the more holistic mode of reason we advocate in this study–whose primary intuition is not the empirical particular, but rather the one over the many which uncovers this intrinsic order[55] –these *ḥaqā'iq*, these objects of mystical cognition, leave their imprint on reality by informing an intelligible order accessible by this henological, experiential reason. A reason illuminated by direct experience of those realities will *experience* that intelligible order; but without the benefit of experience, reason nonetheless remains not entirely bereft, still able to discern that order, however faintly, 'through a glass darkly.' *It is* after all possible for the single effusion of being and truth to overflow into the realm of speculative thought, such that the principles of mystical unveiling become accessible even to that familiar, particularized framework. For human reason constitutes a limitative power of the human spirit, the spirit that with respect to itself possesses a much broader scope of knowledge of reality. Reason is a power which with respect to its temporal unfolding, constitutes the process by which multiplicities are subsumed into unities in accordance with the dictates of causal priority and posteriority. Yet that temporal process thereby uncovers realities that are in themselves timeless; indeed, the structures of reason in themselves are timeless. It is only with respect to their instantiation within our states of physical situatedness that they take on modes of subordinate contingency with respect to individual temporal unfolding. Thus, an elevated form of holistic reason, which recognizes that the appearances of reason are only possible because of prior exemplary forms that grant them intelligibility and rootedness in being, is capable 'from behind the veil', as it were, of demonstrating the truth of certain *kashfī* realities without having yet witnessed them by means of *kashf*. The relation between *kashf* and speculative investigation can also obtain from the opposite starting point. The demonstrative proof corresponding to a *kashfī* reality may also be obtained from the *kashf* experience itself, in so far as the causal priority and subsumption of multiplicities into unities encountered in some mystical experiences possess their analogues in the logical order, after the mystic has 'returned' to more (or less) familiar, ordinary spatiotemporal conditions.

The fact, implied by this 'plenitude of the Divine largesse', that different degrees of access to the same truth exist, corresponding to different philosophical traditions, was widely recognized by a number of ostensibly more mainstream philosophers who mostly lived and worked during the 600 years of the Ottoman Empire, although many of them were in Iran or India. At the end of his broadly Avicennan commentary on Athīr al-Dīn al-Abharī's *Hidāyat al-Ḥikma*, for example, the philosopher, mystic and Shāfiʿī judge, Qāḍī Ḥusayn Maybudī (d. 910/1504) tells enthusiastic students ready to progress to the next level of philosophy

> it is my view that the seeker after the truth must read the books of the two shaykhs, Abū ʿAlī (Ibn Sīnā) and Shihāb al-Dīn al-Maqtūl (Suhrawardī), may God sanctify their secrets. However, beyond their domains there is a domain of elevated standing, like the Red Sulphur (*al-kibrīt al-aḥmar*), and success in attaining to it can only be granted by God, the Greatest (*al-akbar*).[56]

Maybudi makes it clear then, with this unmistakeable reference to Ibn ʿArabī, that attaining to true knowledge involves transcending the level of mere philosophy. It is highly significant that this commentary on *Hidāyat al-Ḥikma*, 'Qāḍī Mīr' as it came to be known, has probably been the most widely taught single textbook on Islamic philosophy of the past several hundred years, in madrasas throughout much of the Islamic world. If the fact that all the students who finished the book must have read the words quoted above does not constitute conclusive proof that the notion of successive degrees of knowledge crowned by the school of Ibn ʿArabī was completely normative in later Islamic civilization, it certainly shows that it would have been a notion that was highly familiar to a great many aspiring ʿulama.

The members of the school of Ibn ʿArabī are the preeminent examples of 'thinkers' who were able to draw on the full scope of both experiential and rational sources of knowledge. It is not difficult to show that the former source in fact demands a much more stringent standard of epistemological warrant than the latter – but space and scope do not allow us to go into this here. For our purposes, the important thing is to affirm that no 'leap of faith' is required in order for the results of this 'mystical' school to be taken seriously as constituents of philosophically meaningful discourse. Their acknowledgement and embracement of the value, though it be carefully demarcated, of 'pure' reason, and their consistent use of both philosophical terminology and speculative arguments to explain or supplement the data of *kashf*, ensures that their positions are almost always intelligible and carefully substantiated even on the 'rational' level.[57] Their openness and receptivity to a higher mode of noetic apprehension simply has the function of making their arguments more credible, rounded and powerful. In our times, in a world that sometimes seems irredeemably agnostic, and in which endless varieties of scepticism and relativism congest the mental scenery of the majority of even 'traditional' Muslims, harnessing the full range of the epistemological apparatuses that our great traditions represent is of the utmost necessity. In providing a new formulation of a broadly 'Avicenno-Akbarian' and higher *kalām* account of the ontological ground of objective truth, that meets the specific philosophical challenges of our times, this short study hopes to provide some idea of how this can be possible.

Chapter 2

The Study of Things as They Are in Themselves: History and Method

2.1 Nafs al-Amr and the Proposition

For students of the Islamic sciences to this day, *nafs al-amr* makes its first, rather innocuous-seeming appearance in the chapter on 'propositions' (*qaḍāyā*), at about the midway point of a number of important standard logic textbooks.[1] The words of the celebrated metaphysician and logician Mulla Fenari (751–834/1350–1431) in his commentary on *Īsāghūjī*[2] are one important example. Commenting on Abharī's definition of a proposition, 'a statement whose utterer can validly be said to be truthful or untruthful', Mulla Fenari explains that 'judgements are annunciations of that which is actual in things-as-they-are (*al-wāqi' fī nafs al-amr*).'[3] Although, as we saw in Chapter 1, the validation of the concept of truth is not part of the subject matter of traditional logic, this short sentence shows how, at times, metaphysical concepts may put in an appearance in the outer regions of a 'lower' science such as logic, exactly in order to guarantee the intelligibility of that science. The judgements supervening on the apprehension of propositions studied by logic are the means by which truths in *nafs al-amr* – that is, in objective reality – are conveyed.

It is significant that Abharī's formulation is identical to the manner in which Avicenna defines propositions in his *al-Ishārāt wa al-Tanbīhāt*[4] because this constitutes another amongst almost innumerable examples of the integration of Avicenna's thought into the Sunni madrasa curriculum. In his chapter on propositions, *al-Shaykh al-Ra'īs* ('the Principal Shaykh')[5] explains that the truth of a proposition is not contingent on its correspondence to particularized essences (*al-a'yān*). 'Affirmation in categorical propositions, like our statement "man is an animal", means that the thing we suppose, in the intellect, to be a man, we must also suppose and judge to be an animal, irrespective of whether it exists, or does not exist, in particularized essences.'[6] In his famous commentary, Naṣīr al-Dīn al-Ṭūsī expands on this: 'existing in particularized essences is not a condition [of the validity] of the subject of a proposition, for we make affirmative judgements on subjects that do not exist in particularized essences (not to mention negative judgements), as in our [judgements] about geometrical figures, even though we do not judge that they "exist"'.[7] By 'exists', of course, al-Ṭūsī means the extramental, individuated existence (*al-wujūd al-khārijī*) of particularized essences (*al-a'yān*).

As a consequence of this principle, merely obtaining distinctly in the intellect affords a thing sufficient eligibility for it to constitute a meaningful component of a true proposition. Indeed, propositions can embody truths entirely without reference to extramental individuated existence. Yet in lieu of any possible empirical reassurance, what could constitute the *guarantor* of the truth or otherwise of such propositions?

In his *Tajrīd*, which as we have noted is a metaphysics textbook of the greatest centrality to later Islamic history,[8] Ṭūsī has a ready answer, which serves as a crucial and fundamental basis for subsequent treatments:

> If the intellect makes judgements upon extramental things with the like of them,[9] correspondence [to extramental particulars] must obtain, in all true [instances] of such propositions. Otherwise, no (such correspondence is necessary); (rather,) true (propositions, that do not correspond to extramental particulars), are [true] in so far as they correspond to that which is in *nafs al-amr* (rather than to the mind), because of the possibility of conceiving of false propositions.[10]

One of the definitive commentators on the *Tajrīd*, Shams al-Dīn al-Iṣfahānī (d. 749/1348), explains that in propositions in which one or both terms *do not* have a referent in extramental particulars,[11] it is correspondence to *nafs al-amr* identified as a broader extramental reality, rather than specifically to extramental *particulars*, that constitutes the guarantor of their truth. This is because if the *mind* in which the terms of the proposition become impressed were to be made to serve as this guarantor (instead of extramental particulars) obviously false propositions would be 'true' simply by virtue of possessing mental forms to which the pertinent judgements correspond.[12] 'Were the truth of a proposition to be [judged] according to its correspondence to the forms in minds (*limā fī al-dhihn min al-ṣuwar*), our statement "man is necessary" would be true, because it has a form in the mind (*li annahu lahu ṣūratun fī al-dhihn*).'[13]

The mind, then, is no warrantor of truth, because it is just as prone to contain false representations and false propositions as it is true forms and true propositions. The mere fact that true propositions like 'man is a possible being' exist in human minds is clearly no guarantor of their truth; and even more evidently, the fact that false propositions like 'man is an impossible being' exist in minds, is no guarantor of their truth. Crucially, then, the fact of existing in a mind is no guarantor of the truth of a proposition, and it is thus clear that the mind cannot be identified with *nafs al-amr*.

The impact of this simple but compelling and powerful argument was a central catalyst for the mature Islamic philosophical tradition's[14] depiction of truth as a relation to a realm or state beyond both the world of extramental particulars and the mind itself. Extramental particulars prove themselves unable to account for the truth of abstract propositions, and moreover, mere existence in the mind is incapable of accounting for our distinction between true and false propositions. We have already noted that one of our main tasks in this study will be to try to show how Islamic thinkers drawing on the broadly Avicennan and Akbarian schools ultimately synthesized important principles and concepts from these two schools in order to discover the identity of this mysterious third domain of reference, *nafs al-amr*. We will also argue that meeting some of the challenges posed by modern, especially post-Kantian philosophy, requires us to draw out certain possibilities hitherto enfolded in the farthest, hidden reaches of our tradition. As we will see in Chapter 4, these allow us to provide the beginnings of a demonstration that the intelligible principles governing particulars (chiefly, the 'transcendentals') are rooted in a hierarchy of prior, exemplary 'metaprinciples', guaranteeing the intelligibility of the world, and hence the possibility of objective truth.

Before embarking upon this weighty task, however, it will be helpful to achieve the somewhat simpler aim of inquiring into the general manner in which the main streams of philosophy both East and West, the broadly Platonic and the broadly Peripatetic, have treated the notion of 'objective truth', and to observe how these basic ideas flowed into Islamic philosophy, via major thinkers like Avicenna, Averroes, Ibn 'Arabī, Fakhr al-Dīn al-Rāzī and Naṣīr al-Dīn al-Ṭūsī, thereby setting up some of the primary tensions that would finally be resolved only by the Avicenno-Akbarian synthesis, also presented in Chapter 4 of this study.

2.2 Truth and Things as They Are: Historical Sketches

Aristotle's (384–322 BC) basic 'correspondence theory', closely mirroring Plato's (427–347 BC) formulation in the Sophist,[15] is simply that 'what is false says of that which is, that it is not, or of that which is not, that it is, and what is true says of that which is that it is, or of that which is not that it is not'.[16] Aristotle in fact held three explicit views on truth,[17] 'the conformity of thought with reality' in *De Interpr.* 9.19a33,[18] 'a connection between concepts inside the judgement', *De anima* 8.432a11,[19] and 'reality itself', *Met.* 10.1051b1.[20] Thoughts and sentences as well as entities that are neither mental nor linguistic (such as individual essences, whose 'truth' is to exist) are all potential 'bearers of truth or falsehood.'[21]

It is something of a platitude that the most far-reaching of Plato and Aristotle's many differences concerns the question of the reality of the Forms or 'Ideas'. Naturally, this difference has a highly significant bearing on their respective conceptions of the ontological grounds that give rise to the phenomenon of truth as capturable in propositions and judgements. For Plato, sense knowledge is irremediably defective; its object is ever in flux, and itself represents only a limited refraction of the reality in which it must participate in order to receive its weak mode of 'being' (really mere 'becoming'). True knowledge pertains by recollection (as per the *Meno*, *Phaedo* and *Phaedrus*) solely to these changeless, incorporeal, timeless and nonspatial Forms,[22] which exist *ante rem*. Yet it is the Good itself (which as later philosophers in Plato's school would affirm, is identical to the One), the first superordinate, superessential principle prior to all the Forms ('beyond being, in rank and power' *Republic* 509B9–10) which constitutes the ground of all truth and knowledge (508e).[23]

Aristotle, on the other hand, rejected the Forms of his old teacher, and while acknowledging the Platonic notion that scientific knowledge pertains only to the universal form rather than any of its particular instances, nonetheless held that the immanent form, which renders sensible particulars intelligible, is the only actual mode of existence which that universal form can ever possess. For the Aristotelian tradition, then, the forms of things, the objects of scientific knowledge, inhere in and inform sensible things, rendering them intelligible; yet they possess no higher degree of existence, *ante rem*, than their instantiations in particular things, *in rebus*. As a certain Boethius (480–524 CE) noted with especial clarity, 'Plato thinks genera and species and the rest are not only understood as universals, but also exist and subsist apart from bodies. Aristotle, however, thinks they are *understood* as incorporeal and universal, but *subsist* in sensibles.'[24] For Aristotle and much of the subsequent Peripatetic tradition, then, universal essences 'in themselves' (that is, without reference to particular individuation), are ultimately mental abstractions; essences only *exist* as particulars. This tension, without exaggeration one of the most fundamental in all of philosophy, also quite accurately depicts some of the key tensions that various synthetical theories of *nafs al-amr* attempt to resolve, as we will see later in this study.

Aristotle's medieval ascendancy notwithstanding, from the third to the seventh centuries CE, Peripateticism had dwelt firmly in the shadow of the Neoplatonist syntheses, which had incorporated much of the former's terminology and classificatory apparatus. For Plotinus (205–270 CE), the immanentism and abstractionism implied by most interpretations of Peripateticism were unthinkable: the intelligible world is radically ontologically prior to the sensible, because 'the sensibles receive their being eternally by participation in [the intelligibles], imitating the intelligible nature to the best of their ability.'[25]

In a similar vein, Augustine (354–430 CE), the first major Christian Neoplatonist, combined Platonic exemplarism with Christian notions in his doctrine of Divine illumination, which 'obviated any need to explain how external things could get into the mind in order to be known. They were already there, since they really existed in the mind's interior light, God himself; indeed, they had a higher type of being in the divine Word than in the external world.'[26] As Augustine tells us in his *Confessions*, 'If both of us see that what you say is true and that what I say is true, then where, I ask, do we see this? I do not see it in you, nor you in me, but both of us see it in the immutable truth which is higher than our minds.'[27]

Since the mutable, phenomenal world by which we are corporeally bound is evidently unable, of itself, to account for or give rise to immutable truth, in order to perceive that truth, we stand in need of being illuminated by an intelligible light beyond the sensible world. 'Though some animals are able to regard this world's light with far sharper eyes than we have, they cannot attain to that incorporeal light with which our mind is somehow irradiated, so that we can judge all things rightly.'[28] Remarkably, given his vital centrality to European scholastic thought, Augustine may have had no intellectual influence on the Islamic world whatsoever.[29]

On the other hand, Proclus (412–485 CE), the most systematic of the later Neoplatonists, was certainly highly influential to early Islamic philosophy. Truth is a phenomenon that obtains in numerous domains. Knowledge of the world of becoming is a necessarily partial and defective type of knowledge, but for Proclus 'even in its ideal actualization human knowledge is still imperfect, knowing the Forms not as they are in themselves, nor even as they are in the Intelligence, but in concepts, which imperfectly reflect them.'[30] Only on the lowest levels of cognition is truth correspondence, 'the agreement of the knower with the known'; at a higher level, truth constitutes the *identity* of the knower and the object of knowledge.[31] Following Iamblichus, Proclus and many other late Neoplatonists considered full obtainment of this true knowledge of the Forms to be conditional on the practice of theurgy. The limited self, drowned in Nature, must be transcended in order that contact be made with the Forms directly, via a higher form of non-discursive intellection (*noesis*) only attainable by theurgy, and not by the intermediary of concepts, as in ordinary, representational discursive thought (*dianoia*).[32]

In this later Neoplatonism of Proclus and his student Ammonius (435/445–517/526 CE), a position which to some degree harmonized Plato and Aristotle became standard, in that it afforded a place both for Plato's transcendent forms, and a version of Aristotle's immanent forms (although, of course, Proclus strongly favoured Plato and remained deeply critical of Aristotle). The wide influence of such synthetical positions would, a thousand years later, help shape some of the theories of *nafs al-amr* that we are shortly to encounter in this study.

Ammonius spoke of natures *i.* 'before the many', *ii.* 'in the many', and *iii.* 'after the many', which corresponded to Proclus' *i.* transcendent forms, which exist prior to particulars, *ii.* universals instantiated in particulars, and *iii.* mental forms of individual things that inform our cognition of those things.[33] Works by Ammonius' own pupil John Philoponus (490–570 CE) were translated into Arabic, alongside, of course, creative paraphrases of works by Plotinus and Proclus,[34] exercising a highly important influence on the formation of early Arabic *falsafa*, and in the case of the latter two thinkers, on Avicenna. As we have said, one germane aspect of this influence pertains to Proclus' and Ammonius' three-fold scheme of the manifestation of natures, as will be seen shortly in our discussion of Avicenna's contribution to *nafs al-amr* theory.

The Arabic term *nafs al-amr* seems to have made its first appearance in Ḥunayn Ibn Isḥāq's (809–873 CE) translation of the Metaphysics of Aristotle, where he used the term in its inverted form *al-amr fī nafsihi*. The term would subsequently be adopted by pivotal philosophical figures like al-Farābī (872–950 CE) and Avicenna. At this stage, the term *al-amr fī nafsihi* was employed to denote 'objective reality', or 'a thing as it is in itself' though without, it seems, the link being explicitly made that *al-amr fī nafsihi* must thus constitute the guarantor of the truth of propositions. As well as in other works, Farābī uses the term at the end of his reconciliation on the question of the Forms of 'Aristotle' (in fact, the doctrine of Forms in question is that of Plotinus, part of whose Enneads were of course misattributed to Aristotle in the Islamic world) and Plato. Farābī humbly tells us that despite his great efforts, he has still fallen short of uncovering and explaining the views of these great philosophers, because discerning their intent 'as [it] really is in itself is extremely difficult, almost to the point of impossibility' (*li'an al-amr fī nafishi ṣaʿb mumtaniʿ jiddan*).[35]

In this early context, it is *al-khārij*, and not *nafs al-amr*, that is employed to denote the truthmaking referents of propositions. As a prelude to a defence of realism and logical first principles against sceptical sophistry at the outset of his *Metaphysics* (1.8), Avicenna sets out a basic definition of this truth-correspondence,

> [By truth], one understands [i.] existence in particularized essences (*al-aʿyān*) [in an] unrestricted [sense], and one understands [ii.] perpetual existence, and one understands [iii.] the statement or belief which indicates the state of something in extramental particulars (*al-khārij*), *if it corresponds to it.*[36]

In the same section, soon after mentioning this explicit correspondence theory, Avicenna turns to the question of how to reform those who deny the possibility of objective truth. This must involve a form of dialogue, such that the sceptic is driven to either accept the evident logical entailment in a true philosopher's words, or simply to resort to silence. Here, Avicenna draws a distinction between a syllogism whose conclusion is truly necessary, and one merely subjectively necessary, that is, because a person has become convinced by its premises, whether or not they are *actually* true. In this context, he implicitly defines *nafs al-amr* (specifically, the earlier usage, *al-amr fī nafsihi*) as a fundamentally epistemological phenomenon, in a manner which Saʿd al-Dīn al-Taftāzānī would later echo:[37]

> The [type of] syllogism which entails its required conclusion with regard to reality (lit. 'the thing as it is in itself' (*al-amr fī nafsihi*)) is the one whose premises are acceptable in themselves, and which are prior to the conclusion.[38]

Of course, in Avicenna's complex system, the ontological conditions for intelligibility and truth are carefully defined. It is merely that he does not explicitly link the term *nafs al-amr* or *al-amr fī nafsihi* to this metaphysical backdrop, an association that would have to wait to be made by later thinkers. For Avicenna, it is the 'Bestower of Forms' (*wāhib al-ṣuwar*), identified with the Agent Intellect, which, having received its own being from the higher intellects' contemplation of the First,[39] effuses into human souls universal forms that render intelligible their sense impressions of particulars.

> The human soul may be an *in potentia* intellector (*ʿāqila bi al-quwwa*), and then become an *in effectu* intellector (*ʿāqila bi al-fiʿl*). Now, everything which goes from potentiality to actuality can only do so because of an action which draws it out. There exists a cause, then, which with respect to the intelligibles draws our souls from potentiality to actuality. It is the cause of the bestowal of intellectual forms, and is none other than an actual intellect possessing all of the principles of the intellectual forms immaterially. Its relation to our souls is like the relation of the sun to our faculties of vision.[40]

Veiled by their bodies, in their multiplicitous, corporeal mode of being, human beings are unable, of themselves, to cognize the forms of things – this is why we require that the forms be 'bestowed' upon us by the Agent Intellect:

> the [human] intellect's inability to form [essential] conceptions of things – which are [however] eminently intelligible – or to abstract [them] from matter, does not stem from [something in] those things themselves, nor from some [deficiency] in the inherent nature of the intellect, but rather because the

soul is occupied, in the body, by the body, and requires the body in a great number of matters; the body thus distances [the soul] from its greatest perfection (i.e. intellectual perception).[41]

It seems intuitive, then, that human knowledge must ultimately 'correspond to' and derive its truth-legitimacy from the Agent Intellect and the higher intellects, because there lie its origins, the ontological grounds for truth. However, as we have said, Avicenna does not appear to have clearly linked *al-amr fī nafsihi* to any of these ontological realities. This is despite the difficulty, posed by true statements involving apparently 'abstract', intelligible terms that do not correspond to anything in extramental particulars, of identifying the realm of truthmaking solely with extramental particulars, as he appears to in the first quote from the Metaphysics above ('by truth one understands ... the statement or belief which indicates the state of something in extramental particulars (*al-khārij*), *if it corresponds to it*'). Perhaps the only way out of this would be to try to interpret Avicenna's '*al-khārij*' as denoting an extramental reality of wider predicative scope than mere particulars, on the basis perhaps of statements in Bk 5.1 of the *Metaphysics*, in which he seems to say that an essence in itself (*fī nafsihi / bi dhātihi*) neither exists in *al-aʿyān* nor in the mind,[42] but is prior to the extramental particular thing in the same way that a simple thing is prior to a composite thing.[43] However, this seems scarcely credible, given the limitation of existence to 'mental' and 'extramental particular' entailed by Avicenna's system, as well as his negation of Platonic Forms, the subsistence of non-existent objects, and of the *ḥāl*.[44]

When in Bk 5.1 Avicenna says that an animal considered in itself is the nature whose existence is prior to the existence of the nature in extramental particulars, and that it is the thing whose existence 'pertains to the Divine existence'[45] he is referring to a mode of existence that he has more fully explained in the *Madkhal* to the *Logic* of the *Shifāʾ*, where he expounds Proclus' and Ammonius' ontology of the nature *i.* 'before the many', *ii.* 'in the many', and *iii.* 'after the many',

> since the relation of all existent things to God and the Angels is like the relation of the objects we manufacture to [our] souls which make them, the true realities of natural [particular] things [as] objects of knowledge and perception, which are in the knowledge of God and of the Angels, exist before the

> many (*qabl al-kathra*)... then they obtain in the many (*fi al-kathra*) ... and then they obtain again after they have obtained in the many, as intelligible to us.[46]

While it is significant, then, that for Avicenna the essences that are the objects of human cognition do enjoy an ultimate grounding in the Divine mind, this still does not clearly solve the problem of how, with his definition of truth as 'the statement or belief which indicates the state of something in extramental particulars (*al-khārij*), *if it corresponds to it*', he can account for purely abstract propositions which are true entirely without reference to extramental particulars, in which, for example, both terms have no extramental particular referents.

Another great Islamic philosopher fabled in the medieval West, Averroes (520–94/1126–98), lays down his important 'correspondence' theory of truth in the midst of refuting al-Ghazālī's ostensibly nominalist views on the nature of 'possibility' in his *Tahāfut*. Reaffirming a type of realism about such concepts, Averroes tells us that

> all intelligible concepts that are characterized by being true require a thing existing outside of the soul, for truth, as it has been defined, is the correspondence of that which exists in the soul to that which is outside of the soul.[47]

One of Averroes' proofs for the eternity of the world is that the very 'possibility' of temporally originated things necessarily requires an eternal substratum – namely, prime matter – making that origination possible. The world must be possible, because the only alternative is that it is impossible (in which case we would not presently be enjoying its existence). Moreover, this possibility must be an eternal characteristic of the world, for to suppose that a particular part of the world has acquired the attribute of possibility only at the moment of its coming into existence is really to acknowledge that it would never have come into existence at all.

Al-Ghazālī had demurred on this necessity; 'possibility' requires no substrate in 'prime matter', and need be no more than a purely mental perspective, which obtains when the mind considers the status of a universal concept (such as judging, by reflecting on the mental form of 'human being', that, for example, 'human being' is a possible rather than an impossible being). Averroes counters that universal mental concepts must exist *in potentia* in their substrates, because otherwise there would be no basis for supposing that these concepts have real application – 'possibility' becomes instantiated in extramental individuals, just as much as any other nature does.[48] Thus reaffirming the necessity of this substratum, Averroes tells us that

> it is indubitably the case that intellectual propositions are no more than the [intellect's] judgement regarding the natures of things *outside of the soul*.[49]

It is of course difficult to exaggerate the importance of the influence of both Avicenna and Averroes on the development and technical refinement as well as the realist tenor of scholastic philosophy in the High Middle Ages. One pivotal example, relevant to the justification of the notion of truth, is that Avicenna's correspondence theory in the *Metaphysics* formed the basis of subsequent scholastic theories, via William of Auvergne (1180/90–1249 CE) and Thomas Aquinas (1225–1274 CE).[50] Whereas the most celebrated answer to the ontological question of *nafs al-amr* in the Islamic world came as a synthesis of aspects of Avicenna and Ibn ʿArabī, developed as the result of the meeting of their broad schools, at a certain stage of Western scholasticism the ontological guarantor of objective truth was standardly identified with reference to Augustine's notion of Divine illumination, which we have already seen. The centrality of aspects of this notion to medieval philosophical orthodoxy is epitomized by the prominence, at opposite ends of the Middle Ages, of figures like Anselm of Canterbury (1033–1109 CE) and Bonaventure (1221–1274 CE), for whom variations on the doctrine constituted the cornerstones of their philosophies. For Anselm,[51] while truth in judgements is, as it is in Aristotle, to state of that which is that it is, the former's account of what this 'is' denotes is thoroughly Platonic and Augustinian. The immutable, timeless quality of truths must be rooted in the eternity of the cause of truth, for 'the truth of a statement could not always exist if its cause did not always exist.'[52] God is the supreme Truth, and so temporal things partake of truth when they conform to the manner in which God intended them to be. 'The supreme Truth as it subsists in itself is not the truth of some particular thing, but when something is in accordance with it, then it is called the truth or rectitude of that thing.'[53]

In Bonaventure's sophisticated system, 'all light springs from exemplarism, and all darkness from the denial of it.'[54] It is futile to seek for the unchanging object of truth in created things ever in flux; this can with propriety be sought only in 'the being of the object as it subsists in the thought of God.'[55] However, in our cognition of truth we do not directly perceive the Divine Ideas. Rather, the Divine Ideas have a 'direct action ... upon our thought ... this direct and immediate action of the eternal principles upon our souls is a regulative action ... Its end is to make our knowledge of truth possible by submitting the restless uncertainty of our thought to an inevitable law.'[56]

When did the West *begin* to depart from this long-established ex-emplarist and realist course? Needless to say, even dedicated specialists cannot hope to encompass the nearly infinite nuances of the history of their period, nor to do justice to their complexity with any single gener-alized account or theory. However, some certainties about the end of the Middle Ages and the early-modern period cannot help but shine through. One of these is a decisive jettisoning, arguably initiated by Aquinas, but certainly settled by Duns Scotus (1265–1308 CE), of the theory of Divine illumination. Within the naturalizing tendencies of his epistemology, Thomas Aquinas set the stage for the subsequent downgrading of doc-trines of Divine illumination. Although illumination is required in order for certain lofty truths to be grasped, in most instances man 'does not need a new light added to his natural light, in order to know the truth in all things, but only in some that surpass his natural knowledge.'[57] It was Duns Scotus, however, who would deal a blow to the doctrine of il-lumination from which it would never fully recover. Writing in response to Henry of Ghent's restatement of the necessity of Divine illumination for the intellection of certain truth, in which he invoked the inherent limitedness and changeability of the human mind, Scotus countered that the combination of intrinsic uncertainty (the natural human mind left to its own devices) and certainty (allegedly provided by Divine illumina-tion) cannot be reconciled as certainty in one locus (the human mind), just as a mixture of contingent and necessary premises produces only a contingent conclusion. For Scotus, 'certain and pure truth' *is* achievable, but by means of our mere natural faculties, chiefly via the reduction of speculative propositions to such as are self-evident. In one fell swoop, knowledge and truth had been naturalized, in an account that would go on to be widely accepted.[58]

After the necessary rootedness of human knowledge in the exemplary forms had been discredited, the next traditional doctrine to be decisively attacked and terrestrialized would be the immanent object of knowledge – the universal nature as manifest in particular substances. The assault on realism, most evocatively associated with the figure of William of Ockham, held that 'there are no universal essences which require to be expressed in matter in order to become individuals ... the singular thing is singular without any addition to it. The singular thing requires no metaphysical "principle of individuation".'[59] One prominent reading of the thought of this subtle and difficult thinker maintains that Ockham dramatically restricted the domain of certain knowledge to the existence of sensations and our minds, and this 'narrowness within which Ockham had confined certain knowledge of reality developed into a subjective empiricism.'[60] The ensuing trajectory of European philosophy, after the breakdown of the scholastic synthesis had been cemented in Descartes, Gassendi, Locke and others, has been aptly described as

> the slow slide of post-scholastic thought toward metaphysical chaos. In place of the entrenched Aristotelian ontology of complete, individual substances, composed out of parts of various kinds organised by a governing substantial form, the seventeenth and eighteenth centuries spin off wildly in all directions. Ordinary objects are rejected as mere phenomena and replaced, variously, with world-sized substances, microscopic substances, scattered substances, or no substances at all. For those who delight in train wrecks, such chaos can serve only to enliven the subject ...[61]

It would be to digress far from our purpose here to attempt a potted history of the descent of Western thought into the extremes of Humean scepticism and Kantian quasi-idealism. Yet what is clear is that the later Middle Ages' rejections of 'form', both 'exemplary' as influencing the human apprehension of eternal truth, and 'immanent' as informing the extramental substance accessible to the collaborative effort of the senses and the intellect, led down the long and meandering road of philosophical history either to a sceptical rejection of the possibility of knowledge altogether, or else to the idealism of man's confining himself and the world entirely to his mind, in order to escape entirely from the now highly problematic notion of an objective world external to the mind. There is no doubt that these two undesirable results are in differing ways both direct and indirect elements of the legacy of Kant. His impact, in shaping the characteristic range of opinion in modern philosophies both continental and analytic on the nature of human knowledge and its relationship to reality, and indeed on almost every other foundational philosophical question, has been uniquely fateful and forceful.[62] Indeed in showing, later in this study, the manner in which our theory of *nafs al-amr* circumvents certain of Kant's key misapprehensions, the need to refute every single modern subjectivist, anti-realist doctrine is largely vitiated, in so far as it is the case that in both of these broad contemporary philosophical methodologies, such doctrines are fundamentally modifications of his thought which, even when highly critical on other questions, often perpetuate some of Kant's most important assumptions about the impossibility of directly cognizing any reality beyond the ultimately subjective.

An even more ubiquitous element of the legacy of Kant's thought has been the rejection of both traditional general and special metaphysics.[63] These often rather tenuously substantiated rejections – indeed, they often have the character of strict assumptions – are widely shared across dividing lines of analytic and continental, and indeed across opposed styles of philosophy internal to these schools of thought; and though they may be sharply at odds with one another on almost every other substantive philosophical position, the untenability of traditional realist metaphysics is a rare area of wide agreement, enjoying something very near to consensus.

A concise but careful consideration of the general features of Kant's theory of truth is thus in order here, and since he is one of our main (albeit antipodal) interlocutors in the theory of *nafs al-amr* proposed in this philosophical study, this requires a somewhat more extended treatment than other thinkers in this section.[64] This is especially the case since opposition to the 'correspondence theory of truth' – which, if once nameless, was only so because it went almost unchallenged – was initiated by Kant. As one of his most prominent exegetes Norman Kemp Smith has suggested, it is really in the *Critique of Pure Reason* that the coherentist theory of truth finds its origins, broadly, the notion that truth obtains not through the correspondence of representations and propositions to extramental objects and states of affairs, but rather via the 'coherence' yielded by the coalescence and reciprocal self-validation of perception and conceptual framework. For Kant, there is no question of the traditional correspondence-theory '*agreement of knowledge* with an extramental object'. This is because he assumes, as we will now see, that the putative necessity that the 'world' can only be rendered fully intelligible via a synthesis of the ontologically (though not epistemologically) contingent *givenness* of the form of sensible perception, and the likewise ontologically but not epistemologically contingent nature of the Categories of our thought,[65] precludes even the merest possibility of our knowing extramental objects as they are apart from the subjective form and order that we have imposed upon them. Since *the agreement of knowledge with the object* is thus precluded, taken in any traditional sense,[66] 'truth' must instead involve the mutual validation, the 'coherence', of sensibility and understanding, the empirical 'given' and the Categories. Kant's 'coherence' point of view has been succinctly expressed thus:

> The proof of a principle is its adequacy to the interpretation of all those appearances that can be shown to be in any respect relevant to it, while the test of the asserted fact, *i.e.* of our description of a given appearance, is its conformity to the principles that make insight possible.[67]

In this circle of justification, the Categories and principles prove themselves 'objective' because they are the necessary framework for any intelligibly ordered account of empirical phenomena, and empirical phenomena prove themselves objective because they conform to the Categories and principles and constitute their sole legitimate spheres of application.

Of course, the subjectivizing undertones of truth as 'coherence' are unmistakeable. Yet the adoption of this epistemological bearing was not without its sincere motivations; and it finds its basis, as indeed does Kant's larger project, in his idiosyncratic account of these two putatively 'coherent' elements, the concepts and principles of the understanding, and the empirical data moulded by sensible intuition, the synthesis of which he considers to be the inescapable *sine qua non* of genuine human knowledge.

Kant held that a strict dividing line must obtain between the concepts and principles of the understanding, and sensibility, rendering them quite separate faculties. This is because the former do not constitute objects, and neither are they immediately related to any objects, but possess only a potential relation to many objects, a relation which may become actualized only when such concepts become applied to an intuition. Intuitions, on the other hand, possess an inherently immediate relationship to the extramental particular;[68] that is, intuitions are always intuitions *of* particulars. The strictness of this division is one of the most fundamental of

Kant's innovated assumptions;[69] another of his assumptions is that it is only via sensation that we can stand in direct relation to an object. That is, the only objects to which we have access are empirical; human beings do not possess a faculty enabling them to have intuitions of any putatively non-sensory, intelligible world.

Kant has thus assumed that knowledge can only obtain in terms of its 'transcendental' (that is, a priori, non-empirical) conditions, as a fusion of intuition (that which is 'given' affectively in the 'pure a priori intuitions' of time and space, which condition sensation) and concept (the necessary, a priori contribution of the mind, by which it renders intuitions intelligible within universal categories), an assumption that also justifies his distinction between appearance and reality;[70] 'reality' is the unknowable given, as it is *beyond* the ordering apparatuses imposed onto it by the human subject.[71]

Let us first consider the reasons that seem to have driven Kant to adopt his distinctive attitude towards the understanding, the faculty of a priori concepts and principles. He had been awoken, on his own account, from his 'dogmatic slumber' by Hume, chiefly the latter's famous repudiation of the self-evidence of the causal principle.[72] Kant's move to redefine 'truth', was motivated by a concerted attempt to reconcile this repudiation of Hume's – and for Kant, 'what is true of this principle must also hold of all of the other principles fundamental to science and philosophy'[73] – with the Leibnizian contention by which Kant's mind was also deeply moved, that all experience must confirm to *a priori* principles, which rather than being dependent upon experience, actually legislate to it.[74] Again,

> If principles are never self-evident, and yet are not arrived at
> by induction from experience, by what alternative method
> can they be established? In answer to this question, Kant
> outlines the position which is now usually entitled the *Coher-*
> *ence* theory of truth. That theory, though frequently ascribed
> to Hegel, has its real sources in the *Critique of Pure Reason*.
> It expresses that modification in the Leibnizian rationalism
> which is demanded by Hume's discovery of the synthetic
> character of the causal axiom.[75]

While Kant concurred, with Leibniz, that the ordered, intelligible-as-distinct nature of experience is only explicable because of its conformity to a priori concepts and principles, Hume's 'discovery' of the non-rational nature of the concepts and principles which govern our experience led Kant to conclude that they are nonetheless inherently contingent with respect to reality (even if they are necessary with respect to subjective experience – we referred to this distinction above with the terms 'ontological contingency' and 'epistemological necessity' respectively). Since we can find no strictly *rational* justification for believing them to apply to the world, but merely find ourselves equipped with them, we are forced to acknowledge that they could have been entirely different. We therefore have no justification for thinking that they objectively apply to any reality beyond our subjective experience of the world. Yet within that self-referential domain, they are universal and necessary in application.[76] With Kant we are thus faced with the paradoxical theory in which, with respect to the 'coherent' intermingling of sensibility and understanding, *a priori* concepts and principles possess strict universality and necessity, and yet simultaneously cannot be known to apply to the unknowable real world of things-in themselves, not universally or necessarily, nor indeed in any other way at all. Despite being epistemologically necessary, then, they remain ontologically contingent.

Yet the conclusion that the universal and necessary a priori concepts must be imposed by the mind – instead of i) being given in the process of abstraction from particulars (*contra* the broadly Peripatetic account) or ii) uncovered via the henological ascent, the intuition of the one over the many with all its systematic and deductive consequences, and thereby revealed as constituting the ontologically prior intelligible structure of reality (*contra* the broadly Platonic account) – is based upon two assumptions. The first, corresponding to i), is a presupposition which, Kemp Smith tells us, is the fundamental one upon which Kant's argument rests, and which Kemp Smith further characterizes as '*a presupposition never itself investigated but always assumed.*'[77] This, namely, is that 'universality and necessity cannot be reached by any process that is empirical in character':

> By way of this initial assumption Kant arrives at the conclusion that the *a priori*, the distinguishing characteristics of which are universality and necessity, is *not given in sense but is imposed by the mind*; or in other, less ambiguous terms, is not part of the matter of experience but constitutes its

form. The matter of experience is here taken as equivalent to sensation; while sensation, in turn, is regarded as being the non-relational.[78]

It is precisely the existence of universally applicable concepts upon which the (apparent) intelligibility of the world rests, then, and the assumption that they cannot be 'given' in sense (or still less, via an uncovering of the underlying intelligible structure of the world)[79] that partially leads Kant to abandon the traditional correspondence theory of truth in which they play an important part; they cannot 'correspond' to extramental reality, because they have in some measure precluded the possibility of our ever knowing such a thing. They must therefore be imposed onto it, or, to put it into other words, interposed between us and it, obscuring our view. We can only ever have 'knowledge of our knowledge'; not knowledge of things as they really are.

The Categories of the understanding such as unity, causality and possibility, then, constitute the forms of the understanding by which we relationally cognize the world; yet they must operate upon 'matter' that is singular and non-relational. Kant was convinced that we must be 'immediately given certain information that cannot be derived from the analysis of concepts'; and moreover that 'our representations of space and time are immediate and singular in a way that none of our general concepts are.'[80] The matter of experience, sensation of extramental reality, is therefore mediated by 'the forms of sensibility', namely time and space, which, like the Categories, do not belong to the extramental object but are imposed upon it.[81]

The second of Kant's assumptions, corresponding to ii) above, is that amongst experience's twin components, that of intuition can *only ever be of that which pertains to the sensible*. Kant rules out the accessibility of intellectual intuitions, and thus, the Platonic notion of insight into the structure of an intelligible world prior to and informing the sensible world, is excluded from the realm of epistemological possibility. At the same time, 'whatever-it-is' (also known as 'the *noumena*') that causes the affections of the knowing subject in sensation, is the only thing that Kant will allow actually exists outside of our minds. Thus, we can never know the true nature of the whatever-it-is that causes this affection, for we know of it only under the subjectivizing, contorting influence of the *a priori* forms.

As the a priori *forms* of sensibility, space and time clearly involve an affective passivity; and as we have pointed out, in further contradistinction to understanding, they stand in direct relation to objects that are *singular*, as constituting their representational arena (rather than the case with concepts, which constitute general predicates that do not inherently pertain to particular objects). Space and time for Kant, thus constitute 'intuitions', and it is exactly because our empirical cognitions are mediated by the a priori forms of time and space that the true nature of their objects can never be known. After all, the intuitions of space and time, which Kant believes must be the sole *forms* of intuition, are not abstracted from sensible objects – which can only ever provide the raw matter, but never the form, of cognition – but are rather *presupposed* by sensible objects and thus, as it were, 'cover over' whatever-it-is that sensible objects *really are* when they are not made subject to the conditions of their spatiotemporal mode of cognition. One cannot see the object-itself *within* space and time, because the object-itself, that is, as it is beyond the forms imposed by our cognitive apparatuses, is definitionally *not* in space and time, which are ultimately mere features of our cognitive apparatuses. Objects *as they appear to us* are nothing more than *intuitions conditioned by their adjustment to the Categories*; yet since both intuitions and the Categories are subjective impositions, again, they veil rather than uncover the nature of things-in themselves. And because true human knowledge can only obtain upon the fusion of the objects of the faculties of sensibility and the understanding, intuitions and concept, the synthesis of which Kant calls 'experience',[82] anything which cannot be 'experienced' in this manner cannot really be known at all.

The general abstractive notion broadly common to Aristotle, the Schoolmen and Avicennan philosophy in the Islamic world, then, that experience involves the sensible particular being rendered intelligible via its abstractive universalization – in for example, Avicenna's thought, this intelligibility having been bestowed both upon the knowing subject (as a universal) and upon the particular (as a substantial form) by the Agent Intellect – is rejected in favour of the assumption that the 'universal' and 'intelligible' must be *imposed onto the sensible* rather than genuinely informing, and thereafter being epistemologically derivable from, sensible particulars.

Yet how does Kant attempt to justify his revolutionary departure from this more obviously intuitive, received philosophical wisdom? We have already seen that Kant *assumes* that the Categories and principles cannot be abstracted from extramental objects, nor known via any form of intellectual intuition in the sense of a direct relation to the Categories and principles; and Kant's certainty that space and time must have a subjectivizing influence in their processing of extramental inputs, is likewise widely viewed as having been founded upon one of his many unproved assumptions. Building on his earlier assumption that 'universality and necessity cannot be reached by any process that is empirical in character', Kant logically infers that, since space and time are the necessary and universal conditions of the sensible representation of objects, they must be entirely contributed by the knowing subject, and thus ontologically contingent (even if as modes of cognition they are *necessary*) since we have no way of grounding them in anything beyond themselves in order to demonstrate that they are objective. Moreover, since sensibility *means* the receptivity of the subject in the presence of individual extramental 'objects', those objects can only be cognized in so far as they enter into that representational framework of time and space; yet since time and space cannot have been abstracted from the extramental objects, they do not reflect their real character. However, as Paul Guyer notes,

> when space and time are then shown to be universal and fundamental characteristics of the sensible representation of objects, it is inferred that they must also reflect the "special character of the subject," that is, of the human being as cognitive subject, rather than of objects themselves. This argument seems open to a glaring objection, however, namely that just insofar as sensibility is described as a kind of receptivity, that is, a form of passivity, it is not obvious why it should in any way modify the appearance of the objects that affect it rather than pass them on to consciousness unchanged.[83]

The clearly unintuitive nature of these assumptions notwithstanding, (especially in the context of the philosophical backdrop we have previously been surveying, whether the provision of first principles via Divine Illumination, the henological ascent, or the effusion of both ontological and epistemological form from the Agent Intellect), for Kant the forms of space and time and the exercise of the Categories do not uncover the real, extramental structure of reality; in fact, they have the contrary effect of veiling it. Although we are given *some form of* data in intuitions, it has been necessarily distorted by the activity our minds bring to bear upon it (by necessarily cognizing that data in terms of the subjective forms of space and time, which do not subsist in extramental reality), and so we will never know what form the given data in fact takes, beyond that subjective imposition. We can never hope to know things-in themselves; we are acquainted only with the appearances of things.

With both intuitions and concepts safely consigned to the realm of subjectivity, the combination of which, again, constitute the necessary elements of any true cognition, it is clear why 'truth' cannot involve any correspondence to extramental states of affairs, but no more than the internal 'coherence' of human cognition, and can be recognized as 'truth', only *on the condition that it is able to recognize its own limitations*, and no longer seeks to correspond to anything beyond *itself*.

This revolutionary theory, which ultimately implies that ordered 'nature' is essentially the inter-subjective creation of the structure of the human mind,[84] governs Kant's entire project in his *Critique of Pure Reason*, even if, as we have suggested, many of his most prominent ex- egetes have acknowledged that the premises upon which he bases this theory ultimately have the quality of unproved assumptions. Regardless of the later reception of his theory, Kant himself believed that concepts and intuitions inform the deliverances of sense experience only, with so great a certainty that in formulating what he calls 'the general question' of his 'transcendental philosophy' (*Critique of Pure Reason*, B73), he presupposes the proven truth of this postulate. This question is 'how is synthetic *a priori* knowledge possible?',[85] and it epitomizes Kant's project of the reordering of the sciences, in which he would crown mathematics and physics the supreme sciences, and demote the previous incumbent, traditional metaphysics, to the status of mere illusion.

The notion of prediction in astronomy provides a clear illustration of the phenomenon, namely the confirmation of the a priori in the sensible, which the notion of the synthetic a priori seeks to capture. How is it that with our mathematical apparatuses we are able to predict a particular solar eclipse with great accuracy, prior to actually *experiencing* the predicted eclipse? For this knowledge is not merely analytic, conceptual, defini- tional knowledge; nor is it knowledge entirely derived from experience, but constitutes, rather, a fusion of conceptual and empirical elements, the success of which seems to confirm the genuine applicability of concepts to sense experience.

The question of the nature of the synthetic a priori asks 'how is it that our a priori cognition matches onto empirical reality?' It is thus another way of asking 'how is it that much that we know about the empirical world presupposes the application of principles that are in no way derived from the empirical world, but that are nonetheless productive of genuinely new knowledge about that empirical world, beyond the mere analysis of concepts?'[86] Kant's conclusion, laboriously ruminated over in the *Critique*, is that synthetic *a priori* knowledge *is* indeed possible in mathematics and physics. This is because neither science purports to extend the Categories of the understanding beyond possible, that is, empirical experience; their proper objects all appear within, or have application within, time and space. Yet synthetic *a priori* knowledge in metaphysics both general and special is chimeric, the result of 'transcendental illusion'. For while the applicability of the conceptual components of mathematics and physics to the world may be confirmed in the coherent intermingling of concept and intuition in experience, for Kant, claims about the general structure of reality in ontology, or, for example, the existence and nature of God and the soul in special metaphysics, possess no corresponding objects in any possible experience.

'Concepts without intuitions are empty' (*Critique of Pure Reason*, A52/B76); Kant has already limited possible intuitions, that is, immediate relations to particular objects, to such as are empirical and mediated by the forms of time and space. The so-called 'dogmatic' metaphysics, that claims to uncover truths that transcend empirical intuitions, is thus discounted, indeed, it is 'a mere grasping amongst concepts.' The traditional contingency argument, for example, that the world is contingent, all contingent things have a cause, and which proceeds through various other premises to the conclusion that the cause of the world must be a necessary being, is discounted by Kant's critical philosophy because 'the world' as the totality of existing things is not an object of experience; moreover, the concept of a cause has no application beyond objects of possible experience, and the idea of a cause of the totality of the world as a whole is thus unintelligible; moreover, the concept of necessity is derived solely from experience, and to try and redefine it outside the bounds of experience – which, as Kant has already decided, can only be of that which pertains to the empirical – is meaningless. The entirety of traditional metaphysics is thus discounted because of Kant's assumptions about understanding and sensibility, and his assumptions about appearance and reality that are consequences of those initial assumptions. In the process of becoming putatively 'real' vehicles of knowledge, mathematics and physics in Kant's hands have become mere sciences of 'appearances'; of course, the possibility of traditional metaphysics, which is definitionally opposed to any notion of being a mere 'science of appearances', is ruled out a priori.

The conclusion that synthetic a priori propositions in metaphysics are impossible – that is, that the real extension of human knowledge via metaphysical demonstration as traditionally understood is impossible – once again turns out to be founded on several of Kant's unproved assumptions which are consequences of those already discussed, most foundationally, that which states that (as the Kantian scholar W.H. Walsh has expressed it) if a proposition purports to be *both factual and non-empirical*, it cannot be true. This is founded on the notion that factual propositions are only such propositions as state a fact of *empirical* experience, that is, the synthesis of sensibility and understanding, as defined by Kant. As Walsh pointed out in his 1939 article, 'Kant's Critique of Metaphysics', this assertion of Kant's is 'unduly dogmatic'. Walsh lists several propositions promulgated by Kant, such a 'there are categories' and 'sense and thought co-operate in knowledge', that both purport to be facts, and must be *a priori* according to Kant's own logic, even though they are undoubtedly non-empirical. Moreover, Kant's assumption rests 'on a *dogmatic* denial of the very thing metaphysics claims–that the senses are not the only source of knowledge.'

> Though all empirical propositions are factual, there is no reason in principle why all factual propositions should be empirical, in the sense of based on sense-experience. For it might be the case that we had some other source of information than the senses, and if we thus had insight into an intelligible world, we could assert propositions about it.[87]

Apart from the many unproven assumptions that constitute the foundation of Kant's critical project, then, there are several instances of what appear to be formal inconsistencies in Kant's first critique; one of the most famous is the question of how things in themselves can be known to have a causal relationship in bringing about the affectivity of the knowing subject in sensation, when this implies the very application of the concept of cause *beyond* possible experience, by which Kant justi-fies his censure of traditional metaphysics. Yet in his later book, *Kant's Criticism of Metaphysics*, Walsh points out perhaps the most glaring in-consistency in all of Kant's work:

> By an elaborate argument Kant seeks to establish that we can have knowledge in some areas and not in others. We can have knowledge in mathematics, pure and applied; we can arrive, in science and in daily life, at many different kinds of truth about things phenomenal ... What we cannot do is know what lies beyond the bounds of possible experience. All our knowledge is ultimately rooted in intuitions as well as concepts, and the only form of intuition available to us is sense-intuition. It follows that knowledge, in its human form at least, is basically bound to sense. But what of the claim that it is? Is that supposed to represent a bit of sense-knowledge?[88]

In the language of our own study, were he to have been fully consist-ent, Kant would have had to have faced the vexed question of whether or not his own theory, that we cannot know things as they are, corresponds to things as they are, to *nafs al-amr*, or not. If it does not, he has wasted volumes of intricate argumentation on a theory he knows to be false. And if it does, then he has achieved the very non-empirical knowledge of things as they are that it has been the purpose of his entire project to prove impossible, which, in its absurdity, also entails the falsity of his point of view.[89] But of course, Kant never confronted this problem.

> How shall we mark off this knowledge of 'reality' which is legitimate from other purported knowledge of the same general kind which is not? How shall we avoid admitting the main results of the Analytic are arrived at by a species of intel-lectual insight which they themselves claim to be unavailable to human beings? It is to say the least unfortunate that Kant does not address himself to these and similar questions.[90]

Kant's subjectivizing project falls victim, then, to the dogmatism of its assumptions, and the inconsistency of its application of its own princi-ples. Although the a priori Categories are not entirely unlike the 'general concepts' or 'transcendentals', the *umūr al-ʿamma*, in that they constitute the universal concepts that necessarily condition all objects of experience, they are in a considerably more important way very much unlike the *umūr al-ʿāmma* in that they do not uncover an underlying intelligible structure of reality; they merely project the structure of our subjective perception onto a world that we cannot truly cognize, precisely because of the shadow that they have cast. The truth, however, is that 'concepts' *are* themselves objects, albeit the mere 'outward tips' of intelligible objects; moreover, in so far as they are also effects, they are able, via the henological intuition, to unveil these exemplary objects, that constitute their necessary substrata. When we perceive the particular, we *are* intuiting the underlying form that renders the particular intelligible, as well as the principles constituting the ontological framework for the appearance of *any* instantiation of a species, concepts that themselves possess prior exemplary realities and are ultimately rooted in the Divine Attributes.

That a particular is intuited directly in sensation, despite being stripped of the species-nature and the *umūr ʿāmma* and superordinate principles that have brought it into relief as a distinct entity, cannot stand up to scrutiny. Intuition (construed as the direct relation of the knowing subject to the fundamental constituents of reality) is fundamentally 'intellectual' (in a sense that embraces the 'spiritual'). Existences are variously distinct but unindividuated, or distinct *and* individuated, but all are *distinct* and therefore subsistent. Both forms of object are intellectually intuited 'before' they can (in the case of physically individuated beings) be sensed. The distinction between intuition and concept, as framed by Kant, is thus false. Although doubtless, *facile* parallels with altogether different philosophical contexts must be avoided at all costs, at risk of anachronism, there is also an unavoidable extent to which quite different philosophical frameworks correspond, to a lesser or greater degree, to *nafs al-amr*, and thus possess a sufficient degree of commensurability to make comparisons genuinely fruitful; and indeed Kant's insight that 'pure' *thought* cannot achieve a great deal on its own without adequate 'matter' is far more satisfactorily framed by Ibn ʿArabī, in his distinction between the receptive and discursive intellects that we have already seen, in which such 'matter' can involve revealed and mystical truths, alongside those yielded by sense.

In every cognition we stand in direct relation to restricted being, which is only cognizable and ontologically possible because of its principle of unity, a superordinate degree of unrestricted being (not restricted, at least, in the manner in which the subordinate degree is restricted); our direct relation to restricted being is, in fact, a direct relation to unrestricted being via the conditions of the intelligibility of that restricted being; and indeed through restricted being, we come into contact with exemplary beings of a lesser restrictedness, which possess a closer relationship to pure unrestricted being; and this does not merely constitute blind inference from effect to cause, 'a mere grasping amongst concepts', but entails direct experience every step of the way. But we will pursue all of these contentions further in Chapter 4.

The naturalizing epistemological trajectory of Western thought, then, from Duns Scotus to Ockham, and on to later Western empiricism, reached a critical juncture in the thought of Kant. Knowledge was first terrestrialized; then it was made into the sole reality, or denied altogether; but let us return now to theories of the ontological ground of truth, from the Islamic world.

Fakhr al-Dīn al-Rāzī, a contemporary of Averroes, would in that Islamic world go on to prove a far more influential philosopher than the Andalusian sage (although, conversely, Rāzī was himself effectively unknown in the West). An eminent Avicennan student and critic, Rāzī recognized the difficulties presented by abstract objects because of his familiarity with Avicenna's demonstration of mental existence, which he initially appears to accept in his *al-Mabāḥith al-mashriqiyya*.[91] The tensions created by these difficulties would prove instrumental to the development of his highly influential and original treatments of truth. Although he does not use the actual term *nafs al-amr* in the following excerpts, Rāzī is nonetheless directly answering the question of what is it that grounds the apparatuses of our cognition – and what it is that thereby guarantees their 'truth', and their utilization in true propositions. In his vast commentary on the *Ishārāt*, the theory is a mere suggestion, meant to form part of his attempt to undermine the theory of 'mental existence' *al-wujūd al-dhihnī*, a doctrine that he seems to have opposed throughout his post-*Mabāḥith* career.[92] In the *Mulakhkhaṣ*, his theory is more clearly defined than in the *Sharḥ al-ishārāt*:

> we know by necessity that awareness (*al-shuʿūr*) cannot become actualized except when a specific relation obtains between the one who has the awareness (*al-shāʿir*) and the thing that

he is aware of (*al-mash'ūr bihi*); [we also know by necessity] that relations do not become actualized except via [the actualization of] the two relata (*al-mutaḍāyifayn*). Moreover, a thing can either know itself, or something other than itself. If it knows itself, it is impossible for this knowledge to become actualized while the object of knowledge does not exist in particularized essences (*al-a'yān*). One's [own] existence, then, must [itself] be sufficient for this knowledge to become actualized. When one knows something other than oneself, one is also able to come to know this thing, which is other than oneself, when it is not directly present to one (*ma'a 'adamihi fī al-ḥuḍūr*). It must then have some other form of subsistence. Those who affirm the existence of mental forms assert that they are impressed in the mind, but we assert, in accordance with Imām Plato's position,[93] that they are self-subsistent Ideas (*wa naḥnu athbatnāhā muthulan qā'imatan bi-anfusihā 'alā qawli al-Imām Aflāṭūn*) ... this is the conclusion I have come to on this topic, after thorough and impartial investigation.[94]

Imām Rāzī's theory arose as a way of accounting for abstract objects. The classic proof for mental existence (*al-wujūd al-dhihnī*)[95] states that there must be an *ontological* basis for our intellection of distinct, abstract entities, which have no extramental existence. These – universal essences, forms recalled in their distinctness in the imagination, and second intelligibles, to take just a few examples – are concepts the ontological statuses of which cannot be ignored, if we are to be able to take at all seriously the notion that the exercise of the sciences leads to objective knowledge, because the functioning of the sciences is entirely contingent upon the ability of these entities to represent the intelligible features of things as they are in themselves. The argument for *al-wujūd al-dhihnī* is that these concepts must enjoy some form of existence, because one cannot 'relate' mentally to something which had no form of existence whatever. Since these concepts do not exist in the world of extramental particulars, they must actually *exist* in the mind.[96] Rāzī does agree with this basic rationale:

if the non-existent entity that is the object of knowledge had no form of subsistence whatsoever, despite the fact that we can distinguish it from that which is other than it, something which is absolutely nothing (*al-ʿadam al-ṣirf*), would be distinct [in itself], such that were [the non-existent thing] to come to exist, it would add nothing [to it], and that is absurd.[97]

The allegedly absolutely non-existent thing is already distinct in itself (which implies its subsistence), and yet in the interests of consistency, because we have stipulated its absolute nothingness, were existence to be superadded to it, no distinct existent thing would obtain, because adding 'existence' to nothing in particular is to cause to exist precisely nothing. In other words, mental entities, which are 'non-existent' in extramental particulars, must nonetheless possess some form of subsistence, because they are distinct, both in themselves and with respect to other such entities. 'Genus' and 'differentia', the universals 'man' and 'horse', the intelligible entities 'unity' and 'possibility' and indeed the fictional objects 'phoenix' and 'unicorn', each have distinct mental forms,[98] and are distinct from one another (unity is *not* possibility, the phoenix is *not* the unicorn). This distinctness must have some form of ontological basis. This is because distinct forms can only be distinct if they possess some form of differentiated being in themselves, that gives rise to their distinctness in cognition; otherwise, the distinctness that 'they' enjoy would be inexplicable. In stating his line of reasoning above, Rāzī has employed a famous argument, associated especially with the Muʿtazila, namely that all non-existent entities are distinct, all distinct things possess subsistence, and that therefore non-existent entities possess subsistence.[99] While opposed by the early Ashʿarīs (who claimed that non-existent 'entities' are 'pure nothingness' (*al-ʿadam al-ṣirf*),[100] modified forms of the argument became widely accepted, utilized by later *kalām* theologians in support of such arguments as those for realism about intelligible entities in the contexts of *wujūd dhihnī* and *nafs al-amr*.[101]

Where Rāzī does *not* agree with the Avicennans, however, is that such entities are in their *fundamental* reality mental, or that sheer mentality can constitute a guarantor of the reliable intelligibility of the distinctness of intelligible entitites. Instead, these entities exist distinctly in 'extramental' reality:

> mental forms only constitute sound intellections if they correspond to the extramental world, and this can only occur if

there is something subsisting in the extramental world [that they correspond to].[102]

Although Rāzī's theory was not widely adopted in *kalām*, in its specific conclusion affirming the existence of separate, self-subsistent uninstantiated Ideas or Forms,[103] it was to become hugely influential in framing the general problematics surrounding 'abstract', intelligible entities. In its exemplarist approach, it also foretokens the approach adopted by the school of Ibn 'Arabī, and later integrated into a higher *kalām*. Rāzī's 'Forms', however, would appear to be in some sense 'self-subsistent', whereas the ultimate Akbarian exemplars arise directly from the Divine Names and Attributes.[104]

This position, which would go on to be widely seen as the experientially and critically verified *taḥqīq* of the question of the ultimate nature of *nafs al-amr*, and the details of which will be explored in some detail in Chapter 4, has its origins in the work of Ibn 'Arabī. Although in the work of the Greatest Master, the problem had not yet been framed in the way it came to be by Ṭūsī, namely, as the answer to the question of what true propositions ultimately *correspond* to, Ibn 'Arabī seems to have been the first writer to identify 'things as they are in themselves' with an ontological realm, namely the distinct non-existent entities in the Divine knowledge.

> Things – that is, possibles, are, in their state of non-existence, distinct in their entities. God, transcendently glorified be He, knows them as they are in themselves (*'alā mā hiya 'alayhi fī nafsihā*) and He sees them and commands them to be existentiated, that is, to exist, and they come into existence at His command. The [knowledge] that is with God is not general, just as the particularized essences of possible beings are not general; rather, in itself and in God's knowledge, all is detailed (*kulluhu fī nafsihi wa fī 'ilm Allāh mufaṣṣal*). It is only with us that this generalized [knowledge] obtains.[105]

Ibn 'Arabī's 'things as they are in themselves' encompass all things – even extramental particulars as they are in their particularized modes of being (namely, that of being temporal, extramental particulars), not only as they are in themselves, in the strict sense of the ultimate, atemporal, eternal essences from which all the 'particularized' modes of their existence are derived. This is because His knowledge is as detailed as are all of His objects of knowledge in each of their various modes of individuated being. Yet His knowledge of essences also possesses dimensions of depth that far transcend those of their individuated manifestations. This point is special to theories of *nafs al-amr* that later arise from the school of Ibn ʿArabī, and contributes centrally to their unique ability to provide all forms of extramental and mental entities an *ultimate* grounding in being.

Writing in the generation after al-Rāzī and Ibn ʿArabī, the philosopher, theologian, astronomer and anti-Rāzian polemicist Naṣīr al-Dīn al-Ṭūsī seems, as we have already noted, to have been the first to have formulated an explicit, ontological theory of *nafs al-amr*, specifically as representing the truthmaking domain that causes, in so far as true judgements correspond to that domain, the truth of true judgements. His positive identification of the objects of non-sensible knowledge with a specific level in the gradation of being, an actual *world* of truth beyond the phenomenal world, is strikingly similar to Rāzī's formulations in the *Sharḥ al-Ishārāt* and the *Mulakkhaṣ*, with which Ṭūsī was so intimately familiar.

Ṭūsī is however a dyed-in-the-wool Avicennan, firmly set against any notion of 'Platonic' Forms, and so for him, it must be the Agent Intellect[106] that takes up this truthmaking mantle – it is their correspondence to the Agent Intellect that renders true mental propositions 'true'. Ṭūsī elaborates this theory in his treatise *Establishing the Existence of the Separate Intellect* (*Ithbāt al-ʿaql al-mufāriq*); according to al-Ṭūsī, the intelligibles must be impressed in some extramental yet incorporeal entity, in which the changeless intelligibles are contained *bi al-fiʿl* (*in effectu*). Since Ṭūsī's argumentation is pivotal to later discussions, (despite the fact that his precise conclusion was almost universally rejected), it is important that we look at his intriguing argumentation in relative detail. His argument might be paraphrased in the following way.

Premise 1: We have no doubt that the apodictic judgements made by our intellects correspond to that which is in *nafs al-amr*, and we know that those believed by the ignorant do not correspond to *nafs al-amr*. P2: We know moreover that correspondence cannot obtain except between two entities that are distinct with respect to individuation, but united with respect to that shared factor due to which correspondence is able to take place. P3: We know that true and false propositions are equivalent in sharing in mental existence. Conclusion 1: Therefore, true propositions, but not false propositions, must possess a form of subsistence external to our minds, namely, *nafs al-amr*, to which correspond true propositions existing in our minds. P4: This extramentally subsistent entity is either self-subsistent, or impressed in something else. P5: Entities which are subsistent extramentally either possess physical position (*waḍʿ*), or do not. P6: The first alternative (that is, the possession of physical position) is impossible, because those judgements do not pertain to any particular direction, nor a particular time, whereas everything that has a physical position necessarily pertains to these. P7: Their being self-subsistent is also impossible, because it is tantamount to upholding the reality of the Platonic Forms. C2: Therefore, these judgements are impressed in something that has no physical position. P8: The entity wherein the judgements are impressed cannot be merely potential, because correspondence between that which is actual or is capable of becoming actual, and that which is merely potential, is impossible. P9: Moreover, this entity cannot disappear, change, or move from potency to act, for the subsistence of judgements impressed within it is necessary in beginningless and endless eternity, and their substrate must be likewise. C3: Therefore, a self-subsistent thing exists extramentally, with no physical position, that contains all intelligibles *in effectu*. However, C4: 'that existent [entity] cannot be the First of all "firsts", that is, the Being Who is Necessary in His Essence, glorious are His Names, and this is due to P10: the fact that that entity must contain an actually infinite multiplicity; and P11: It is impossible that the First of all "firsts" contain multiplicity within Himself.' C5: We call this self-subsistent thing, which exists extramentally, with no physical position, and that contains all intelligibles *in effectu, al-ʿaql al-kull*.[107]

Despite the power and undoubted perspicacity of many of its premises, the specific conclusion was, again, not generally well received. The first to raise serious objections was al-Ṭūsī's own student, al-Ḥillī, which he tells us he raised with his teacher directly. Discussing the notion that true mental propositions correspond not to their mental existence itself, but to something beyond this, Ḥillī says in his commentary on Ṭūsī's *Tajrīd al-iʿtiqād*,

> During some of my sessions benefitting from [al-Ṭūsī], this point came up, and I asked him the meaning of their[108] saying that true mental judgements are [only true] in so far as they correspond to *nafs al-amr* – but that by *nafs al-amr* either mental subsistence or subsistence in extramental particu-

lars [and nothing else] is understood – [this] given that he [al-Ṭūsī] had rejected [the correspondence of mental judgements] to either category in this part [of the *Tajrīd*]. He said 'by *nafs al-amr*, the Agent Intellect is meant. Every form or judgement that subsists in the mind and that corresponds to a form impressed in the Agent Intellect is true, and if it does not [correspond to a form in the Agent Intellect] it is false.' I then brought up the fact that one of the implications [of the Avicennan theory] that the philosophers [are compelled to accept] is false judgements being impressed in the Agent Intellect. This is because they sought proof for the [existence of the] Agent Intellect by pointing out the difference between failing to recall and actually forgetting, because failing to recall is the intelligible form being lost to the cognizing substance and its being impressed in its repository, whereas forgetting is its being lost to both of them. Now, this argument comes off regarding sensible forms, but the cause of forgetting when it comes to intelligible [forms] is the cessation of the [relevant] capacity, resultant of the cessation of that which gives rise to knowledge, this in conceptions and assents. Both of these circumstances, [that is, in conceptions and assents pertaining to non-sensible, intelligible forms], are exposed by false judgements. He [Ṭūsī] had no convincing response to this.[109]

Ḥillī's argument is that false judgements are just as liable to be unremembered, and then to newly appear, as true judgements. This appearance must be ascribed to the activity of the Agent Intellect, because such judgements, though false, are still intelligible, and the Agent Intellect is the source and guarantor of intelligibility. Thus, maintaining that the Agent Intellect is *nafs al-amr* involves the same problem as positing that it is the mind, for the Agent Intellect and the mind are both host to false propositions, just as much as they are to true propositions. The Agent Intellect's status as *nafs al-amr*, as the ontological guarantor of the truth of true propositions, is thus rendered highly questionable, because the original argument for the Agent Intellect dictates that false propositions must also have corresponding forms in the Agent Intellect; thus, if correspondence to the Agent Intellect entails truth, false propositions must all be true, which is absurd.

Early Ottoman philosophers like the Akbarian Dāwūd al-Qayṣarī also raised serious objections to this type of theory, although often for reasons distinct from al-Ḥillī's. Important later thinkers, like al-Sayyid al-Sharīf al-Jurjānī, Ibn Turka (d. 835/1432), Ibn Bahā'uddīn, Ibrahim Kūrānī (d. 1101/1690), Abū Thanā' al-Ālūsī and others, adopted the alternative to the Agent Intellect (the Akbarian 'Immutable Archetypes') suggested to them by Qayṣarī, the exposition of whose pivotal theory will occupy much of Chapter 4. One of the greatest philosophical theologians of the fourteenth century, Sa'd al-Dīn al-Taftāzānī, would also write against al-Ṭūsī's theory – we will consider his theory in Chapter 3. The notion that *nafs al-amr* is the Agent Intellect was also rejected by 'Alā'uddīn al-Ṭūsī (d. 877/1473) in his *Kitāb al-dhakhīra*,[110] and later by Mīr Zāhid, in his commentary on Quṭb al-Dīn al-Rāzī's (d. 766/1365) *al-Risāla al-ma'mūla*.[111] Taşköprüzade uniquely followed *both* Qayṣarī and the post-Rāzian *kalām* theologians just mentioned, in his rejection of Ṭūsī's theory. In the interests of intellectual precision and not necessarily because he endorsed the theory, the renowned Jalāl al-Dawānī did at least come to al-Ṭūsī's aid about al-Ḥillī's objection, in a manner which convincingly renders Ṭūsī's theory consistent,[112] but the identification of *nafs al-amr* with the Agent Intellect never became a popular answer to the question of the identity of 'things as they are.' Most fundamentally, this was due to difficulties that had their roots in serious errors, diagnosed by later thinkers, in some of Ṭūsī's metaphysical presuppositions, particularly those pertaining to his assumptions about the Divine knowledge in P11 above.[113]

Taftāzānī, who represents the tendency to reduce the question of *nafs al-amr* to its epistemological dimension,[114] seems to have been the first thinker in the broadly Peripatetic (*mashshā'ī*)[115] tradition to have formulated a credible alternative to Ṭūsī's theory. We will meet with his theory in some detail at the beginning of Chapter 3. Yet it was in the developed ontology of the school of Ibn 'Arabī – which because of its frequent ability to find answers to previously intractable problems, revolutionized Islamic thought – that a more enduring answer was found. It is this answer which forms the central topic of this study (particularly its culmination in Chapter 4), and which, we contend, constitutes the most explanatorily powerful of all theories of *nafs al-amr*, and the least susceptible to sceptical challenges. Certainly in Islamic history, the answer ultimately attributable to Ibn 'Arabī would become *the* solution to the difficult problem of the ontological guarantor of knowledge, and the case of *nafs al-amr* would prove another of the positions adopted (or at least very seriously considered) by the scholarly establishments in the Ottoman and Mughal periods because of the direct influence of the Akbarian school.[116] The Ottoman savant Taşköprüzade's (d. 968/1562) sophisticated *kalām* formulation of the Akbari doctrine (which forms one of the centrepieces of this monograph) was part of a larger synthesis that we are still at the very beginning of being able to understand, but that may well prove the defining intellectual characteristic of later Islam. Some of the greatest thinkers of the later period of Ottoman and Mughal Islam, like Ibn Baha'uddīn, Ibrāhīm Kūrānī, Gelenbevi, Abū al-Thanā' al-Ālūsī, and 'Abd al-'Aliyy Baḥr al-'Ulūm contributed significantly to *nafs al-amr* theory, most of them working within the rubrics of broadly Akbarian conceptual tropes. In this later period, this often involved a tendency to explain the Akbarian view through common Avicennan and *kalām* concepts. Kūrānī, for example, discusses his theory of *nafs al-amr* in the context of the Avicennan notions of restrictively conditioned (*bi sharṭ shay'*), unconditioned (*lā bi sharṭ shay'*) and negatively conditioned (*bi sharṭ lā*) quiddities.[117] Similarly, Ālūsī shows the direct pertinence of *nafs al-amr* to the question of the subsistence of non-existent entities, a philosophical point of contention since the age of the Mu'tazila, (the question of whether 'non-existent entities are "things"', *al-ma'dūm shay' am lā*, that we have alluded to above).

We have now briefly considered some of the most general, overarching themes informing the history of the notion of 'objective truth' and of *nafs al-amr* more specifically. Although the details are complex, it might nonetheless be possible to simply reduce these to a fundamental difference of opinion about how broad our notion of reality should be. Is it limited to particularized, individual reality informed by solely immanent intelligible forms, as in the broadly Peripatetic view, and if so, how are we to account for entities that do not seem to fit into this framework, and yet are indispensable to science and to the coherence of our view of the world? Or alternatively, is it in fact the case that 'uninstantiated' exemplary forms – that is, distinct in themselves, but not instantiated as particulars – underlie the immanent manifestations of these forms in phenomenal reality, and thereby make possible a credible account of an ultimate ontological groundedness that must be possessed by abstract, universal and other metaphysical entities? In the coming sections and chapters, we will present some of the logical and metaphysical apparatuses that we will need to be able to wield, in order to properly understand and explore this fundamental tension, as well as to defend what we will argue are the most developed and successful theories concerning the actual identity of *nafs al-amr*.

2.3 *Logical, Epistemological, and Metaphysical Propaedeutics*

2.3.1 THE PREDICATIVE SCOPE OF *NAFS AL-AMR*

Al-Sayyid al-Sharīf al-Jurjānī beautifully epitomized *nafs al-amr*'s central logical dimension in his *Critical Verification of [the Meaning of] Things as They Are In Themselves (Risāla fī taḥqīq nafs al-amr)*. We have already alluded to his alignment with the Akbarian tradition as regards the ultimate identity of *nafs al-amr*. Yet in this short treatise, *The Meaning of Things as They Are In Themselves*, he is primarily writing in his very formidable capacity as a logician. However, although his intention is to illustrate points which are fundamentally logical in character – particularly the question of predicative scope – a number of metaphysical insights cannot help but shine through. In what follows, we will attempt to draw these out, in order to demonstrate the logical basis of certain properly metaphysical concepts that we will be treating later. Al-Sharīf al-Jurjānī first contrasts the real entities in *nafs al-amr* with 'suppositions'.

> Know that the actualization (*taḥaqquq*)[118] of things is either
> as intellectual supposition (*farḍ ʿaqlī*) – and these are what
> exist only in the faculty of cognition (*al-quwwa al-darrāka*)
> or 'real' (*ḥaqīqī*), and these obtain outside of the faculty of
> cognition, regardless of whether the supposition is [also] to
> be found [affixed to it] or not. These are those which are said
> to exist in things as they are in themselves (*fī nafs al-amr*).[119]

While a supposition may pertain to something existing in *nafs al-amr*, with respect to itself, that something nonetheless continues to exist, regardless of whether or not the supposition continues to accompany it. 'Black, negatively conditioned' (*bi sharṭ lā*), that is the pure quiddity of black in itself, on the condition that it is considered completely separately from its possible or actual instantiation in any individual or instance in a mind, represents a *farḍ ʿaqlī* that exists only in the mind (in fact, as we will see in Section 4.4, in its standard, non-Akbarian construal, only the *idea* of *al-māhiyya bi sharṭ lā* exists in the mind, and not the *māhiyya bi sharṭ lā* itself, because according to its own stipulation, it must be without reference to a mind – in this sense, it thus represents a very eminent example of a *farḍ ʿaqlī*). A different example of a *farḍ ʿaqlī*, similar to one that Jurjānī will soon proceed to supply, could be represented by 'The possible instance of black that does not exist in extramental particulars'. This is a combinatorial concept, that exists only in *al-quwwa al-darrāka*, and which like 'black negatively conditioned', is thoroughly mind-dependent. 'Black' however, continues to exist as it is in itself, as do the rest of the elements that have rendered these combinatorial concepts intelligible. The actualization of the suppositional concept is contingent upon the act of conceiving the 'supposition'; conversely, the *elements* of the proposition enjoy 'real' actualization (*taḥaqquq ḥaqīqī*) in themselves.

Having made this apparently simple point, Jurjānī quickly dispels any false implication the reader might infer from this distinction between suppositional and real actualization. The possible misunderstanding is to think that what we usually associate with 'outside of the mind' is limited to the sensible world of individuated entities. In fact, there is more than one ontological mode of 'real actualization'. This is to say that entities capable of being 'pointed out' (in the most familiar cases, 'physically' pointed out), namely, individual entities, by no means enjoy reality to the exclusion of entities of a different order.

> [Entities with] real [actualization] are either so with respect to themselves, or with respect to the objective realm outside of themselves, which is called 'extramental particulars' (*al-khārij*). Now, things as they are in themselves (*nafs al-amr*) exists outside of the faculty of cognition, but is of wider predicative scope (*aʿamm*) than the realm of extramental particulars, and extramental particulars than the mind, but in a different sense [to the usual],[120] namely that it is true in the realm of extramental particulars (*yaṣduq fī al-khārij*) that 'that which exists in the mind' exists in the mind, but not [true] that it exists in extramental particulars.

That is, since individual minds are individuated (and therefore exist in extramental particulars),[121] that which exists in the mind exists in a mind which is *in* extramental particulars, but – and this is the crucial point – that which *itself* exists in the mind - that is, has the mind as its proximate locus (such as purely abstract concepts) – does not *itself* exist *in* extramental particulars. Relations, to give a type of example that we have already discussed, exist in the mind, and do not exist as extramental particulars, yet *it is nonetheless true*, in the realm of extramental particulars, that they exist in the mind.[122]

In its metaphysical application, this subtle formulation is exceedingly fruitful in drawing our attention to the fact that the proximate locus of first principles, second intelligibles and other abstract mental concepts, can be considered quite independently of *al-khārij*. This in turn strongly suggests the existence of a distinct ontological substratum able to account for the existence and truth-value of these types of non-*khārijī* entities, and that can moreover account for the fact that they can be employed in scientific activity, and, indeed, meaningfully spoken about at all. After all, how is it that we can meaningfully speak 'about' an entity that does not exist in extramental particulars, if our definition of existence is strictly limited to existence in extramental particulars? Such entities must enjoy some form of independent being other than *khārijī* existence, which is ordinarily time and space bound,[123] and this form of being must also be something that transcends individual minds, since individual minds cannot account for the evident truth-value of these types of non-*khārijī* entities. Although in this logical context Jurjānī is not ontologically committed (unlike in the Akbarian definition of *nafs al-amr* that he offers in his *Taʿrīfāt*), he goes on to expand further the implications of *nafs al-amr* being of 'wider predicative scope' than *al-khārij*, in a way that further illustrates the distinction between extramental particulars and a thing as it is in itself.

> If things in themselves is of wider predicative scope than extramental particulars, then whenever something is true in extramental particulars, it is also true in things as they are in themselves. For example, if it is true that bodies are composite in extramental particulars, then it is also true that they are composite in the realm of things as they are in themselves. However, if [a thing] is true in things as they are in themselves, in the sense that in itself it is a certain way, yet it does not exist in extramental particulars, [the appropri-

ate proposition] will not be true in the realm of extramental particulars. This is because a thing that does not exist in extramental particulars cannot be characterized by any properties *therein*; however, it may well be [characterized by those properties] with respect to itself. For it is true that [a particular mental instance of] 'black' that does not happen to exist in extramental particulars is [nonetheless] in itself a colour, yet it is not true that it is a colour in the realm of extramental particulars.

Here, in order to illustrate the distinction between *al-khārij* and *nafs al-amr*, Jurjānī elegantly utilizes an example that would seem on the face of it to belong firmly to '*al-khārij*': a colour. It would *not* be true, in an 'extramental-particular proposition' (*qaḍiyya khārijiyya*), that an imagined instance of black, pictured mentally, is itself 'black in the realm of extramental particulars', yet *it is* black 'in itself'. Indeed, basic truths about 'black', such as 'black is a colour', are to be made without any specific reference to any *individual* instances of black in the realm of extramental particulars – their epistemological justification lies rather in things as they are in themselves.

This is in affirmative judgements; conversely, in negative judgements the realm of things in themselves is of narrower predicative scope (*akhaṣṣ*) than the realm of extramental particulars. For if it is true in the realm of things as they are in themselves that black is not white, it is [necessarily also] true in extramental particulars, but not *vice versa*, like in the case of '[this instance of] blackness is not a colour' being true in the realm of extramental particulars, in the event that that [particular instance of] blackness does not [in fact] exist in extramental particulars, whereas this [proposition] is not true in the realm of things as they are in themselves.[124] This fact obtains in accordance with the principle that you know well, which is that the contradictory of that which is of wider predicative scope[125] is of narrower predicative scope than the contradictory of that which is of narrower predicative scope.[126]

An imagined colour is not a colour in extramental particulars, although it would be false to say that it is not a colour in *nafs al-amr*. A smaller number of negative propositions are true in *nafs al-amr* exactly because there are more objects in *nafs al-amr* than in extramental particulars, in that *nafs al-amr* surpasses *al-khārij* by containing non-*khārijī* entities about which it is possible to make true statements.

Al-Sharīf al-Jurjānī ends his short treatise by drawing the important conclusion that all scientific statements pertaining to entities of different types, that are not merely observational statements about the purely sensible features of individual instances thereof, pertain to beings *as they are in themselves*, not to their individuals *qua* individuals. Red is not a colour because the shirt belonging to John or Zayd is red, but their red shirts constitute instances of a colour because the universal judgement 'red is a colour' corresponds to things as they are.

> Now, the modalities that essences undergo, dependence, independence, concomitance, entailment, having accidents and essential properties and real and perspectival properties, only become actualized and known with respect to themselves (*bi ḥasabi anfusihā*) [that is, in terms of the realm of things as they are in themselves], and most mistakes [in the philosophical sciences] come about simply as a result of confusing the logical entailments of judgements related to things as they are in themselves for the logical entailments of judgements related to things in extramental particulars.

That 'man' is a species, for example, pertains to 'human being' in itself, not to individual human beings, for individual human beings are not 'species'. Individuals merely *partake* of second intelligible universal properties (like being a species) that characterize the essence in which they participate, *in itself*, and only from the perspective afforded by that participation – but not with respect to their specific individuality.

Understanding the meaning of *nafs al-amr*, Jurjānī says, is the fundamental *sine qua non* of philosophical competence – presumably because it involves the ability to distinguish between essential natures on the one hand, and accidental, perspectival and relational modifications post-individuation on the other. After an essence has become instantiated in an individual, many predicates that apply to the essence in *nafs al-amr* no longer apply to it *qua* individual. Zayd, for example, is not a universal, nor, as we have said, a species, although 'man' is. Moreover, an individual is subject to change; if Zayd loses his capacity to move, or feel or think, it makes no difference to the definition of 'rational animal', namely that a human being is capable of cognizing and manipulating intelligibles in a logically structured fashion (*nāṭiq*), and of experiencing sensations, and moving by volition (*ḥayawān*).

> Whoever masters the [distinctions] that we have here conveyed will find it easy to become acquainted with [philosophical] realities and subtleties. In fact, coming to intimate knowledge of the philosophical sciences without knowing [these distinctions] is effectively impossible. The meaning of the realm of things as they are in themselves and the distinction between it and the realm of extramental particulars has here been critically verified.

One of the metaphysical results implied by al-Sayyid al-Sharīf's short logical tract, is that there exist objective truths which are true without reference to the obtainment of a correspondent state of affairs in extramental particulars. *Nafs al-amr*, therefore, cannot be considered synonymous with *al-khārij*, but *al-khārij* is, as it were, contained within *nafs al-amr*. This means that it is not merely first intelligible judgements, such as 'this stone is white' – judgements both the subject and predicate of which have referents in extramental particulars – that are objectively true. Judgements made entirely without reference to extramental particulars possess truth value in themselves, and this includes diverse species of statements, like 'genus is a second intelligible', 'nothing comes from nothing', 'the phoenix is a mythical cyclically regenerated bird', 'abstract objects are distinct and therefore subsistent' and the example presented by al-Sayyid al-Sharīf, namely that every instance of black that does not exist in extramental particulars, and is thus not a colour therein, is nonetheless a colour in itself.

The importance of this apparently simple logical distinction – that *nafs al-amr* is of wider predicative scope than extramental particulars and yet encompasses extramental particulars – lies in the fact that it clears logical space for a science of metaphysical first principles that *govern* extramental particulars, whilst not being dependent thereupon. While these are certainly some of the metaphysical implications of the principles outlined in the treatise, Jurjānī's fundamentally logical treatment does not of course broach the question of the ontological statuses of these abstract propositions, entities and first principles at all, a question that we will be treating in Chapter 3 and especially Chapter 4. Ad interim, however, there is some further propaedeutic that requires investigation; namely, the metaphysical topic of real and relational quiddities, which brings into sharper relief the need for a theory of *nafs al-amr* able to account for certain special facts about even the world of everyday experience, and provides further evidence of the insufficiency of extramental particulars and the mind as complete guarantors of truth. Broadly, this amounts to the fact that the relationality of the world, that is, the relational framework and configuration, one thing to another, of that which constitutes 'the world', is inconceivable without this relationality having been defined in a prior level of intelligible being, and this is shown, as we will see, via the analogy of man-made objects.

2.3.2 REAL AND RELATIONAL COMPOSITE QUIDDITIES

In Chapter 1, we saw an almost universally accepted definition of the most rudimentary meaning of *nafs al-amr* as a universally employed term in the sciences – a thing itself, in itself (*nafs al-shay' fī ḥaddi dhātihi*). This definition would appear to be wholly valid for its own purposes, as a statement expressing the most general notion of a thing in its objective, putatively 'perspective-neutral' state of being, the thing as it is in itself. This definition does not answer, however, or even begin to broach the question of the ontological identity of *nafs al-amr*, although it is granted that there is nothing to prevent it being fully compatible with various such identifications, if and when they are made. Nonetheless, it faces yet further metaphysical difficulties. Certain of the results of the post-Avicennan, post-Rāzian treatments of the varieties of quiddity seem to make highly problematic this definition's stipulation that a 'thing as it is in itself' must not involve 'the perspective of a subject' – indeed they seem to question the very possibility of perspective-neutrality. In fact, in numerous cases a thing 'as it is in itself' *includes* the perspective of a subject, that is, that perspective forms *part* of the thing as it is in itself. This has important implications for the broadness of our notion of objective reality; it implies that there must be instances in which an objective state of affairs is *informed* by an apparently 'subjective' state of affairs. Before we proceed to explore the difficulties summoned up by such implications, let us look at our original definition again:

> [*Nafs al-amr*] means a thing itself, in itself (*ma'nāhu nafs al-shay' fī ḥaddi dhātihi*) and so were you to say that a thing exists in itself (*mawjūd fī nafs al-amr*), this would mean that its existence is not contingent on the perspective of a subject (*i'tibār mu'tabir*) or someone's supposition (*farḍi fāriḍ*), regardless of whether that supposition is fabricated [out of nothing], or has been abstracted [from extramental entities]; indeed, were any [attendant] hypothetical conceptions and mental perspectives to be ignored, the thing would still exist.[127]

As we have said, this standard basic definition faces considerable philosophical difficulties, raised by the notion of 'a thing itself, in itself', *irrespective of any knowing subject,* as well as the existence of certain entities that call into question the clause in this definition of *nafs al-amr* which states that *were any [attendant] hypothetical conceptions and mental perspectives to be ignored, the thing would still exist.* The transcendentals (*al-umūr al-'āmma*)[128] do not pose these difficulties; although being, individuation, quiddity, unity, possibility, causality and so on constitute the necessary conditions through which *the thing qua-existent* achieves actuality, these apply equally to all things, and do not constitute *parts* of particular essences. In order to exist, after all, an individual human being must be possible, participate in the quiddity 'human being', be individuated, constitute both an essential and individual unity, and be related to and embody various forms of causality. Yet none of these general concepts forms a part of the essence of 'human being'. Their 'perspectival' nature cannot thus pose a problem for this clause in our definition.

However, in the context of the main, post-Avicennan strand of later Islamic philosophy and metaphysical *kalām*, the tensions to which we are alluding do come into unmistakeable relief as soon as the distinctions between different types of composite quiddity (*al-māhiyya al-murakkaba*) are set out, as treated in the great books of post-Rāzian metaphysical *kalām*. In order to understand the difficulties posed by certain types of existent composite quiddities to the notion of a 'perspectiveless' essence, we must first determine what is meant by 'composite quiddity'; then, we will look at what it means for such a quiddity to have 'real composition'. This will enable us to discover the fact that although a very familiar category of quiddities possesses the surprising characteristic of being partially constituted by mental perspectives (*i'tibārāt dhihniyya*), they yet nevertheless exist in extramental particulars, and thus, in *nafs al-amr*. In turn, this fact will throw into question the apparently common-sense notion that the intelligibility of 'sensible' reality is always traceable to properties existing as particulars in 'concrete' physicality; indeed, it may even render such a notion untenable. This will provide crucial support for our main contention concerning the identity of *nafs al-amr*; that it is an actual realm of objective truth that constitutes the foundation and ground of the possibility of all human knowledge, and even for the intelligibility of the familiar concrete particulars of everyday sense experience.

Composite quiddities are to be contrasted with simple quiddities, namely those which, like 'unity' and 'existence', are not made up of parts. On an epistemological plane, this simplicity arises from the self-evidence of such concepts, as well as their (putative) irreducibility to better-known concepts, which makes them unsusceptible to necessarily multiplicitous 'essential' definition (*al-ḥadd*), via genus and differentia. On a straightforwardly ontological plane, their simplicity arises from their priority to all composite quiddities; the latter presuppose the existence of simple quiddities, as constituting the fundamental principles allowing them to arise. Composite quiddities, conversely, like 'body' and 'human being', are constituted by parts. That such quiddities in fact possess real parts is known via their evident participation, with quiddities other than themselves, in essential properties, whilst being distinct from those other quiddities with respect to other essential properties, or with respect to necessary concomitants of their quiddities.[129] A man and a parrot for example, clearly share in being 'sensitive growing bodies that move by volition' (*jism nāmī ḥassās mutaḥarrik bi al-irāda*) (the traditional definition of 'animal'). They are also distinct, however, in that man evinces a capacity to put abstract reasoning into practice, whereas parrots do not appear to share in having this capacity. Indeed, parrots have other essential properties, like the imitation of sounds including speech, but purely through imitation, and not as arising from an understanding of intelligibles, nor as an expression of rationality.[130] Evidently, then, both 'man' and 'parrot' must be composite, for they both possess an essential property in which they each participate, and another essential property which they do not both participate in.

'Unity' and 'existence', on the other hand, do share in, for example, the property of 'being an accident,' yet have distinct essences. This does not imply that they are composite, because unlike, for example, horses and human beings, they *do not* participate in essential properties, and then differ in other essential properties – the decisively indicative test of a thing's constituting a composite of real parts. Rather, they simply share in some accidental properties, while each constituting, in themselves, unique and distinct simple essences.[131]

Real composition (*al-tarkīb al-ḥaqīqī*) is the real interdependence of the parts of a quiddity; if one were to surgically attach a stone to a human being, no new essence would obtain, constituting a composite of a stone and a human being.[132] The material and formal elements of a tree, on the other hand, come together to make a single unitary reality. The existence of certain quiddities requires the real interdependence of the genus and differentia. The genus requires the differentia, because in itself the genus cannot be instantiated as an extramental individuated essence; 'before' this happens (of course, the 'process' is atemporal), it must be unified with the differentia, in order that it be actualized as a particular species and rendered subsistent.[133] After all, there is nothing in the individuated extramental world that is an animal but no particular species of animal; this general concept must be differentiated in order to be actualized, by differentia such as, perhaps, 'rational', or 'flying'. Although it is true that with respect to extramental particulars, the genus and differentia refer to a single entity, an intellectual distinction nonetheless exists between them, which is fully real, often because it arises from the extramental constituents of (for example) 'human being', in so far as those extramental constituents are analysable into 'matter' and 'form' – the genus corresponding to the physical substrate or 'matter', and the differentia to the distinguishing, essential nature or 'form' that informs that matter.[134]

In perspectival composition (*al-tarkīb al-i'tibārī*), however, (the opposite of 'real' composition) the parts that make up the quiddity in question do not depend upon one another in order to exist:

> [like] an army ... a multiplicity of elements that the mind considers to be one thing, even though they may not in reality be one thing ... one may give this a name ... [as constituting the name] of all of the individuals [of which it is composed] ... the

> configurational form (*al-ṣūra al-ijtimāʿiyya*) in perspectival
> composites (*al-murakkabāt al-iʿtibāriyya*) is purely a perspec-
> tival [entity] of the mind, which possesses no actualization
> (*taḥaqquq*) in individuated extramental existence, because
> the only elements of an 'army' that actually exist in individu-
> ated extramental existence are those individuals (that is, the
> individual soldiers) - this unlike in the case of real compos-
> ite [quiddities] (*al-murakkabāt al-ḥaqīqiyya*), for they have
> forms which effuse onto their *matter* in things as they are
> in themselves (*ṣuwar tufīḍu ʿalā al-mawād fī nafs al-amr*).[135]

Essential properties can have distinct *foundations* in the world of extramental particulars, such that they are separable, like a human being
– at death, the rational soul leaves the body, and the dead body remains
for a time, both of their existences continuing independently. Some essential properties, however, do not have extramental origins in the same
sense; whilst 'colour' serves as the genus of all of the sensible colours, it
is not an independently *sensible* quality, yet 'colour' itself is still distinct
in *nafs al-amr*. This is because mental differentiation *does* entail differentiation in *nafs al-amr*,[136] but not necessarily in extramental particulars.
On the other hand, although an 'army' does have an essential nature in
nafs al-amr, in extramental particulars there are only individual men;
the configurational form (*hayʾa ijtimāʿiyya*) that provides the army with
an intelligible unity is not abstracted from any specific extramental particular. In *nafs al-amr*, then, the individual soldiers in an army depend
upon one another in order for the actualization, with respect to *al-khārij*,
of an 'army' to take place; yet the individual soldiers do not depend upon
each other in order to exist themselves in extramental *particulars*, where
there are in any case only particular beings, and no armies as such. Thus,
individuals exist in extramental particulars and armies exist in *nafs al-
amr*, but human minds actualize concepts, such as 'army', that intelligibly
inform individuals existing in extramental particulars, such that it is as
if such concepts *do* have extramentally instantiated referents, and that
they do have 'forms which effuse onto their matter', when in fact strictly
speaking, they do not.

The most striking and significant example of this might be the cosmos or universe itself; for purposes of practicality, we might invoke a
fairly standard contemporary definition, namely 'all of existing matter

and space considered as a whole'. Yet this totality itself is surely not an individuated entity, but rather consists of the unimaginably vast array of individuated entities that we *consider* to be a whole (although we cannot *experience* the whole). Must we then conclude that the universe does not exist, since it does not exist *in al-khārij*? Surely not; although it is not a single individuated entity, we can certainly deduce that it exists in *nafs al-amr*. The same goes for countries, cities and groups of adherents of religions. Indeed, any of the 'relational' Categories not deemed to 'exist' in particulars (the position widely associated with *jumhūr al-mutakallimīn* is that these are the 'relational' Categories of quantity, relation, time, position, possession, action and affection)[137] exist in *nafs al-amr*, but not in *al-khārij*, despite being conditions of the intelligibility of *al-khārij*.

Another vital distinction to be made in the uncovering of the difficulties certain types of essences raise for the traditional definition of *nafs al-amr*, is the division of the constitutive parts of composite quiddities. These parts are either 'relational' (*iḍāfī*) – which is to say that their essence is to designate a particular type of relationship between two things – namely, that their constituent parts amount to relations[138] – or 'real' (*ḥaqīqī*), which is to say that their intellection does not involve any relation. These relational parts do not constitute distinct things 'in themselves', independent of other things, or irrespective of that relationship between the two parts that make up the quiddity. 'The nearest' (*al-aqrab*), a commonly cited example[139] of a relational composite universal quiddity, is not *wujūdī* in the metaphysical sense,[140] for relations are mind-dependent, although its constituents are *wujūdī* in the sense that their concepts do not involve negations (a specific logical sense of '*wujūdī*'). As al-Sayyid al-Sharīf al-Jurjānī says, its 'concept is a composite of "near" (*al-qurb*) and an augmentation (*ziyāda*) thereof, both of which are relational (*wa kilāhumā iḍāfiyān*).'[141]

With this example, we are ready to discern the main difficulties affecting Tahānawī's definition above, namely the notion that 'were you to say that a thing exists in itself (*mawjūd fī nafs al-amr*), this would mean that its existence is not contingent on the perspective of a subject (*i'tibār mu'tabir*)', as well as the stipulation that 'were any [attendant] hypothetical conceptions and mental perspectives to be ignored, the thing would still exist.' 'The nearest', to take one of our examples, is an objective concept that might be validly predicated of one individual in each of numerous possible sets of relations. Yet it is not predicable of an independent physical object. It is, rather, contingent upon both the relation of the object it describes to the object which that object is near to, and the relation of that nearness to the degree of nearness of at least one other object existing at some degree of proximity to it – a comparison which certainly depends upon the cognitive activity of a knowing subject in order to be actualized.

Even more clearly problematic for Tahānawī's definition would be a quiddity that *does* firmly exist in extramental particulars, but that is nonetheless contingent upon abstract entities for its actualization. An example under the rubric of real composite quiddities, but one which is a composite of real and relational elements,[142] is a 'bed' - a classic representative case. Elucidating the significance of these elements, al-Sharīf al-Jurjānī says,

> [a bed] is a composite of pieces of wood, which are individuated extramental entities, and of the particularized arrangement (*tartīb makhṣūṣ*) between them, in terms of the perspectival relationality of which, the bed is resultant - and this [latter component] is a relational entity, that is not independently intelligible (*lā yastaqill bi al-maʿqūliyya*).[143]

His teacher Mubārakshāh similarly tells us,

> 'real' parts, like the pieces of wood, are not sufficient to actualize the quiddity; rather, the particularized arrangement [of the wood] is necessary, which is a relational entity that does not of itself exist independently.[144]

In his supercommentary on the same page of *Ḥikmat al-ʿAyn*, Jurjānī comments,

> perhaps someone might bring up the objection that a bed is undoubtedly a substance. How then could a type of relation be taken to be [the determining factor] in that quiddity's actualization? For this entails that a substance be caused to subsist by an accident [which is impossible]. The answer to this is that it is [only] a substance being caused to subsist by an accident subsisting *within it* that is [in actual fact] impossible.

The white colour of a cat could not possibly have caused that cat to be instantiated; however, unlike the whiteness of a cat, the accident 'particularized arrangement' does not subsist 'within' a bed; rather, it constitutes the external cause of its actualization, which nonetheless constitutes a 'part' of the form that it gives rise to. The obtainment of this particularized arrangement is merely the occasion for the effusion of a form from *nafs al-amr* to become manifest through this composite, an effusion that ensures that it instantiates a single, individuated essence distinct from other essences. Yet how, again, can the evident fact that perspectival or partially perspectival entities–armies, beds, relations, events, groups of co-religionists, countries, intellectual schools of thought, and indeed, the very cosmos–are nonetheless objective, distinct entities, 'in *nafs al-amr*', be harmonized with Tahānawī's stipulations 'not contingent on the perspective of a subject (*i'tibār mu'tabir*)', and 'were any [attendant] hypothetical conceptions and mental perspectives to be ignored, the thing would still exist'?

In actual fact, all the foregoing has been leading up to a perhaps surprising conclusion, which is that Tahānawī's stipulation is perfectly sound. Yet this is only because thinkers working in the later, metaphysical *kalām*, such as Jurjānī and Taftāzānī, adopted a classificatory scheme which carefully made the crucial distinction between perspectival (*i'tibārī*) and relational (*iḍāfī*) concepts and judgements that are 'objective' in the sense of corresponding to *nafs al-amr*, and those that are purely subjective. It is only the latter that are precluded on Tahānawī's definition. This distinction was to become well-established in Islamic thought; in his famous supercommentary on the classic principles of jurisprudence (*uṣūl al-fiqh*) textbook, *Jam' al-jawāmi'*, for example, 'Abd al-Raḥmān ibn Jād Allāh al-Bannānī (d. 1198/1783), shows how intimately questions regarding perspectival entities are intertwined with those of *nafs al-amr*.

> It is established and well known that '*perspectival* entity' (*al-amr al-i'tibārī*) has two meanings. The first of them is 'something which possesses, regardless of anyone's perspective, actuality (*taḥaqquq*) in itself, but is not an extramental particular,' and the other is 'that which becomes actualized by means of someone's perspective; were this perspective to be disregarded, it would possess no actuality [at all].'[145]

Thus, certain types of 'perspectival' entities, while *constitutive* of human perspectives, in fact possess distinct actuality *in themselves*, regardless of anyone's perspective! Anyone passably familiar both with the developed, unreduced tradition of intellectual sciences (*'aqliyyāt*) in Islam, and with their modern, often radically simplified and truncated manifestations, will know that *kalām* can sometimes be proudly portrayed, particularly by some of its neo-advocates, as dismissing anything that is classed as *i'tibārī* –and that thereby falls off the edge of an austere 'objective' world populated solely by atom-substances and certain kinds of accidents – as 'subjective'. The most profound questions about the fundamental structure of reality are therefore liable to be passed over, in implicit favour of a linear, didactic natural theology that dismisses all metaphysics as dangerous but ultimately irrelevant.[146] It would be a great shame – indicative of the pervasiveness in philosophical history of a confusion of epistemology for ontology – if these great thinkers of the great age of *kalām*, utilizing this sophisticated language of the extramental individuated and the mind-dependent, were to be accused of relativizing the great majority of the world around us and dismissing it as 'perspectival' (and therefore not truly real),[147] simply because of their acknowledgement of the mental elements that inhere within it. Whereas it is true that thinkers using this language rightly question whether a quiddity's *relational* elements can in any real sense be said to *exist within* extramental particulars (*fi al-khārij*), it is difficult to see how anyone could doubt that they have a form of existence in *nafs al-amr*. The 'particularized arrangements' of our houses, for example, irrespective of whether we are always dwelling in them,[148] certainly seem to exist in some sense; yet at the same time, it is an unquestionable fact that relations *qua* relations cannot exist in extramental individuated form.[149] Taftāzānī's formulation of real composite [quiddities] (*al-murakkabāt al-ḥaqīqiyya*) as having 'forms which effuse onto their matter in things as they are in themselves' indicates a solution to this problem, for houses and beds are also 'real composite quiddities.'[150] However, the guarantor of their unquestionable objectivity seems to be neither *al-khārij* alone (because of the relational aspect of the quiddities) nor *al-dhihn* alone (because the 'particularized arrangement' of the individuated materials of the house or bed, really *has* become manifest 'out there'), but a combination of the two that simultaneously transcends them both[151] – *nafs al-amr*.

If such perspectival entities are to be reduced to their relationality and thus effectively made to disappear from 'reality', it is only because we cause them to be smothered by their apparent human relativity and obliterated by their utility, such that the evident teleological directedness, towards the gracious assimilation of man into his environment, inherent exactly *in their relationality,* is liable to be lost. That is, man's encountering the idea of 'a house' in the realm of conception (*taṣawwur*) as a distinct manifestation of his simultaneous rationality and creaturehood, in so far as that rationality and creaturehood unfold 'in the world'. Moreover, his containing within himself the physical apparatuses necessary to bring it into the realm of assent (*taṣdīq*) as the possible subject in an extramental proposition (*qaḍiyya khārijiyya*). The like of a 'house', then, is indubitably relational, and intimately bound up with and contingent upon the mental world, but also possesses a profound dimension of fixity, in its constituting a distinct manifestation of human rationality *vis-a-vis* the world, and one that is, teleologically speaking, necessary. Its presence as a seed, as it were, in man's mind, is after all *known* and created by the Creator of man: one of the innumerable indications that its reality - though contingent on man's, and though a branch, as it were, of his reality - is in a certain manner just as fixed, and just as 'real', as his own.

Granted, in the ontology shared across most forms of Islamic thought, in which quality (*al-kayf*) but not relational accidents enjoy existence, it can on the surface appear difficult to account for the ultimate rootedness in being of numerous entities and concepts. In dominant strands of the earlier *kalām* tradition at least, the act or fact of knowledge *itself* is perspectival (*i'tibārī*), in that it is considered to come under the category of relation (*al-nisba*). Yet as we have just explained, this by no means implies that the objects of our knowledge do not correspond to *nafs al-amr,* nor even that our knowledge itself does not enjoy some form of subsistence in itself (after all, maintaining that relational accidents have no extramental particular existence (*wujūd khārijī*) only negates the *individuated* extramental existence of these abstract, *i'tibārī* objects).[152] Yet a clear danger nonetheless exists in the sheer fact of the intricacy and sophistication of the later *kalām* tradition – if the notion of 'perspectival' is misunderstood as a necessarily ontological rather than a merely epistemological classification, the ultimate value of our scientific knowledge – all of which depends procedurally on representational intelligibles and other abstract entities – is called into question. That is, 'perspectival' is liable to be misinterpreted as 'relative' and 'subjective', yet this would be a dangerous error,[153] for these 'perspectives' of course constitute the fundamental ingredients of scientific knowledge. After all, intelligibles, not sensibles per se, are the proper objects of science,[154] in both the traditional sense of 'certain knowledge' applying to all particulars and to essences in themselves, and the modern sense which, speaking very broadly, amounts to the study of theoretical models and inductive statements purporting to represent the various constants that can been garnered from the observation of sensible phenomena. Generalized accounts of particular phenomena are perspectival, and do not exist in extramental particulars. Likewise, modern science presupposes the notion of natural laws, which are purely intelligible, perspectival entities. Another example is to be encountered in the manner in which physics must assume that mathematical representation of reality is able to capture real extramental features of reality. Yet this would be impossible should the perspectival status of mathematical models consign them to the realm of subjectivity. Likewise, traditional sciences and philosophy; their operation is contingent upon the universalization of particular phenomena (regardless of whether this universalization is construed as abstractive or not), and presupposes that logical form as well as general-metaphysical principles and concepts, that do not become instantiated extramentally, possess forms of distinct subsistence and a verifiable grounding in objective reality, that justify their forming the basis for our scientific appraisals of particularized entities, or, indeed, of the intelligible structure of reality. The distinction between such perspectival entities as correspond to *nafs al-amr*, then, and such as do not, saves the notion of science from ontological unjustifiability. Yet while it is easy to affirm that perspectival objects, whether abstract, universal or otherwise, possess some form of objective reality, it is less easy to identify precisely what it is about reality that makes this so. How, and in what, or as what, can perspectival, intelligible, 'abstract' entities be ontologically grounded *beyond individual minds*? In Chapter 4, we will provide the foundations of the answer.

In the broader intellectual context it is notable that the *majority* of the later *kalām* critical verifiers would in fact go on to maintain that knowledge itself, in the broader sense of perception rather than the strict sense of science (that is, not as *ṣifatun tūjibu tamyīzan lā yaḥtamil al-naqīḍ*, 'an attribute that necessitates [an act] of discrimination, the contradiction of which is inconceivable'),[155] is from the non-perspectival category of quality (*kayf*), thereby affirming a form of mental existence;[156] its reality cannot be reduced to a relation, because, according to Taftāzānī's formulation in his *Tahdhīb al-kalām,* a relation must be a relation *to something,* whereas the fact is that

> we intellect that which does not have extramental individuated subsistence (*nataʿaqqal mā lā thubūta lahu fī al-khārij*), for we pass affirmative judgement on impossible entities, and also encounter universal concepts and real propositions (*qaḍāyā ḥaqīqiyya*);[157] now, if that intellection occurs because [those concepts] obtain in the mind, that (constitutes exactly the conclusion we are seeking to prove, that is, the mental existence of these abstract objects); and otherwise, [intellection] necessarily entails a relation between the knowing subject and the intelligible object, and [the notion of a relation] to a pure negation (that is, if such abstracted objects are not afforded any form of existence) is not meaningful. Thus, if this [necessary] subsistence is not extramental and individuated (since this is impossible), it must be in the mind [itself].[158]

Let us look now very briefly at a concluding example, which presents an example representative of another of the most serious difficulties posed to the notion of 'a thing itself, in itself, irrespective of the perspective of a subject', *even when the 'thing itself' in question is an extramental particular.* Blind people of course exist outside of our minds, and yet 'blindness' as a concept is mind-dependent, in that it constitutes a privation, simply an 'absence of sightedness' – formed by affixing a negation to the intelligible form of 'sight' that has obtained in the mind.[159]

Yet irrespective of whether or not there are other knowing subjects to perceive it,[160] people that are blind really do *lack* sight, and the epistemological fact of the manner in which we process 'blindness' (that is, by negating 'sight') is quite irrelevant to this fact in the external world. That the person who approaches us in the street *is blind* rather than sighted is, after all, not a fact that has been caused by our minds. This is really the crux of the matter when we discuss a potential confusion of epistemology for ontology. Were 'blindness' *ontologically* mind-dependent, our minds would constitute the *cause* of the phenomenon of the absence of sight. Yet in the real world, it is merely *epistemologically* mind-dependent: that is, we only intellect the phenomenon of 'blindness' through acknowledging the absence of a concept, 'sightedness', which unlike 'blindness', presents an *independently intelligible* form to us, such that its intellection requires no negation, nor the affixation of a foreign concept, in order to obtain in the mind. On the other hand, privations certainly cannot *exist* (in the sense of physical individuation) in the external world, and so it is quite out of the question that a blind man should be blind *fi al-khārij*; and yet it is equally clear that blindness, though epistemologically mind-dependent, is not ontologically so.

Up until the fall of the Ottoman Empire, Ismail Gelenbevi (1143–1204/1730–90) was widely acknowledged as one of the most important philosophers and theologians of the latter centuries of Islam. Muṣṭafā Ṣabrī described him as 'the greatest of the Turkish critical verifiers of the latter centuries', and Abū Thanā' al-Ālūsī called him 'the greatest of the later scholar-sages.'[161] Gelenbevi was also the founder of the latest major school of logic in the Arabic tradition.[162] In his *Taḥqīq 'ilm Allāh bi al-maʿdūmāt* (Critical Verification of [the Nature of] God's Knowledge of Non-existent Entities), he cites this problem to point to the insufficiency of the simple division of *nafs al-amr* into *al-khārij* and *al-dhihn* (we might call this 'the objective blind man')):

> The fact that the subsistence[163] of 'blindness' *in* extramental particulars possesses actuality in things as they are in themselves, and [the further fact that] this [subsistence] *neither constitutes mental existence nor extramental particular subsistence*, annuls their [the *mutakallimūn*'s] confinement of intrinsic existence (lit. things as they are in themselves-existence – *al-wujūd al-nafs al-amrī*) to actualised[164] extramental particular and mental existence (*lammā kān al-thubūt al-khārijī li al-ʿamā mutaḥaqqiqan fī nafs al-amr wa lam yakun thubūtan dhihniyyan wa lā wujūdan khārijiyyan faqad intaqaḍa bihi ḥaṣruhum al-wujūd al-nafs al-amrī fī al-wujūd al-khārijī wa al-dhihnī al-muḥaqqaqayn*).[165]

If as a privation 'blindness' cannot become instantiated in particulars, 'where' is the objective blind man we meet in the street 'blind'?

The questions that we have treated up to this point in this section have shown that as traditionally defined, the realm of extramental particulars (*al-khārij*) cannot provide an adequate ontological account or serve as the guarantor of the existence or truth of numerous entities and propositions, which would however seem at first sight to belong firmly to the category of extramental particular entities. This includes i) extramental particulars like beds and houses, the differentia of which are contingent on the prior activity of minds, subsequent to which, these intelligible entities become 'fixed' in extramental particulars, ii) extramental entities the intellection of which involves the negation of a concept (like the blindness of an extramental particular blind man and the darkness of an extramental particular room), and iii) the genus and differentia of any given extramental essence. Although the form of the essence represented by the genus and differentia truly exists, it does not do so in the same mode of differentiation internally. An extramental particular man is with respect to his intelligible form a real and simple unity; the multiplicitous and *universal* forms of 'animal' and 'rational' that constitute his definitional essence are *grounded* in the extramental particular, and *arise* from the extramental particular, yet extramental particulars is not 'where' the genus and differentia exist *qua* universals.

Nafs al-amr, on the other hand, constitutes this complete guarantor; it informs even extramental particulars and renders them intelligible. 'Rational animal' is the multiplicitous form in the mind, grounded in *nafs al-amr*, that is instantiated by the individual human, and represents the proper mode of the intellection of an individual human being in its relational context; but in the individual distinctness of its isolated extramental form, each human being is a unitive essence.

The purpose of this necessarily detailed exposition of the 'perspectival' aspects of quiddities and intellection has been to uncover the fact that human perspectives are objective, '*nafs al-amrī*' elements of the world – indeed, they are indispensable mental elements without which the world could not be intelligible to human beings. Accurate human representation of the world is a part of the world quite as 'objective' as the rest of the world, as is the human contribution to the world's intelligibility. *Nafs al-amr*, or 'objective reality' is partially thus a human reality, though not a 'subjective' human reality. The reason for this will become clear when we explore an altogether deeper region of philosophy in Chapter 4; suffice to say, it pertains to two momentous principles that underlie all that is most distinctive about Akbarian and certain late-*kalām* conceptions of truth and objective reality. The first is that intelligible reality is ontologically prior to physical and sensible reality; the second is that the being of the entire cosmos is radically contingent on cognition, and in a different way, on human beings – yet this is strictly not a form of idealism, as that word is usually understood. Rather, it is a recognition that the very being of the world constitutes a branch of the Muhammadan Reality, the perfect form of humankind, from whose light it has been created,[166] and who is simultaneously its final cause.[167] And as we will see, it is moreover a recognition that the meaning of the 'created' being of that ultimate created essence and most perfect locus of manifestation of the Names of God –and likewise, the meaning of 'creation' as pertaining to all other essences, the exemplary realities of which arise from that Muhammadan Reality–can be no other than their own self-consciousnesses. Thus, although some of the statements we will encounter in Chapter 4 will seem identical in expression to the idealist *esse est percipi*, we will see that they arise from a very different context;[168] moreover, even if apparently inanimate objects exist *through* the Muhammadan Reality, through their own modes of self-consciousness they can still exist independently alongside human beings, irrespective of whether they are being actively perceived by individual human beings.

For now, we will return to somewhat more sober matters, and outline the development of *nafs al-amr* theory within the broadly Peripatetic traditions of Islamic theology and philosophy up to the time of Taşköprüzade, who, we contend, is one of the key crossover figures. To show the manner in which he combined our different Akbarian and Avicennan streams of thought, we will need to provide a somewhat detailed exposition of the Akbarian position in Chapter 4; and at the end of that chapter, we will meet with Taşköprüzade's marrying of the two positions.

Chapter 3

Abstract Objects and Metaphysical Necessity

3.1 Taftāzānī on Nafs al-Amr Known and Unknowable

The widespread adoption of the powerful Avicennan logical and general metaphysical apparatuses amongst post-Rāzian *kalām* theologians and their integration into the normative curricula, and the simultaneous necessity many of these theologians saw in opposing some aspects of Avicennan special metaphysics, such as the affirmation of the Ten Intellects, ensured that later *kalām* theologians would often use Avicennan intellectual tools to fight Avicennan conclusions. In this chapter we will look at a particular such debate that pertains to the question of *nafs al-amr*, drawn from the period from the 14th to the 16th centuries, the age of one of the greatest of all flowerings of post-Avicennan, post-Razian philosophy and theology, whose three most fructuous seeds may have been those from the rich supercommentary traditions yielded by al-Jurjānī's *Sharḥ al-Mawāqif* and al-Ṭūsī's *al-Tajrīd*, as well as Taftāzānī's *Sharḥ al-Maqāṣid*. At the end of this period, these post-Avicennan intellectual traditions in all their subtleties were married to the luminous insights of the Akbarian school in early works like Dāwūd al-Qayṣarī's *Muqaddima*, and Mulla Fenari's *Miṣbāḥ al-uns*, which later found further expression, this time within the context of the ordinary *'ulūm*, in the synthetical aspects of the work of thinkers like Ibn Kemal, Ibn Bahā'uddīn and Taşköprüzade. This Akbarian component will be considered briefly at the end of this chapter, and chiefly in Chapter 4. In this section, we will examine some important 'Avicennan' elements of that synthesis.

When it came to the intricate and pivotal question of *nafs al-amr*, it fell to al-Sayyid al-Sharīf al-Jurjānī's arch-rival Sa'd al-Dīn Taftāzānī,[1] to formulate what was perhaps the first theory within the post-Avicennan, broadly *mashshā'ī*[2] tradition that could serve as a real alternative to Ṭūsī's invocation of the Agent Intellect as guarantor of the truth of propositions.

In the *matn* or 'basic text' of his classic *Sharḥ al-Maqāṣid*, Taftāzānī sums up his agreement with Ṭūsī's formulation in the *Tajrīd*, and disagreement with the latter's ontological identification in his *Ithbāt al-ʿaql al-mufāriq*

> The truth of a judgement is not conditional on its correspond-
> ence to particularised essences (*al-aʿyān*), for both of the terms
> [of the proposition involved] might not exist therein; and
> correspondence to that which is in minds is not sufficient [for
> truth], for false propositions may become impressed therein.
> Rather, the recognised criterion [for truth] is correspondence
> to things as they are in themselves (*nafs al-amr*), the meaning
> of which is the denotation of our statement 'this thing is in
> itself such-and-such' – that is, in and of itself, irrespective
> of anyone's judgement. Its construal as the Agent Intellect is
> extremely dubious.[3]

This passage again raises a question which, thus far in our exploration, has continued to come to the surface. Does construing *nafs al-amr* as 'a thing as it is in itself' not simply repeat a terminological commonplace? This definition appears to have little bearing on the ontological dimension of the whole affair, and, on the Ashʿarī and Avicennan schools of thought in which 'thing' is co-extensive with 'existent' (with some qualification in the case of Avicenna), this definition appears to limit *nafs al-amr* to extramental particulars (alongside the mind, in the cases of the Avicen-nans and *kalām* theologians who affirm mental existence).[4] Does it not simply ignore the fundamental challenges and tensions posed by purely intelligible, 'abstract' entities, the mere existence of which has necessitated that questions of the ontological nature of *nafs al-amr* be confronted? Taftāzānī has anticipated this objection

> Should it be said, 'how can [*nafs al-amr*'s construal as "a
> thing (*shayʾ*) as it is in its own entity" (*dhāt*)] be conceivable
> with respect to things which have no entity, and no thing-
> ness (*shayʾiyya*) in particularised essences, like non-existent
> entities, and especially impossibles?', the general answer is
> that we know apodictically that 'the conjunction of contra-
> dictories is impossible' corresponds to *nafs al-amr*, and that
> our saying '[the conjunction of contradictories] is possible'

does not, even though we do not know the manner in which this correspondence takes place in its innermost essence (*bi kunhihā*).[5]

The essence of this apparently transcendent relation is inaccessible to us, but this is of no consequence. This is because, for Taftāzānī, the *necessary certainty* of the like of these abstract truths is exactly what we actually *mean* by 'correspondence to *nafs al-amr*'. The point can nonetheless be pushed a little further, and he now gives us what he called the 'detailed' answer to the objection,

> Correspondence is a relation in order for which [to occur], the actualization, in the intellect, of the two relata (*al-muḍāfayn*) is sufficient; and it is clear – regardless of whether they are existent or non-existent entities – that when the intellect considers the two meanings concerned and evaluates them with respect to one another, it finds, in accordance with the [particularities] of each instance, an affirmative or negative relation entailed by logical necessity or demonstrative proof. Now, this relation – in so far as it is, with respect to that particular intelligible, yielded by logical necessity or demonstrative proof, without [reference] to a specific subject or reporter – is what is meant by 'actuality' or that which is in things as they are in themselves (*hiya al-murād bi al-wāqiʿ wa mā fī nafs al-amr*).

It seems that for 'al-Saʿd', as Taftāzānī is affectionately known in the *kalām* tradition, there is no need to go beyond studying our *direct experience* of having knowledge to make the idea of correspondence to *nafs al-amr* fully intelligible. This is because correspondence to *nafs al-amr* is something eminently accessible to us. It constitutes exactly the affirmative or negative judgement regarding the truth of a given proposition, in so far as this judgement directly rests upon ('corresponds to') logical necessity (the epistemological import of each of the *yaqīniyyāt* amounts to 'logical' necessity) or a demonstrative proof, both of which are necessary regardless of the particularities of a given subject; that is, logical necessities or demonstrative proofs yielding certainties that thereby rest upon objective factors, not on a given person's subjective state of mind or imagination.

This theory was not appreciated across the board. The great Mīr Zāhid (d. 1101/1689) had it that 'the position stating that *nafs al-amr* is tantamount to that which is entailed by necessity or demonstrative proof is one that conflicts with anything suggested by the expression [i.e. '*nafs al-amr*'] or indeed anything manifest to the understanding.'[6] There is no doubt that Taftāzānī's theory involves an ingenious analysis, but this notwithstanding, it may well seem to simply amount to explaining away the question of *nafs al-amr*, or even to merely begging the question.

It is the affirmative or negative relation itself (that is, the relation of judgement, of the abstract proposition, to the affirmation or to the negation), *in so far* as it is yielded by the appropriate demonstrative proof as pertaining to the proposition in question, which for Taftāzānī constitutes 'correspondence to *nafs al-amr*', and as he himself stipulates, 'Correspondence is a relation in order for which [to occur], the actualization, *in the intellect*, of the two relata *is sufficient*.' The domain of the mental need not be transcended – both the proposition itself, and the logical necessity or demonstrative proof that for Taftāzānī take on the role of 'truthmakers', exist only in the immanent domain of the mind. On the face of it, this may seem to constitute a coherent view; but its strictest logical and metaphysical consequences are surely to entail that any philosophy adopting such a position as its account of 'objective' truth, must inevitably end up as a philosophy of mere outward semblances. It *appears* to be the case that our abstract concepts apply to things in *nafs al-amr*. And it *seems* to be the case to us, as knowing subjects equipped with certain logical apparatuses and acknowledged patterns of assent, that the judgements borne by propositions constructed out of those concepts, are true or false in terms of their relationship to logical necessities or demonstrative proof. Yet all the while, we remain on the level of the mental; a proposition *in the mind* is validated by a proof *in the mind*. Ṭūsī's interdiction of the identification of *nafs al-amr* with the mind (which we have already seen at the beginning of Chapter 1) applies, even here. In the case of conceptions, Taftāzānī's theory fails to be coherent, even on its own terms. Where is the 'necessity' which Taftāzānī invokes as our justificatory recourse, when it comes to the particular array of concepts that we happen to be equipped with, say, the *umūr ʿāmma*? They could have been entirely different (should we hypothesize, for example, a creature with entirely different cognitive apparatuses looking upon the world, and thereby seeing an entirely different world to the one we are accustomed to seeing when we look upon it with our own cognitive apparatuses) *unless* we are able to uncover their true status as features of *all* of the domains and degrees of reality, *beyond* appearance (a feat that Taftāzānī has certainly not even attempted to achieve). Similar problems obtain for Taftāzānī's account of assents. The productivity of the figures and moods of formal logic is derived neither from individual minds, nor extramental individuals, and demands the existence of distinct, uninstantiated, intelligible states of affairs deeply embedded in the structure of reality, both temporally and essentially prior to particulars, and that give rise to these truth-relations. Even more fundamentally, the principle of non-contradiction (to use Taftāzānī's own example) is not *validated* by logical necessity, as Taftāzānī claims, but is rather *constitutive* of logical necessity, unless we are content to demote 'necessity' to the status of a merely psychological phenomenon, which would represent a still more decisive condemnation of the viability of the theory. *Truth* cannot be identified with logical necessity, for it is not logical necessity that makes a proposition true, but rather its being found to genuinely capture the constitution of the intelligible mode of being or beings *as they are in themselves*. Logical necessity must be rooted in metaphysical necessity (and its truth thus validated by correspondence to that which transcends the immanent domain of the mind) or it is nothing but mere convention, in the final analysis scarcely more compelling a designator of truth than animal instinct. Figures like Kant were able to see the inadequacy of the broadly Peripatetic 'abstractionist' account of universally applicable concepts and principles (which are meant to arise from an extramental particular object that shows no extramental sign of them whatever), but as we have seen, Kant replaced one deep inadequacy with an even greater web of confusion. Yet long before Kant, the Platonic and Akbarian schools had perceived the dismal contradictions that must inevitably and inexorably attend any metaphysical doctrine purporting to render logical principles and intelligible frameworks of representation ontologically subordinate to the instantiated particulars that must presuppose them. And moreover, they had perceived this in virtue of the light shed by an alternative account of the degrees of reality, that could provide a comprehensive depiction of these phenomena altogether immune to such fatal challenges to the possibility of objective truth.

Of course, one might venture, in Taftāzānī's defence, that he is evidently well aware that the question of the grounds for the *existence* of these objective but purely intelligible truths remains a mystery; individual minds constitute the loci of these judgements, but cannot be their ultimate source. This is precisely why he has emphasised that 'we do not know the innermost essence of the manner in which this correspondence takes place (*bi kunhihā*).' It could be argued, then, that his choice of this type of solution is not to be understood as a form of untempered reductionism, of the notion of truth to our *experience* of its necessity. It is rather to be understood in the context of his commitment to a particular methodology within the dominant form of late *kalām* theology, one firmly *mashshāʾī* in that it tends to spontaneously rein in any attempt to use reason to arrive at transcendent, or 'exemplary' forms, or uninstantiated natures in themselves. The ultimate status of the principle of non-contradiction, as in Taftāzānī's example, is a mystery; we do not perhaps know *precisely* what it is about reality that makes it true; nonetheless, assent to it is evidently necessary, and for Taftāzānī this is after all what we really mean by 'correspondence to *nafs al-amr*'. From this Peripatetic *kalām* perspective, there is no use speculating about any putatively transcendent state of affairs or entity which generates the truth of, or ontologically 'underlies', a particular individuated or intelligible object of experience, because these transcendent states of affairs are not objects of experience; in any case, the notion that instantiated entities are contingent upon ontologically prior uninstantiated exemplars, or that there are extramental Forms underlying intelligible mental objects, of course goes against some of the most important tenets of broad 'Peripateticism'. In many (especially earlier) forms of *kalām*, this tendency is even more pronounced than it is in Avicennan philosophy. In this Peripatetic vein, natures exist, but only as individuals; we have no evidence that they have any other sort of subsistence, and in any case, Fakhr al-Dīn al-Rāzī in his *al-Mulakhkhaṣ* and a few other authors notwithstanding, the majority of broadly Avicennan philosophers and *kalām* theologians maintain that the doctrine of Platonic Forms is contradictory.[7]

Regardless of the particularities of this argument of Taftāzānī's, it can certainly be argued that the prevalence of similar forms of ontological parsimony within much of *kalām* arises from the simple faithfulness, in the moment of their engagement with it, of *kalām* authors to their subject as it is normally understood. A prototypical example would be Jurjānī himself; in his *kalām* works, he often explains anti-exemplarist stances similar to those of Taftāzānī – yet in his *Risālat al-Wujūd* he explicitly adopts an Akbarian epistemology which is in many ways diametrically opposed to that of *kalām* in its strictly demarcated form. In his *Taʿrīfāt*, Jurjānī defines *nafs al-amr* as 'the essential knowledge that contains the forms of all things, universal and particular, great and small, as a whole and as distinct, whether they be particularised or sciential essences'[8] - a verbatim quotation from Dāwūd al-Qayṣarī's Akbarian treatment of *nafs al-amr*, which is the subject of Chapter 4.

Of course, Taftāzānī famously rejects the Akbarian framework that underlies Qayṣarī's account, and he is even more ill-disposed to invoking the overcrowded and doctrinally problematic universe of the Ten Intellects dreamt up by 'the philosophers' (*al-ḥukamā*'). From this *kalām* perspective, Ṭūsī's theory of *nafs al-amr* is one very good example of the deep problems that these philosophers can at times become entangled in, as the result of their general approach; after all, Ṭūsī feels compelled to identify *nafs al-amr* with the Agent Intellect only because, by his own admission, it is the first level of reality in which eternal truths in their full multiplicity can become objects of knowledge; according to Ṭūsī, if God were to know them in Himself, a multiplicity utterly contrary to His nature would have to obtain in His Essence.[9]

Taftāzānī concludes the main argument for his theory of *nafs al-amr* exactly by alluding to the Avicennan identification of the Agent Intellect with the 'Preserved Tablet' and the 'Manifest Book', which Ṭūsī interprets as the locus of the Qur'anic, *With Him are the keys of the Unseen; none knows them but He. He knows what is in land and sea; not a leaf falls, but He knows it. Not a grain in the earth's shadows, not a thing, fresh or withered, but it is in a Manifest Book* (Qur'ān 6:59).[10] 'You will be aware' says Taftāzānī, 'of the fact that his theory, quite apart from the weakness of certain of its premises, is incompatible with the explicit sense of the words of the Most High, *with Him are the keys of the Unseen*, to the end of the verse.'

The dominant interpretation of 'the Manifest Book' (*al-kitāb al-mubīn*) is that it refers not to the Preserved Tablet, but to the knowledge of God Himself.[11] However, even if it be interpreted as the Preserved Tablet – a widespread and valid interpretation – Allah nonetheless clearly knows all things *in and of* His own Essence, for the keys of the Unseen – matters which, like destiny, are hidden from men – are 'with Him', and 'none knows them but He'. That He would require the mediation of the Preserved Tablet in order to know them is thus rendered quite out of the question. Moreover, some major exegetes such as Rāzī,[12] have also interpreted the 'keys of the Unseen' as referring to all the possible entities in God's knowledge, to which His power can pertain.

Given the prevalence of these interpretations, perhaps there is after all a slight implied possibility that Taftāzānī could have held that *nafs al-amr is* in some sense the knowledge of God Himself. However, he does not explicitly make this identification, much less attempt to demonstrate it, and again, it is conceivable that this is because he does not deem the demonstration of such a notion to be within the ken of *'ilm al-kalām*.

At the end of this chapter and in Chapter 4, we will meet both with a more expansive view of the scope of *kalām* (that unlike Taftāzānī will have no qualms about explicitly specifying the ontological identity of *nafs al-amr* within an alternative non-Avicennan and non-classical-*kalām* ontology), as well as with a group of thinkers who do so working within an altogether higher science. In the meantime, let us look briefly at how theories of *nafs al-amr* in the glorious formative century or so of intellectual figures of the statures of Rāzī, Ibn 'Arabī, Tūsī, Qayṣarī and Taftāzānī were discussed and developed in the century or so that succeeded it, by major thinkers like Qūshjī, 'Alā'uddīn al-Tūsī, Jalāl al-Dīn al-Dawānī, Taşköprüzade and Ibn Bahā'uddīn.

3.2 *The Road to Taşköprüzade's Synthesis: Qūshjī, 'Alā'uddīn, and Dawānī*

The next generation of thinkers in the Taftāzānian and Jurjānian traditions of *taḥqīq* contributed significantly to the formulation of the problematics of *nafs al-amr,* for example, the great Ottoman astronomer and philosopher 'Alī al-Qūshjī (806–79/1403–74), and 'Alā'uddīn al-Tūsī (d. 877/1473), both of whom worked under the patronage of Sultan Mehmet the Conquerer.[13] The latter chose 'Alā'uddīn, alongside the great Hocazade (838–93/1434–88), to take part in a competition to compose the best philosophical work adjudicating between broad (Avicennan) 'philosophy' and Abū Ḥāmid al-Ghazālī's refutation thereof in *Tahāfut al-Falāsifa*.[14] Despite his consummate philosophical mastery, 'Alā'uddīn was perceived to have lost (competition was stiff: Hocazade was not only one of the Sultan's personal tutors,[15] but was also recognised as perhaps the preeminent philosopher of his age by, amongst others, such acknowledged luminaries as Qūshjī and Dawānī);[16] but 'Alā'uddīn's *al-Dhakhīra* is nonetheless an often subtle and rewarding work.

He clarifies the argument against *nafs al-amr* being confined to extramental particular and mental existence by saying that this would involve the absurdity, in the case of abstract mental propositions, of their truth being guaranteed by their 'correspondence' to *themselves*. Moreover, since false propositions obtain in the mind and thus also 'correspond' to themselves, the theory asserting that mental existence is *nafs al-amr* would also have the function of entailing the truth of false propositions, 'for they too obtain in the mind and therefore correspond to themselves, without thus being distinguishable from true propositions.'[17] 'Alā'uddīn then turns to his namesake Naṣīr al-Dīn al-Ṭūsī's theory of the ontological identity of *nafs al-amr*, showing (albeit within the trap of immanentist assumptions about the equivalence of *thubūt aṣlī* and 'extramental particulars') that rather than providing a real solution as to its identity, it simply raises the original question of correspondence,

> Should it be said, 'all true propositions subsist in the Agent Intellect, and those that obtain in our intellects correspond to it (and this is exactly what the correspondence [of true propositions] to *nafs al-amr* means); false propositions, however, do not correspond to it, such that the difference [between true and false propositions] becomes established' we would say, 'their subsistence therein (in the Agent Intellect) is either substantial existence (*thubūt aṣlī*) – that is, existence in *al-khārij*, in which case impossible beings would exist in extramental particulars, and non-existent beings would certainly exist therein – or, umbral subsistence (*thubūt ẓillī*) – that is, [a form of] mental existence, which would itself have to correspond to *nafs al-amr*, the original ambiguity thereby entirely repeating itself.[18]

It is an acknowledged principle that impossible 'entities' (like, for example, a square circle) and abstract and non-existent entities (respectively, the universal concept of 'relation', and fictional beings like 'sea of quicksilver')[19] *cannot* exist (in the case of impossible entities), and *happen not* to exist (in the case of fictional beings), in extramental particulars.[20] Their necessary subsistence in the Agent Intellect, then, (necessary in order to validate true propositions like 'relations are intelligibles') is either extramental particular existence, which is absurd, or umbral – 'shadow' or derived, representational existence, in which case these propositions in the Agent Intellect would also themselves need to correspond to something beyond themselves, just as propositions in minds derive their truth from correspondence to something beyond minds.

In some similar lines of thought in his renowned commentary on the *Tajrīd*, al-Qūshjī offers an especially clear explanation of the acknowledged principle that the mind cannot serve as a truthmaker,

> it is possible for judgements that do not correspond to actuality (*al-wāqiʿ*) to become impressed in the mind, such that were the truth of a judgement to obtain as the result of its correspondence to the contents of minds, our statement 'the world is eternal' would have to be true and correct, since it corresponds to what it is in the minds of the philosophers – but this would be indisputably absurd. Moreover mental judgements differ; the philosophers believe the world to be eternal, and the theologians that it is existentiated *ex nihilo*, so which [of these judgements] would be corresponded to?[21]

Correspondence cannot be to beliefs, because then, quite simply, all beliefs would be true, which they are evidently not. Having established this, however, al-Qūshjī alludes to a more serious problem: that of how to account for a posited correspondence – one that seems logically necessary – to something that is *neither the mind, nor extramental particulars.*

> Here there is an even more difficult problem, which we have previously alluded to, which is that *nafs al-amr* must be distinct from the [affirmative or negative] judgement-relations (*al-nisab al-ḥukmiyya*) that exist in minds, for the criterion, in order that their truth or falsity be known, is that they correspond to *nafs al-amr*, and that which corresponds to something must be distinct from that [thing] which is corresponded-to ... Now, it is well known that [an existent thing] that is not in minds must [exist] extramentally (*fī al-khārij*), since there is no intermediary state [between them].[22] [Moreover], what is meant by *al-khārij*, is 'outside of the mind', such that if something is not in the mind, it must of necessity be outside of the mind. What then does it mean when [philoso-

phers and theologians] say 'if both the two terms involved in a proposition do not exist in extramental particulars, the truth [of that judgement] depends on its correspondence to *nafs al-amr*, not to what exists in extramental particulars (*al-khārij*), nor to what exists in minds?'[23]

With great clarity, Qūshjī has accentuated the central motif of our study – if objective abstract objects and propositions cannot be *ultimately* mental, where do they exist in their ultimate and original state? The only option, on the binary Avicennan and *kalām* ontology of 'mental' and 'extramental particular' existences, would seem to be that they exist in extramental particulars. But the purely intelligible, abstract and non-individuated nature of the referents of the terms of such propositions makes this impossible. Qūshjī rejects Ṭūsī's theory of the Agent Intellect, but nonetheless does not seem to make any attempt to resolve this apparently insurmountable problem.

In the logical sphere, the most influential contribution of the middle period came from the renowned philosopher Jalāl al-Dīn al-Dawānī, in his commentary on Taftāzānī's logic text, *Tahdhīb al-Manṭiq,* as his answer to the old question of what it is that guarantees the validity of a subject of predication.

> All concepts that can be formed are on a level footing, in that they all exist in *nafs al-amr*, for of necessity they can all constitute the subject in a true affirmative proposition; the least [justification] for this is that [each of these concepts] is distinct from all others.[24]

This important formulation would come to be standard, and was later to be employed by Taşköprüzade, Mirza Jān, Gelenbevi, Baḥr al-'Ulūm and others; without the subject of a proposition enjoying some form of subsistence, that is, by being absolutely nothing (*ma'dūm ṣirf*), it would of course be impossible to say anything about it at all – that is, it would not be capable of serving as a term in a meaningful proposition. This saving of some basic semblance of ontological dignity for abstract mathematical and logical and even non-existent fictional objects is, again, of central importance to the central argument of this study, as we will soon have occasion to explain.

However, it was in the *al-Shuhūd al-ʿaynī fī mabāḥith al-wujūd al-dhihnī* ('The Eyewitnessing: Topics in Mental Existence') of Taşköprüzade that the most truly significant leap forward for *nafs al-amr* theory in a *kalām* context really came.[25] His treatment is particularly enlightening, firstly because, in the course of constructing a remarkable synthesis of *kalām*, the Avicennan doctrine of abstraction, and Akbarian metaphysics, Taşköprüzade draws a distinction between and then reconciles the more terrestrial, 'epistemological' identification of *nafs al-amr* with 'the mind' (*al-dhihn*) on the one hand, and its true ontological identity on the other. This reconciliation is of the most pressing importance if a truly viable theory of *nafs al-amr* is to be uncovered. Without it, the epistemological problem of how we can possibly match our judgements onto entities that few people have direct experience of (that is, the Immutable Archetypes in the knowledge of God as the ontological guarantors of true judgements) can seem insurmountable, as we will see in Chapter 4.

The critical verification of the answer to the question of the real essence of *nafs al-amr* is, Taşköprüzade says, 'a very difficult matter, one that the perspicacious have been unable to achieve, and a rough and uneven road, that even the great ones have rarely taken.'[26] Before we look at the ultimate answer he arrived at – which, we argue, is the definitive *taḥqīq* of the question achieved in the *kalām* tradition – we must examine as far as possible in logical sequence how it is that he got there. Certainly, before presenting his final synthesis, we will have to set forth al-Qayṣarī's classic exposition of the broad Akbarian view, but this must also wait until Chapter 4. In the meantime, we will briefly examine some of the logical and metaphysical considerations that Taşköprüzade presents in order to serve as the necessary background to his own theory.

After presenting the standard definition of *nafs al-amr* in its distinctness from *al-dhihn* and *al-khārij*[27] (and he implies that this is where most treatments of the problem have stopped), he first provides a summary of seven arguments from previous generations of philosophers for and against the identification of *nafs al-amr* with the Agent Intellect, as well as a few that appear to be his own.[28] Perhaps the most striking objection Taşköprüzade offers, broadly following Taftāzānī and Qūshjī, is that were *nafs al-amr* the Agent Intellect, the Divine knowledge itself would have to correspond to it, which seems a clear metaphysical category mistake.

It would then be impossible to characterise knowledge that has even *essential*[29] priority over [the Agent Intellect], like the knowledge of the Necessary Being, Exalted is He, as 'true' or as corresponding to 'things-in themselves', [and this is] due to the [logical] impossibility of something corresponding to a thing the actualization of which is posterior to it. [30]

Before elucidating his positive theory of *nafs al-amr*, Taşköprüzade briefly considers another important theory of *nafs al-amr*, which attempts to explain the correspondence of second intelligibles to *nafs al-amr* by reducing them to concomitants of extramental particulars (*al-khārij*), and ostensibly making it possible for *nafs al-amr* to be reduced to *al-khārij* alone (thus conveniently disencumbering us of the difficulties, necessitated by abstract entities and uninstantiated essences, of identifying *nafs al-amr* with some mode of being distinct from *al-khārij*).

Some have said that *nafs al-amr* is merely extramental particulars, because all mental quiddities are extracted therefrom (*muntaza'a minhā*); true judgements correspond to it either through an intermediary or through [numerous] intermediaries. The detailed exposition of this, as expounded by the author of the *Ta'dīl*,[31] is that the meaning of truth in the affirmative relation (*al-nisba al-thubūtiyya*) is for something to have obtained in particularized essences (*fī al-a'yān*) that [also] arises mentally when the relation [is affirmed]. This could be without an intermediary, if both terms in the proposition are first intelligibles, like one's saying 'Zayd is a writer', and it could be by means of an intermediary, if one of the terms or both of them are intelligibles that arise from first intelligibles (*nāshi'a 'an al-ma'qūlāt al-ūlā*),[32] which themselves[33] arise from extramental existents, like your saying 'man is a universal.' It is in this way that the gradations of mediation increase, in accordance with the gradual increase in the gradation of intelligibles, from second and third [intelligibles], and so on.[34]

On this view, the 'first intelligible' form of, for example, a human being ('man') – the form of the essence proper – arises directly from extramental particulars, and the second intelligibles predicated of man (for example, 'man is a universal') arise directly from those first intelligibles, which are themselves rooted in extramental particulars. Second intelligibles are almost made, thus, into a kind of epiphenomenon, deprived of ontological status except in terms of their relationship, through the intermediary of first intelligibles, to extramental particulars; they are in some sense really 'just' extramental particulars. Ṣadr al-Sharī'a also has a distinctive method of accounting for the correspondence of true negative propositions to *nafs al-amr*,

> the meaning of truth in the negative relation (*al-nisba al-salbiyya*) is that its contradictory does not arise from anything in extramental particulars, like your saying 'the conjunction of contradictories does not exist' (*ijtimā' al-naqīḍayn laysa bi mawjūd*). This [proposition] does not mean that this relation arises from something that exists in extramental particulars, because the conjunction of contradictories is not an existent, and it is not possible to say 'its non-existence exists', because it is impossible for something non-existent to 'exist'; rather, what is meant is that its contradictory, which is the affirmative relation in our statement 'the conjunction of contraries exists', does *not* arise from something in extramental particulars.[35]

This theory, which might seem almost reminiscent of the method of some forms of reductivist analytic philosophy, is deemed by Taşköprüzade a thoroughly inadequate approach by which to account for the correspondence of abstract entities to *nafs al-amr*. This is because of the existence of certain classes of rational judgements which are simply irreducible to extramental particulars. He tells us that Ṣadr al-Sharī'a's words are

> good details, which will benefit you in many different contexts, but they are of no avail here, because some rational judgements are not founded in extramental particulars at all, neither essentially nor by means of an intermediary. For example, your conceptualizing 'mental existence' and 'not-mental-existence', and then judging that they are distinct, is [a judgement that] corresponds to things-in themselves, although it is not founded in extramental particulars essen-

tially – this is clear – nor by means of an intermediary, because
'not-mental existence' cannot be supposed to [constitute an]
application of any one of the intelligibles.[36]

The purport of the theory that is here so adeptly refuted, is that all
intelligible judgements, and all 'mental quiddities', are simply abstracted
from extramental particulars, and merely constitute concomitants necessarily supervening upon these particulars, in the event of their obtaining
in a locus of intelligible representation, that is, a mind. Properly speaking
then, their reality is reducible to extramental particulars, and thus, when
mental judgements correspond to *nafs al-amr*, this is ultimately no more
than their correspondence to extramental particulars, even be it that this
correspondence obtains via numerous intermediaries, as in the case of
a statement which includes even *third* intelligibles, for example 'element
of proper classification' in the proposition "genus" denotes an element
of proper classification.' Nonetheless, in Ṣadr al-Sharī'a's theory, such a
statement still ultimately corresponds to states of affairs in extramental
particulars, because even third intelligibles are merely ways – albeit more
distant and abstract ways – of *referring* to extramental particulars.

This theory is untenable, says Taşköprüzade, and is of 'no avail' in answering the question as to the real identity of *nafs al-amr*, simply because
of the profusion of examples of intelligible entities that are not ascribable
to extramental particulars even by the most resourceful stretches of the
imagination. The *distinction* between mental existence and 'not-mental
existence' (*al-lā wujūd al-dhihnī*),[37] for example, is one that corresponds
to *nafs al-amr*, but clearly cannot in any way be founded in any given extramental particular. Moreover, 'not-mental existence' can in no way be
described as a first or second intelligible, since these by definition arise
as the mental forms and concomitants of extramental particulars. For
example, in 'this individual particular is a not-mental existence', 'mental
existence' is evidently not a first intelligible arising from an *extramental*
particular qua *extramental* particular, and even more eminently, 'not-
mental existence' is not a first intelligible but a negation (first intelligibles
cannot involve negations, for otherwise negations would exist in extramental particulars, which is impossible). The individuated form that
constitutes the partial grounds for the truth of '*this individual particular
is a not-mental existence*' is a positive and distinct form, the intellection
of which is not contingent on negating anything.

Amidst an illimitable array of other examples, Taşköprüzade might also have mentioned the productivity of syllogistic figures and moods to illustrate the broader irreducibility of abstract truths to extramental particulars, an example which we have previously alluded to. While this productivity mirrors an intelligible structure that underlies particulars, its universality and the framework of relationality that it presupposes[38] clearly preclude its being rooted in any given individual particular.[39]

3.3 'Where Then Are They?' Ibn Bahāʾuddīn on Intelligible Entities

With this section, we bring to a close our discussion of the fundamental notions that have required some degree of exploration, in order for the most fundamental logical and metaphysical backdrops to the substantive theories regarding the identity of *nafs al-amr* (which we will finally explore in Chapter 4) to have emerged into sharper relief. It is metaphysically necessary that human knowledge correspond to a 'third' realm, beyond our ordinary sense and mental experience; this is because:

(i) The sense objects of extramental particulars cannot provide warrant for the truth of abstract propositions that do not correspond to anything in extramental particulars; nor can abstract truths be reduced to extramental particulars.

(ii) The fact of being a mental entity or obtaining in a mind cannot provide warrant for the truth of abstract judgements, because false abstract judgements are also mental entities and also obtain in minds, but have not thus been rendered true.

(iii) Even many features of extramental particulars are entirely informed by and depend upon elements that are *objective*, despite being fundamentally mental.

Nafs al-amr cannot be fully accounted for by anything we encounter in the realm of the strictly 'concrete' nor in the realm of the strictly mental, and more than this, its identification with any entity ontologically subordinate to the Divine, constitutes a rather extreme category mistake. It is clear 'where' the referents of judgements concerning extramental *particulars* in some sense exist – in the guise of individuated entities themselves, a part of which (this world of ours) we are able to perceive with our ordinary rational and sense faculties. However, even this correspondence to extramental particulars provides no ultimate ontological grounds for the *relation* of minds to extramental particulars (nor indeed does it explain the existence of extramental particulars themselves). This coaxes forth the fundamental question with which this study is concerned; we will tarry no further in the realm of the merely propaedeutic. 'Where' do things exist, as they are in themselves?

Fascinating words from the great but little-known Ottoman mystical theologian Ibn Bahā'uddīn reveal that this question was treated even in works of *kalām*, and furthermore seem to suggest that some sort of relative consensus may have been achieved regarding its answer:

> the prior innate capacities by which the realities of things are characterised in the first of the degrees (*marātib*) [of manifestation] ... is designated as the world of [Immutable][40] Archetypes, and identified by all of the different groups of intellectuals as *nafs al-amr*.[41]

This excerpt from *al-Qawl al-faṣl*, wherein, as Taşköprüzade has it, Ibn Bahā'uddīn 'combined the way of theology with that of Sufism'[42] utilises several Akbarī concepts. In order to provide an answer as to the true nature of *nafs al-amr*, Ibn Bahā'uddīn first alludes to the *marātib al-ẓuhūr*, or degrees of manifestation of the Divine Names. He then invokes the *a'yān al-thābita* or 'Immutable Archetypes', which constitute images of the Divine Names and the objects of God's beginninglessly eternal knowledge.[43] Finally, he speaks of the 'innate capacities' or *isti'dādāt* by which those essences are characterised, as entailments of the specificities of their entification in the Divine Knowledge. Earlier on in his magnum opus, Ibn Bahā'uddīn had delimited the exact tension inherent in the question of *nafs al-amr*, and highlighted some of the profound implications contained in the position he deemed the only intelligible one:

> *Nafs al-amr*, which everyone talks about, but the true nature of which is not understood [by most], is the existence of the realities of all things; that is, their subsistence through Absolute Existence, as we have critically verified; otherwise, it is not possible to conceive of [*nafs al-amr*] having an intelligible meaning, for many things that do not exist in extramental particulars have properties in *nafs al-amr*, irrespective of [the existence of] minds and knowing subjects. Where then are they? Allah's encompassing of all things and His 'with-

ness' (*ma'iyya*), pronounced by scripture, with respect to all things,[44] is not intelligible except on this basis.[45]

Nafs al-amr, then, constitutes the subsistence of all things in a mode of existence unconfined to the mind and 'extramental particulars' as usually characterised. Ultimately, this is their subsistence in the Divine knowledge, where God is 'with' us. This doctrine appears in an Ottoman tome that might on the face of it be characterised as a work of broadly Māturīdī *kalām*, since it is a commentary on Imām Abū Ḥanīfa's *Fiqh al-Akbar*. In fact, Ibn Bahā'uddīn's book constitutes, alongside aspects of the work of Taşköprüzade himself, clear and remarkable evidence of an Ottoman synthesis[46] of metaphysical Sufism or 'the science of spiritual realities' (*'ilm al-ḥaqā'iq*) with the 'critically verified' later tradition of *kalām*.[47] In the next chapter, we will enquire into both the Akbarian origins and subsequent history of the basic formulations eminently exemplified by the treatments of Ibn Bahā'uddīn and Taşköprüzade, and then meet with the latter's final synthesis. Moreover, we will set forth our own *taḥqīq*, which with an approach hitherto unseen (that nonetheless builds upon many of the positions presented in this study), treats the most fundamental challenges that the encounter with modern thought has raised for the question of *nafs al-amr*.

Chapter 4

Nafs al-Amr and the Exemplary Forms of Cognition

4.1 Qayṣarī and Nafs al-Amr as the Immutable Archetypes

The theory of the ontological identity of *nafs al-amr* appearing in Dāwūd al-Qayṣarī's (d. 1350 CE) *Prolegomena* to his commentary on Muḥyī al-Dīn Ibn ʿArabī's *Fuṣūṣ al-hikam* went on to become probably the most influential of all such theories. The *Prolegomena*, often published and studied independently of the actual commentary, is one of the most incisive, penetrating and authoritative original works in the Akbarian tradition. Following the method and principles of Ibn ʿArabī's son-in-law and spiritual and intellectual successor Ṣadr al-Dīn al-Qūnawī (605–673/1207–74), in works like *Miftāḥ al-ghayb* and *Tafsīr Sūrat al-Fātiḥa*, the *Prolegomena* confidently ventures a critique and synthesis of *kalām*, Avicennan philosophy, and Akbarian metaphysical Sufism, in which these epistemological modes are restored to their rightful places in an order of intrinsic hierarchical complementarity, at the apex of which, of course, stands metaphysical Sufism. Qayṣarī's work is also significant as evidence of the intellectual circumstances of the early Ottoman State, and therefore of the intellectual backdrop to the particular milieu in which thinkers like Ibn Kemal, Ibn Bahāʾuddīn and Taşköprüzade found themselves in the 1500s, an Istanbul in full cultural bloom.

From the very beginning, the intellectual character of the Ottoman polity had been intimately bound up with the thought of Ibn ʿArabī.[1] Granted, everyday *medrese* education in the philosophical and theological sciences was dominated by the new-fashioned post-Rāzian *kalām* of Jurjānī and Taftāzānī, and by the advanced post-Avicennan logic of the commentators, Quṭb al-Dīn al-Rāzī and others, but such was the enthralling, lightning impact of the nascent Akbarian mystical philosophy that it could not help but immediately challenge and influence its philosophical surroundings. This was the case even when that influence was largely negative, as in Taftāzānī's critique of aspects of Akbari thought in *Sharḥ al-Maqāṣid*, aptly rebuffed by the Ottoman *şeyhülislam* Mulla Fenari in his *Miṣbāḥ al-uns*.[2] Almost all of the major figures in the development of the new post-fourteenth century philosophical and theological orthodoxy[3] were bound up in varying degrees of intimacy with the burgeoning school of Ibn 'Arabī. Al-Abharī (d. 663/1265) corresponded with al-Ṭūsī, and had himself been a student of Fakhr al-Dīn al-Rāzī. Al-Kātibī and al-Ṭūsī were students of Abharī, and al-Ṭusī and al-Kātibī (d. 675/1234) are also known to have studied with one another. Quṭb al-Dīn Shīrāzī (637–710/1236–1311) was a student of both al-Kātibī and al-Ṭūsī,[4] and also, fascinatingly, of Ṣadr al-Dīn al-Qūnawī,[5] the supreme architect of systematic Akbarianism (of course, Ṭūsī also maintained a highly important correspondence with Ṣadr al-Dīn al-Qūnawī).[6] Shīrāzī would also go on to be one of the most influential authors in the Suhrawardian Illuminationist tradition, due to his famous commentary on *Ḥikmat al-ishrāq*,[7] where he also alludes approvingly to Ibn 'Arabī. Quṭb al-Dīn al-Rāzī would subsequently study with Shīrāzī, and go on to write the influential *Muḥākamāt*, in which amongst a plethora of other philosophical matters, he discussed the respective merits of the commentaries of Fakhr al-Dīn al-Rāzi and al-Ṭūsī on *al-Ishārāt wa al-Tanbīhāt* (he tends to favour Fakhr al-Dīn al-Rāzī).

Quṭb al-Dīn taught Mubārakshāh,[8] the teacher in the *'aqliyyāt* of two important figures in the early reconciliation of Akbarianism and post-Avicennan philosophy and *kalām* – al-Sayyid al-Sharīf al-Jurjānī and Mulla Fenari. Mulla Fenari had also been a student of Jamal Al-Dīn Aksarāyī (d. 776/1374), the great-grandson of Fakhr al-Dīn al-Razi;[9] moreover, according to Taşköprüzade, Mulla Fenari's father had been a disciple of Ṣadr al-Dīn al-Qūnawī himself, and had studied his *Miftāḥ al-ghayb* with him directly. In turn, Mulla Fenari had studied the book with his father, thereby establishing a direct chain of transmission to Qūnawī. We already know of al-Sharīf al-Jurjānī's Akbarianism through his *Ta'rīfāt* and especially his *Risālat al-wujūd*, but it is now emerging that he had also studied the new Akbarian *''ilm al-taḥqīq'* firsthand in Konya.[10]

Akbarian works like Qaysari's *Prolegomena*, Kāshānī's Qur'anic exegesis, Mulla Fenari's *Misbāḥ al-uns*, and Mulla Jāmī's (d. 897/1492) *al-Durra al-fākhira* would come to be widely revered amongst some of the most well-known *'ulamā* in the Ottoman and wider Islamic world.[11] This is despite the fact that they contained 'experientially verified' positions (*taḥqīq*, in the Akbarian sense) on the whole range of the Islamic sciences that at times appeared to diverge, at least in their formulation, from commonly accepted Ash'arī and Māturīdī positions.

Dāwūd al-Qayṣarī commences the first chapter of his *Prolegomena* with a statement that provides a very fundamental theoretical foundation for his theory of *nafs al-amr.*

> Know that existence in itself (*min ḥaythu huwa huwa*) is distinct from both extramental individuated existence and mental existence.[12]

Here Qayṣarī is elucidating the *taḥqīq* position on 'existence' (*al-wujūd*) for post-Akbarian writers after al-Qūnawī. This position was strongly opposed by some extremely influential *kalām* writers like Taftāzānī, who wished to preserve the traditional, broadly Avicennan view that considered purely with respect to itself, existence can be no more than a perspectival entity that arises out of its particularised substrata as a second intelligible.[13] However, al-Sayyid al-Sharīf al-Jurjānī, alongside Taftāzānī possibly the most influential theologian of the last six centuries of Islamic thought, sympathetically expounds the Akbarian position in his supercommentary on the *kalām* work *al-Tajrīd*,[14] and in his *Risālat al-wujūd*, Jurjānī explicitly endorses it.

Existence in itself is not merely *conceptually* distinct from existence in extramental particulars and existence in the mind. As referring to God Himself, as the sole possessor of 'true' existence and the bestower of 'qualified' or 'restricted' existence (*al-wujūd al-muqayyad*) (that is, everything other than God in Himself), it is prior to both extramental particular and mental existence, and the source of them both: it is 'Absolute Existence' (*al-wujūd al-muṭlaq*). This Avicennan term took on a significance within Akbarianism that it largely lacked in its original context. In post-Avicennan philosophical terminology and *kalām*, *al-wujūd al-muṭlaq* chiefly denotes a perspectival mode of considering the concept of *al-wujūd* without any *particular* qualifications or restrictions, for example like 'mental' or 'extramental' existences. In the Akbarian context it presupposes the negation of *all* 'qualifications' (*quyūd*); and these negations *reveal* the reality of the One God, as the ultimate principle of unity of all particular beings. God's reality, in Himself, is not conditioned by *limitary* determinations,[15] nor is His existence *derived*, unlike qualified existence, which *derives* its existence from being rendered determinate.

In the post-Avicennan tradition, on the other hand, it might be more accurate to translate *al-wujūd al-muṭlaq*, 'unqualified existence' as it is a mere perspectival entity (*amr i'tibārī*). Mubārakshah provides an especially clear statement of this essential 'perspectivality' in his commentary on Najm al-Dīn al-Kātibī's *Ḥikmat al-'ayn*:

> extramental particular existence is something's being *in* extramental particulars (*kawn al-shay' fī al-a'yān*), and mental existence is something's being *in* the mind (*kawn al-shay' fī al-adhhān*), whereas unqualified existence (*al-wujūd al-muṭlaq*) is the unqualified [fact of] being (*muṭlaq al-kawn*)[16] (that is, without it being specified whether this is extramental or mental existence).

The Akbarian concept of *al-wujūd al-muṭlaq* on the other hand, identifies unconditioned and absolute reality with God. All qualified and particularised 'existence' is necessarily contingent, for its determinate form and the specific conditions of its reality, on the One who is the source of all finite being.[17] The nominal 'existence' of created beings is existence contingent, subordinate and derivative.[18] It is 'conditioned' existence, in that it has been qualified by limitary specifications. These qualifications, restrictions or conditions might be illustrated in the following manner. 'Weak, short, green tree', for example, is of a more limited scope with respect to existence than 'green tree', the possible individuals of which could also be tall and strong. 'Tree' is more restricted than 'body', which could be a tree, but many other things besides. 'Body' is more restricted than 'substance', which could be a body, but could also be a spirit or a mind. A person wise, generous or beautiful only to the degree of his particular individuation is similarly restricted; higher beings may possess these qualities more maximally, but this characterization will remain restricted and qualified by its finite relationality to other degrees of these qualities. It must not be imagined, however, that in Himself, God as 'Absolute Existence' denotes the being that exemplifies all qualities in their states of uninstantiated[19] maximality; rather, in the infinite plenitude of His entirely non-composite, simple reality, He constitutes the transcendent *source* of the effusion of those qualities in their true maximality and quasi-infinity, but cannot be restricted, and cannot be limited, by any of these qualities; He infinitely surpasses them.

Radically unlike His creation, God is not restricted by any familiar condition, limitation or mode of individuation; even 'absoluteness' and 'non-restrictedness' are strictly speaking artificial intellectual restrictions that cannot do true justice to the ultimate principle of unity, who alone requires no principle of unity, for He is, in Himself, Transcendent beyond multiplicity or thought or perception. However,

> It [should not be understood] that, in the degree of non-determination, He is not Knowing, Almighty or Willing, nor [characterised by] the rest of the Attributes. Rather, it is that there [in that degree], there is no name or description.[20] That is, [it is] our considering the Pure Essence in the capacity of being beyond all Attributes and Names, and unconditioned by any restrictions or perspectives, even from the restriction 'unconditioned' (*ḥattā ʿan qayd al-iṭlāq*), [and] does not [mean] that He does not have these Attributes and Names in Himself ... this is what is meant by their statement 'the Necessary is Absolute Existence' (*al-wujūd al-muṭlaq*) – that is, pure existence unconditioned by determination by qualifications ... [they do not mean that] He is 'existence' as a universal, which has no existence except in its individuals, which is the position of heretics.[21]

Although He is in Himself transcendently unlike His creation, in His infinite plenitude God is the origin and His creative power the wellspring of the essences of all created beings. These can only come 'into existence' through His volitional self-revelation, in the act of creation. This self-revelation is the Divinely generated, particularised entification and determination, in the worlds of creation, of perspectival aspects of His Eternal Knowledge of the infinite possible *representations* or 'images' of His own knowledge of His nature[22] – these images are the 'Immutable Archetypes' (*al-aʿyān al-thābita*).[23]

God is *necessarily* omniscient; His knowledge of the Immutable Archetypes is thus eternal. Yet by God's free creative act, these Immutable Archetypes become manifest in diverse loci of manifestation – different 'worlds' in which the same essence will appear in different forms and under different individuation-conditions. In his dictionary of Akbarian terminology Kashānī tells us that by

'Existence manifest in the degrees of cosmic being' (*al-wujūd al-ẓāhir fī al-marātib al-kawniyya*) is meant '[Existence's] appearing in the degree of the spirits (*martabat al-arwāḥ*), of imaginal representations (*al-mithāl*), and of sensible being (*al-ḥiss*); each of these entifications of Existence is necessarily 'creation' and 'other [than God].' The meaning of the 'existence' of those degrees is *the experience that the form of every entified thing has of itself* as an existing spirit, imaginal being, or sensible being.[24]

Kashānī is telling us that by the 'existence' of these worlds of manifestation, exactly their self-perception is meant; this is what has been 'created'. The radical philosophical repercussion of this is that the rigorous distinction between 'being' and 'knowing' becomes thus highly questionable. All things ever are in God's uncreated knowledge; though He perceives them, they cannot yet perceive themselves. What it means for a thing to *exist* in the created degrees of being, on the other hand, is for it to constitute a locus of self-knowledge – that is, a limited, qualifying *perspective*, on objects of knowledge that God knows eternally in their fullness. As 'Abd al-Wahhāb al-Sha'rānī (d. 973/1565) asks:

If the entire world [already] exists in the knowledge of the Real, what could the world have gained from appearing as the visible world (*'ālam al-shahāda*)? The answer is, as the Shaykh [Ibn 'Arabī] said in the seventeenth chapter of the *Futūḥāt*, that through its having appeared as the observed world, the world *gained knowledge of itself* that it did not have before, not that it gained an [essential] state it did not have before [in God's knowledge] ... the Real perceives all possible beings both in their states of non-existence and existence, as well as the variegations of their states, but possible beings [in the knowledge of God] do not perceive themselves, nor their existence, nor the variegations of their states. When the vision of their own selves was unveiled for them, they perceived in their imaginal faculties the variegations of their own states. Thus, God only brought particularized essences (*al-a'yān*) into existence in order to unveil to them, stage by stage, their [own] essences and states in succession, one after the other. This is the meaning of our saying 'He derives no new knowledge from the [appearance] of new beings, because they are all [already] known to the Real.'[25]

This unveiling or 'expansion' of the potential already actual in the Immutable Archetypes – which are the primary objects of God's knowledge, but which have, in that purely sciential (*'ilmī*) state of being, no self-knowledge[26] – is exactly the existences of an essence, in

> the world of spirits (*'ālam al-arwāḥ*), which is its obtaining there (*ḥuṣūluhā fīhi*), and in the world of imaginal representations, which is its becoming manifest there (*ẓuhūruhā fīhi*) as a corporeal body, and existence in the sensible world, which is its becoming actualized there (*taḥaqququhā fīhi*), and sciential existence in our minds, which is its subsistence therein (*thubūtuhā fīhi*).[27]

Distinct existence in the mind, that is, human knowledge, is therefore simply the final stage of the effusion, from the One, of created being, itself defined exactly as self-reflexive apperception.

> The forms of quiddities in our minds are the shadows cast by those sciential forms [in God's knowledge].[28]

Let us now go on with the task of providing the necessary context, within Qayṣarī's *Prolegomena*, of his theory of *nafs al-amr*, having provided some of the key backdrop to that theory, chiefly in the Akbarian account of the unfolding of contingent reality as creative *taqyīd* (qualification, limitary restriction), arising from *al-iṭlāq* (absoluteness, unrestrictedness), and resulting in the degrees, the 'worlds', of distinct entification.

'[Existence] is not a perspectival entity' Qaysarī says, '[contrary to what] the unjust (*al-ẓālimūn*) maintain, [and this is shown] by its having actualization in itself without [depending on] any knowing subjects being there, let alone [depending on] their *perspectives*.'[29]

Qaysarī alludes here to a theme that runs throughout his *Prolegomena* – the *kalām* theologians adhere to a relatively reasonable *epistemological* understanding of concepts like 'existence' in understanding them to be '*i'tibārī*' in so far as they tend to become known via the mind's processing of extramental forms; yet they confuse this epistemological understanding with an ontological truth. That is, in the main they possess no clear way of accounting for the ontological status, if any, of these entities (or non-entities). Were it indeed the case that 'existence' can become actual solely in the perspectives of human beings, that is, by being abstracted from extramental particulars, surely none of us would be here in the first place? After all, we would presumably still exist, even were we not able to formally abstract the concept of 'existence' from extramental particulars! Particularized entities must bear a relation to a context of prior reality that constitutes their principle of unity, whence they indeed derive their own share of reality. Otherwise, on the broadly Peripatetic *kalām* account, essences simply languish in ontological obscurity, that is, without any ontological status at all, until 'existence' is superadded *to* their essences, which is merely another way of saying that they become individuated; and yet unless there *is* already a prior principle of unity, the exemplary reality in which all instances thereof partake, there would surely be no 'they' at all *to* become individuated. Moreover, while 'existence' as a second intelligible is certainly a perspectival entity, the notion that this and other perspectival entities possess no deeper roots in reality than the fact of the details of an essence's individuation, is from the Akbarian point of view untenable. Individuation is after all only possible because there *are* prior degrees of reality, with their own, superordinate individuation-conditions. It is not sufficient to merely call the superaddition of existence, the 'effect of the Agent' (*athar al-fāʿil*) as the *kalām* theologians do, as if this constituted an explanation; for although individuated entities certainly exist, and were certainly created by the Agent, 'where' is this individuated state taking place? If it is not taking place 'in' reality, and as a determination of prior essences that already exist as distinct degrees of reality, this would seem to imply that things, though individuated, have no prior ontological context at all, which is unintelligible.[30]

Qayṣarī next turns his attention to another lamentable confusion of ontology and epistemology that is a partial consequence of the question we have just considered. While deeming existence 'perspectival' may be somewhat defensible if one claims that 'existence', though a mental concept, does have an extramental *foundation*, namely particulars in their individuated extramental states,[31] (even though this too ultimately falls prey to the criticisms of the Akbarian *taḥqīq* that we have just alluded to above, in that it fails to account for the prior ontological context of individuated particulars), the notion we are about to discuss seems entirely indefensible. This is the foundational Peripatetic assumption we have already seen several times in this study, standard amongst both the post-Avicennan philosophers and later *kalām* theologians, which maintains that the essences of things, that of, say, 'man', only have reality *within* their individuations in extramental particulars. In other words, essences only have extramental existence *qua* concrete individual[32] – otherwise (for 'the philosophers') they are mere undifferentiated concepts impressed in the Agent Intellect, a locus devoid of the conditions necessary to enable the manifestation of their *distinct* multiplicity[33] and for many of the *kalām* theologians, their status seems even less clear, as we will see in more detail below. In affirming exemplarism against these immanentist approaches to the ontological status of natures, Qayṣarī tells us,

> We do not accept that the actualization of the natural univer-sal is contingent on an [individuated] substrate coming into existence ... for if this were the case, a circularity would be entailed ... [for] anything that becomes speciated (*tanawaʻa*) or individuated (*tashakhkhaṣa*) is intrinsically posterior to [its] generic and specific nature (*al-ṭabīʻa al-jinsiyya wa al-nawʻiyya*) and the posterior cannot be the cause of the actualization (*taḥaqquq*) of that which is prior.[34]

This luminous insight underlines the major difficulty inherent in the contention that the realm of individuated particulars is, in some ultimate way, *nafs al-amr* to which all true propositions correspond – even be it that for the purposes of this theory *nafs al-amr* be bifurcated into *al-dhihn* and *al-khārij*, and even be it that *al-khārij* is posited as the '*nafs al-amr*' pertaining solely and exclusively to propositions whose terms have indi-viduated, *khārijī* entities as referents. This is because the identity of each particular in the external world is exactly the result of the particularized individuation of a 'universal' nature, the existence of which can neither be purely mental – for the resultant individual would then be ultimately perspectival and relative, as a mere branch of something putatively per-spectival and relative – nor purely *khārijī*, because of the inherent and necessary priority, explained by Qayṣarī above, of essences with respect to the individuated particulars that instantiate them. Thus, there is more than one factor that challenges the notion that *al-khārij* (understood in the standard *kalām* sense, as effectively confined to sensible extramental particulars)[35] can constitute 'the *nafs al-amr*' even of *khārijī* propositions. From the discussion in Chapter 2, we are already aware of the fact that the intelligibility of propositions about individuals in *al-khārij*, 'Zayd is atop the mountain in a woollen robe', for example, are often contingent upon mental elements. This first point, that for example 'being atop', a relation, is a mental, perspectival predicate (but also exists in *nafs al-amr* because it would still apply to the world *in potentia* if there were no actualized minds at all), makes it difficult to ascribe a large number of even ostensibly 'extramental particular' propositions to extramental particulars alone.[36] Moreover, and also pertaining to this first point about the mentalness of many extramental particular propositions, our discussion in Chapter 2 also showed us that human creations like beds, houses, or woollen garments, are indeed extramental particulars, but are nonetheless *ontologically* contingent upon relational, mental properties like a 'particularized arrangement', that can serve as universals, capable of instantiation in innumerable identical woollen garments of exactly the same specification. A third realm in which objective yet *purely* intelligible, unindividuatable principles inhere, *nafs al-amr*, must thus constitute the embedded framework rendering strictly *particular* reality intelligible (the framework nonetheless remaining of a greater scope than its special manifestation amongst the particular individuation-conditions of the given world in question),[37] a framework that is, as it were, 'interposed' 'between' the individuatable elements of extramental particular reality, so as to be constitutive of, for example, the *relationality* of extramental particular reality. This is another way of simply saying that *al-khārij* exists *within* a larger reality, *nafs al-amr*, merely constituting its outermost tip.

Yet as Qayṣarī's words above show, the problems do not stop here for the notion that *al-khārij* (construed as confined to sensible extramental particulars) can serve as the 'things as they are' *even for extramental particular propositions regardless of any possible mental elements*.[38] This is because even the unequivocally *khārijī*, non-mental elements of such propositions (in our example, these are limited to 'Zayd' and the 'mountain'), do not derive their intelligibility from *al-khārij* per se, that is from their individuated, particular instances, but rather from the prior existence of exemplary forms, the one over the many that renders Zayd an instantiation *of* 'man' (rather than of something else), and the mountain an instantiation *of* 'mountain' (rather than of something else). An extramental individual is an instantiation *of* an essence, and utterly contingent upon that essence-itself. Yet on the Peripatetic, Avicennan and most widespread late *kalām* view, that essence can only be said to exist when at least one individual that depends upon it has already come into existence. This is a manifest contradiction, and continued to be seen as such in the subsequent writings of the school of Ibn ʿArabī. While for extramental particular propositions *al-khārij* certainly serves as one aspect of *nafs al-amr*, no given immanent *manifestation* of a thing as it is can ever account for the ultimate mode of being of the essence-itself; for that immanent manifestation is utterly contingent upon, and *only rendered intelligible by*, the prior existence of the essence-itself, and the former cannot thus be fully cognized in isolation, without reference to the latter. While an extramental particular proposition is certainly *meant* to refer to the *particular* Zayd and the *particular* mountain,[39] the respective essences of 'man' and 'mountain' are nonetheless inescapably essential (*dhātī*) elements of the particulars in question (an individual, after all, is made up of the essence alongside particular individuations). Thus, no given particularizing instantiation, considered with respect to itself, of 'man' or 'mountain' – the extramental instantiation of Zayd on the mountain for example – could ever serve as the ontological grounds making it possible for there to be (for example) a 'Zayd'-man on the mountain in the first place. The result of this is that particularizing instantiations *considered in isolation* can never serve as any form of *nafs al-amr*,[40] if *nafs al-amr* is to be understood in its real sense as the fullest, truthmaking, distinct reality underlying the truth of any judgement that corresponds to it, rather than the mere *appearance* of that reality, which is all extramental particulars *qua* extramental particulars could ever be.

It is not widely known today that one of the two or three most original and influential representatives of *kalām* theology in all of its later history, Fakhr al-Dīn al-Rāzī, defended the existence of Forms in some of his most important works. In Chapter 2, we saw some of his positive arguments for exemplary Forms. In order to see how serious Rāzī was about the viability of the doctrine of Forms (his keen awareness of certain difficulties involved notwithstanding), and to provide further support for our own affirmation of the reality of Forms and the importance of their place in any renewed *kalām*, let us look here at his remarkable refutation of some of the classic Peripatetic arguments against the consistency and possibility of Forms.

Aristotle sought to prove the absurdity of these Forms by saying that that uninstantiated [entity] is either shared, exactly as it is, by all individuals, or it is not; the first [possibility] entails that that uninstantiated entity be characterized by all of the properties that have obtained for these individuals, such that what Zayd knows, ʿAmr must also know and moreover contrariwise, and this is impossible. The second [possibility] is also impossible, because the concomitant (*lāzim*) of one nature must also be one; [either] independence from matter, or requiring it, must be uniform across all of the individuals of a species, and ʿwe [speaking in Aristotle's voice] have provided proof that individuals – of any species that is not confined to one individual – can only obtain via matter.' The answer to [Aristotle] is to choose the second [possibility] (that is, that the uninstantiated entity is not shared exactly as it is by all individuals). [Aristotle's] saying that the individuals of a single nature must all share either in being independent from a [material] receptacle (*qābil*), or in requiring one, is refuted by existence, and indeed by genera and differentia. Moreover, his saying that the individuals of any species not confined to one individual can only obtain via matter is founded on [affirming] the first possibility (i.e., that the uninstantiated [entity] is shared, exactly as it is, by all individuals, a notion that Rāzī has just rejected).[41]

For Rāzī's notion of Forms, then, the exemplary Form exists aloof and uninstantiated; yet individuals exist through the Form, and derive their intelligibility therefrom. However, the absurd simultaneous predication, of the timeless, spaceless Form, of the corresponding individuals' contradictory, contingent properties, is not entailed by Rāzī's theory of Forms, because he rejects the contention that the manifestations of a given nature must be strictly confined to particulars individuated by matter, unless the nature in question entails its own individuation, in which case the sole individual yielded must be incorporeal.[42] The nature, 'existence', for example, possesses both corporeal and incorporeal individuals. Likewise, in the cases of genera, like 'substance', and differentia like 'rational' – each possibility being instantiated (on a conceivable account) respectively by men (corporeal) and angels (incorporeal). Incorporeal, uninstantiated essences untainted by contingent, changing properties are thus shown to be possible.

In his magisterial *Misbāḥ al-uns*, the first Ottoman *şeyhülislam* Mulla Fenari (to whom the substance of the synthetical achievement hitherto credited to Mulla Sadra must in justice be ascribed)[43] tells us that the demonstration of the existence of exemplary Forms (*al-muthul*) as well as Imaginal Forms (*al-muthul al-khayāliyya*) constitutes the whole basis of 'the science of experiential verification' (*'ilm al-taḥqīq*).[44] Affirming the Forms provides 'a foundation for proving that the Real is Absolute Existence'; indeed, affirming them 'leads one to affirm [the notion of] Absolute Existence'.[45] Moreover, by proving the existence of the Forms, 'harmony between revealed religion and the intellect obtains.'[46] Fenari has taken especial care to provide detailed intellectual arguments to demonstrate the existence of exemplary Forms, rather than merely invoking arguments from mystical experience, because 'rendering [the Forms] familiar to the intellects of the veiled ones' that is, *kalām* theologians and speculative philosophers, by expressing Akbarian metaphysics in their own philosophical language, 'in order to stave off their persistent delusions' is of 'pressing importance', in order that this harmony be actualized.[47] Fenari offers several proofs for the existence of exemplary forms, that evoke Qayṣarī's objection to the notion that an essence's existence depends upon its becoming extramentally individuated. Some of his most basic and fundamental formulations:

> universal quiddities like 'humanness' exist extramentally, because the existent [individual] 'Zayd' is composed of [the universal quiddity] and of individuation; now, the non-existence of a part entails the non-existence of the whole.[48]

That is, if the essence rendering 'Zayd' intelligible did not exist in itself, a basic principle of mereology would ensure that the individual that is partially composed of it would not be able to exist at all. Even more vividly,

> Another [proof] is that a thing's essence is that thing by means of which its existent individual becomes actualized; and that which brings about actualization must itself be actual.[49]

Before offering positive proofs for exemplary Forms, Mulla Fenari had, like al-Rāzī, needed to deal with the immanentist claims of the broadly Peripatetic school, that the notion of uninstantiated exemplary Forms must be ruled out a priori, as entailing a violation of the principle of non-contradiction:

> The [supposedly] most [cogent proof] that the repudiators of the Forms have held onto does not [actually] apply, [namely] that were a single nature to be shared [by many individuals] in extramental particulars, a single entity would have to be characterized by contradictory properties. This [does not apply] because the impossibility only pertains to a singular thing that is extramental-particular and sensible, not to an exemplary or spiritual singular thing. Moreover, [it does not apply] because its characterization by contradictory properties obtains with respect to its loci of manifestation, and its individuals, and with respect to its unity in itself [in a different manner in each], and it is possible for mutually exclusive things to come together when they pertain to different perspectives; and moreover, because although [it is true that affirming the Forms] entails that [the single exemplary entity] would have to be characterized by [contradictory properties], this is only in a *universal* manner, whereas it is its being characterized thereby in a *particular* manner that is impossible. Moreover, [the Peripatetic proof does not apply] because extramental participation in a spiritual or exemplary entity is akin to the participation of [universal] quiddities in [different] minds, which the repudiators [of the Forms] affirm. For just as participation in different minds does not entail the quiddity [itself] being characterized by contradictory properties[50] ... so is the same true of participation in extramental particulars. [Finally], there is nothing far-fetched in the notion of the conjunction of the incorporeal and the material, and this does not entail the materiality [of the former], for this is akin to the conjunction of the human rational soul with its body – which [the Peripatetics acknowledge], for this is not comparable to physical conjunction, even though by means of it a particularized, singular new mode of being obtains.[51]

According to the later Ottoman thinker Ibn Bahā'uddīn, those who limit the meaning of an essence's 'existence' to its sensible appearances in the world of ordinary experience, thereby rejecting the Akbarian notion that these sensible appearances are derived from Forms in the ontologically prior worlds of the Imaginal Representations, the World of Spirits and the Immutable Archetypes, 'become so entangled in [intellectual] difficulties that every time they try to extricate themselves from one, they tumble into another.'[52] Only exemplarism can solve these problems. As Ibn Bahā'uddīn tells us,

> [the doctrine that] the sciential forms are the essences [of things], and the forms of extramental particulars shadows thereof, subordinate (*taba‘*) thereto, is the terminator of all difficulties, and the guide against all misguidance; not as the philosophers have reversed things, [saying] that the extramental particular forms are the fundamental principles, and the intellectual forms representations and shadows thereof.[53]

Qayṣarī's Akbarian teaching on *nafs al-amr* as identified with the ultimate exemplary forms of all possible objects of knowledge, may be the first explicit such formulation, although the doctrine is certainly contained *in potentia* throughout the writings of Ṣadr al-Dīn al-Qūnawī, al-Kāshānī and of course in those of Ibn ‘Arabī himself, (the passage from the *Futūḥāt*, for example, quoted at the beginning of this study). Immediately before making his identification of *nafs al-amr*, Qayṣarī feels it necessary to rule out once and for all the notion that God's knowledge of the world obtains *via* the Intellect, a notion he ascribes to some of the 'later philosophers', although he is evidently referring to Naṣīr al-Dīn al-Ṭūsī. Amidst numerous other arguments, Qayṣarī tells us that '[this would] entail His Essence, in its most noble of attributes, standing in need of that which is other than Him and that emanates from Him, and that He not know particulars and their modalities in so far as they are particular, far Exalted be Allah above such a notion!'[54]

Qayṣarī then pre-empts the Ṭūsian (though not genuinely Avicennan) argument underlying this notion, namely that placing the ultimate locus of multiple objects of knowledge in the Divine knowledge would entail the existence of real multiplicity in the Divine Essence, which is impossible. In his *Ishārāt*, Avicenna had unequivocally stated that 'the First's apprehension of all things is from His Essence, and in His Essence.'[55] He then tells us that since these objects of knowledge are concomitants of His Essence and posterior to it, they do not subsist *in* His Essence, which remains unsullied by multiplicity. That is, the First's objects of knowledge are *essentially* (though not temporally) posterior to His Essence, and cannot thus be considered part of His Essence, although He knows them in and of His Essence.[56] Somewhat unusually, Ṭūsī takes clear exception to Avicenna here, arguing that the latter's position entails that God constitute the substrate of His effects, multiplicitous possible beings (*maḥallan li maʿlūlātihi al-mumkina al-mutakaththira*). 'Far Exalted be God above such a notion!' says Ṭūsī. As an alternative to Avicenna's position, Ṭūsī somewhat infamously argued that God's knowledge of His creation in all of its multiplicity is exactly His apprehension of the knowledge of the Intellects that emanate from Him.[57]

Qayṣarī provides an Akbarian explanation of the presence of this apparent multiplicity:

> He Who brought all into existence, from non-existence to existence ... knows all things in their realities, and in their concomitant extramental particular and mental forms, before His existentiation of them. Otherwise, it would not be possible for Him to bestow existence upon them (...).[58] The position maintaining the impossibility of His Essence, and Knowledge - which is identical to His Essence – being the locus of a multiplicity of things, would only be sound if [the multiple things] were other than Him, as is the opinion of those who are veiled from the truth. However, if they are identical to Him in existence and reality, and other than Him in particularization and restriction, this [impossibility] is not logically entailed. [59]

The Immutable Archetypes are in themselves *iʿtibārī* entities, possessing no independent reality, and as 'images' of His Names and Attributes, entirely subsumed in the nature of the Real. As Ibn ʿArabī tells us, they have 'never scented the fragrance of existence' (*mā shammat rāʾiḥat al-wujūd*). In terms of their particularization and as 'non-existent', but 'subsistent' entities, they are, in their specific identities, particularly 'themselves', and cannot thus be God. Yet the notion of a 'multiplicity' obtaining in

God's Essence has no application, for the Immutable Archetypes are a perspectival, rather than real multiplicity.

> Things as they are (*nafs al-amr*), then, is the Essential Knowledge that encompasses the forms of all things ... whether particularized or sciential (*'ilmiyya*): *the Knower of the Unseen, not so much as the weight of a mote escapes from Him, neither is aught smaller than that, or greater, but that it is in a Manifest Book* [Qur'an 34:3].[60]

This is the ultimate degree of *nafs al-amr*: it is the state of subsistence in which things, in an ultimate sense, *are*, as they are 'in themselves', unrestricted by the modifications entailed by the particularities of instantiation in one or another of the worlds averred by the Akbarians, or by the perspectives of contingent knowing subjects.[61] Here, the essences of things subsist directly through their ultimate Divine origin, for the Immutable Archetypes possess two aspects. The first aspect is their constituting 'the images of the Names (*ṣuwar al-asmā'*).' The second aspect is their constituting the most primary exemplary Forms of created reality – 'the aspect in which they are the realities [underlying] extramental particularized essences (*ḥaqā'iq al-a'yān al-khārijiyya*).' In this first aspect, 'they are like bodies to spirits, and in the second, like spirits to bodies.'[62] Yet because *nafs al-amr* possesses ontologically posterior loci of manifestation, it can admit of degrees:

> some of the gnostics have made the First Intellect (*al-'aql al-awwal*)[63] tantamount to *nafs al-amr*, for it is the locus of the manifestation of the Divine Knowledge with respect to its encompassing the universals that contain all of their particulars, and because its knowledge corresponds to that which is in Allah's knowledge. From this perspective, the Universal Soul (*al-nafs al-kulliyya*), which is named the 'Preserved Tablet' (*al-lawḥ al-maḥfūẓ*) is also tantamount to *nafs al-amr*.[64]

This accounts for the ontological grounding of assents, and the conceptions of real existents, but God's knowledge also pertains to contradictory notions (the existence of which are impossible) 'in terms of His knowledge of [the human] mind and imagination, and the concomitants [of mind and imagination], of the one who imagines that which [in fact] has no existence and no essence.'[65] Second intelligibles, and the *umūr ʿāmma* (like unity and multiplicity, essence, individuation, necessity and possibility, causality and so on) are also ontologically rooted:

> Existence possesses loci of manifestation in the mind, just as it has loci of manifestation in extramental particulars. Amongst these [loci] are the transcendentals (*al-umūr al-ʿāmma*), and the universals which do not have existence except in the mind.[66]

At length we have arrived, with these words of Qayṣarī's, to the most telling tension with which we have been concerned in this study, and that has most pressingly entailed an identification of objective reality with something beyond both individuated particulars and minds. This is the problem of the rootedness in things as they are, or *nafs al-amr*, of special varieties of primary abstract, intelligible entities, that do not merely constitute both terms in certain true propositions – many of which are indispensable to the operation of the sciences or entailed by such as are thus necessary – but moreover constitute, as we shall argue, the ontological grounds of the intelligibility (in the sense of objective knowability) of our world. Conversely, if (as dominant strands of modern, post-Kantian thought contend or assume) such entities possess no deeper roots in reality than their appearances in individual minds, the obtainment of objective truth about metaphysical reality, and indeed, even regarding 'ordinary' experience of individual-particular reality, is placed beyond our reach. In the next section, in setting forth our account of the actuality and fundamental nature of this prior intelligible framework, we delineate a way to cut off, at source, the (ultimately very meagre) argumentative force of the most fundamental and widespread doctrines incessantly dictated to us by subjectivist philosophical fashion. It is a way rooted in the richness of the resources bestowed upon us by the broad traditions of Islamic philosophy and theology, as well as kindred traditions of philosophy to which some of our revered forebears did not perhaps have access; and the creative adaption of this grand heritage to meet the challenge of our times, has yielded and will continue to yield fresh possibilities for its renewal.

4.2 Transcending the Transcendental: 'Metaprinciples' and the Henological Ascent

Construed as the Divine knowledge as in Qayṣarī's formulation, *nafs al-amr* does not merely play host to the intelligible forms of species, like 'man', 'angel' and 'river', but furthermore to the *umūr ʿāmma* and other primary intelligible entities, without which the world would be devoid of order, indistinct and unrelatable, an inchoate, unintelligible murkiness.

'Possibility', to give one example amongst the *umūr ʿāmma* (and we might quite as easily have taken 'unity', 'causality', 'essence' or others, as examples in its stead) exists in, and 'corresponds' to *nafs al-amr*, whether it is construed as a pure self-evident concept or as abstracted from an intelligible or sensible substrate. Were 'possibility' and 'contingency', and further subordinate, cognate notions, to be somehow entirely ousted from the armoury of our cognitive apparatuses, the intelligibility of the world would be severely impaired. We would no longer be able to perceive an important dimension of the richness of non-essential properties possessed by individual things and states of affairs. The apprehension of facts as basic as 'my son may become a doctor one day, but the same will not be possible for my cat', 'human beings can ride bikes' (that is, *in potentia/ bi al-quwwa*), or even 'a pandemic may one day emerge, that will force the entire world into lockdown', would simply exceed our capacities, as would knowledge of more foundational, elevated truths, such as the fact that the extramental particular existence and non-existence of any item in the world of time and space, are both possible with respect to the essence of that given thing.

Were we to be deprived of the inclusion of 'possibility' amidst the array of cognitive apparatuses that we recognize as both our own, and as distinctively human, we would no longer be able to apprize ourselves of the contingencies of life, and no longer able to plan to procure the good or to ward off harm. For if, per impossibile, 'possibility' could somehow cease to be a feature of the intelligible structure of the world, all would be necessary, or, perhaps, modally neutral. Yet precisely because there really are possible things, our inability to cognize 'possibility' would entail, in the unhypothetical world we do in fact experience, that the world cease to be fully knowable.

What, then, does it mean for 'possibility' to exist within and correspond to reality, to things as they are? On a somewhat sparse but in some sense 'standard' account, its correspondence or non-correspondence thereto is necessarily contingent on the predicative truth-value of 'possibility' with respect to a particular substrate, that is, in terms of assent to propositions the like of 'this human individual is possible'. This is because when we examine any given human individual, we find that neither existence nor non-existence necessarily pertains to him; John or Zayd might never have existed, and the universe would have proceeded perfectly admirably without them. This account of the 'truthmaking' of possibility, ultimately amounts to the Taftāzānian view that we have already seen, that the correspondence of a true proposition to *nafs al-amr* (and thus, the 'truthmaking' activity of *nafs al-amr*) is no more than the relation resultant of the ascription of this proposition to the pertinent logical necessity or demonstrative proof of its truth. Ultimately, our direct assent to the merely possible nature of the existence of any given human individual, granting the acknowledged relation of the concept to self-evident ones like necessity, accounts for the validity and applicability of the concept to all manner of particulars.

Yet while this immanentist view is attractive to those committed to the impossibility of uninstantiated essences (of whatever type) it suffers from a not insubstantial failing: that of begging the question as to why 'possibility', or any other abstract predicate, can apply even in potentia (to bring in a further immanentist circularity) to illimitable varieties of subjects. This question stands, regardless of whether in the self-referential context of the synthesis of the logically self-evident and necessary empirical foundations of knowledge, with the demonstrative, syllogistic procedure, we can prove that 'possible' (or 'a unity', 'exists', 'has such-and-such an essence', 'stands in relation to', 'is the cause of' and so on) can, in a true proposition, be predicated of a given entity. For how, other than because it just seems that way to us, do we know that such abstract terms –none of which denote even a possible particular[67] – genuinely characterize the entities that they are predicated of? The fundamental question is not 'what leads us to believe a thing "possible"?' The answer to this question would provide no more justification than any provided by the simple observation that a given entity's essence does not necessitate its own existence or non-existence in a particular domain; thereby resting merely on the assumption that a further concept, that of necessity, is understood to us. That is, such attempted justification merely begs the further question of whether the concept of necessity is itself embedded in reality. Yet in fact, all immanent 'definitions' of possibility are merely circular – possibility, impossibility and necessity can only be defined in terms of one another. The question cannot thus even be deferred to 'necessity'; if 'possibility' is a self-evident concept that we simply happen to be equipped with, how are we to deal with claims that it is ultimately an ontologically contingent feature of our cognitive apparatuses, that possesses no relation to any reality beyond subjective experience? If we can find no strict reason why the application of such concepts to intelligible or sensible objects should be productive of genuinely objective knowledge, physical or metaphysical, why should we think that it in fact is?

The appropriate question, instead, is 'what is it about reality that gives rise to a class of entities that regulate, define and necessarily attend all particulars, and without which those particulars would not be intelligible?' Moreover, what accounts for the distinction in specific nature between each of these entities, whether it is 'possibility', 'existence', 'unity', 'multiplicity', 'necessity', 'causality', or others? It is doubtless the case that the epistemological procedure by which anything at all is rendered intelligible to us, is founded on the intuition of the self-evidence of a vast array of foundational concepts. Yet the intuition of unity, the most primary intuition of them all, and that of the one-over-the-many, which the former entails when confronted by the manifold of individual unities with which the world presents us, compel us to question how it can be that evidently purely intelligible concepts nonetheless order, regulate, apply to, and (using the demonstrative method uncover hidden depths of), all particulars (the aggregate of which putatively constitutes our world), unless those concepts are actually embedded in reality in a manner fundamentally intertwined with sensible reality, yet simultaneously independent of it,[68] an embeddedness that is moreover ontologically prior to the particular appearances that such concepts make in individual minds.

4.2.1 A SHORT EXCURSUS ON UNITY AND BEING

The observant reader may have noted that we do not adhere to broad Avicenno-Thomist and Neoscholastic doctrines of the primacy of 'being',[69] in the orders of reality and of knowing, and a short digression is required, not merely in order to justify this possibly unfamiliar departure,[70] but more fundamentally, because the deduction of the exemplary metaprinciples underlying the transcendentals is an entailment of the primacy of unity, not that of being. In terms more general than this particularity of application (which, nonetheless, possesses vast systematic consequences for the deductive structure of reality), it is our view that the doctrine of the primacy of being is a considerably less coherent or philosophically fertile position than has often been presumed. The tension cannot be assuaged by invoking the rather anodyne objection that 'surely the One exists.' Of course, the One does exist.[71] The One is the supremely Real, the source of all being and the ultimate principle of unity of all things, itself requiring no principle of unity. The nub of the question, however, does not reside in this, but rather, whether some construal of being itself is the ultimate and primary reality underlying all possible determinations, and whether a (presumably rather downgraded version) of being itself subsequently becomes our 'first principle' of cognition. Perhaps the most fundamental difficulty for the primacy of 'being' takes the problem of non-being as its main point of departure, and this is admirably encapsulated by Jens Half-wassen in his pellucid and incisive article, 'The Metaphysics of the One'

> As the *basis* for Being and Thought, the One precedes both. This absolute priority of the One also shows itself in the fact that while we can think all entities and even Being itself only as a unity, we must on no account always think the One as connected to Being. We can of course conceive of non-Being. So, for example, we can think of non-Being as different from Being, Becoming as the intermediary between Being and Nothing and even of Nothing itself as the complete lack of Being; and by this means we think of Non-Being, Becoming and Nothing, in each case, as a unitary constitution. In contrast, we cannot think of anything, without simultaneously thinking of it as a unity. The One is therefore prior to Being, just as it is prior to Thought. The One is the Absolute and is not contingent upon Being or Thought and it is presupposed in and before all Being, just as in and before all Thought, and does not allow itself to be thought away.[72]

Under every possible construal, the 'existent' is only possible if it is a 'one' thing, whereas it is not possible to find a broad enough notion of 'existent' enabling us to non-tautologically state that 'the one is only possible if it is existent' (that is, that does not simply amount to saying 'the one is only possible if it is one'). The non-existent is also one, and this ensures that 'the one is only possible if it is existent' is false if 'existent' is to be predicated of 'one' non-tautologically, and redundant if it is taken as a synonym for 'one'.

If 'existence' and 'subsistence' are contrasted, as in the general scheme of the Akbarian school, with subsistence (*al-thubūt*) denoting determinateness without individual consciousness (as with the Immutable Archetypes), and 'existence' the self-consciousness of their successively unfolding loci of manifestation (*maẓāhir*) in the worlds of creation, we have a case in point. Neither of these varieties of being, 'unqualified determinateness' (subsistence), nor 'determinate self-consciousness' (existence) arise from any mysterious substratum 'being', but rather constitute the means by which some intelligible sense for the term 'being' can be garnered. They both have their principles of unity, however; (let us say, for example, within an Akbarianesque scheme, 'determinateness' in the Name *al-muqaddir*, and self-consciousness in the Name *al-'alīm*). The Names 'exist', of course, in the broad sense that they are prior and more real than their participants, which depend upon them; but can we make sense of the notion that the Divine Essence that is their principle of unity is, in itself, 'pure being'?

If we turn to the broadest Avicennan and later *kalām* notions of existence, either as the necessarily individuated *mabda' al-āthār al-khārijiyya* (the principle of extramental effects), or as distinct mental existence, we face similar problems. A phoenix possesses a type of determinateness (it is a phoenix, not a unicorn), and therefore possesses a type of 'being', mentally, in that it is distinct (again, being = determinate distinctness), but has no being in particulars (*fī al-khārij*), because it is merely a distinct thing, not a distinct thing that is also individuated. Yet what is the positive content of the term 'being', such that it can intelligibly divide into the solely mental, which is merely distinct, and the extramental particular, which is not only distinct, but moreover individuated and the 'principle of its extramental effects'? The determinateness that allows us to say that a phoenix in some sense 'exists' is identical to, rather than caused by 'being' (because its 'being' = determinateness, which in a relational context entails distinction); its cause lies, rather, in the fact that the multiplicity within the concept 'phoenix' is governed by a principle of unity rendering it determinate (a phoenix, not a unicorn), just as things which are not merely distinct but moreover possess individuals (such as man), are determinate because their multiplicitous elements are gathered into a principle of unity such that 'it is a man', not a horse, or 'it is a horse', not a man (and as individuals, they are determinate not only in terms of being what they are qua individual, but also in so far as they determine 'man'). Being a 'principle of extramental effects' also fails to irreducibly capture the meaning of extramental being in terms of something that arises from any intelligible construal of 'being itself'. The sun 'exists' extramentally, for example, because it constitutes the principle and starting point of its palpable effects of light and heat, but any such definition fails to be *māni'*, that is, to exclude individuals that it should not embrace in its definition – what of my particular, entirely mental conception of a beautiful house, which motivates, constitutes the formal cause and the 'principle of effects', the 'effect' here being the extramental house itself? Although the mental 'house' exists in my mind which 'exists in extramental particulars', the mental house itself does not exist in extramental particulars, for otherwise it would not be mental.[73]

If it be said that we can all discern the self-evident difference between the being of an individuated horse in space and time, and that of a merely mentally distinct 'unicorn', we would answer that this is certainly so! However, although invoking 'in space and time' as the differentia of this mode of 'extramental' existence might have the benefit of motivating an investigation into the nature of space and time, it tells us nothing further about what 'existence' itself could mean, especially if that 'existence' is meant to be the same univocal concept that also applies to God's existence, given that God expressly exists 'outside of space and time'. Nonetheless, surely 'man' and 'horse' possess greater 'degrees' of being than 'phoenix' or 'unicorn'? Indeed, this would appear to be so; but it is unity, not 'being', that can provide an account of 'grades' of lesser and greater reality. The mental image of a particular man, thought by an individual man who is his friend, possesses less reality than the individual man he is thinking of, and moreover, less even than the mind of the man thinking of his friend, which constitutes the principle of unity synthesizing the sensible, imaginal and intelligible elements of the concept into a unity of particularity-in-universality; both are thus 'prior in reality'. The exemplary Form of 'human being', in turn possesses greater reality than the individual man, because it is the principle of the unity of the determinateness of immanent 'man' within the proliferation of individual men, and the rubric in accordance with which all individuating characteristics must obtain. In a similar manner, 'horse' contains more reality than 'phoenix' although both exist in the sense that both are determinate; but 'horse' is the principle of unity for individual horses, whereas 'phoenix' fails to be the principle of unity of anything, resting rather on a principle of unity which is itself subordinate (for the purposes of this argument, the individual man in its creative activity, itself subordinate to the Form of man).[74] In each case, we could say that the prior possesses 'more existence', but this contention is not rendered intelligible by any construal of 'being itself', but rather, by the notion of the greater participation in unity of the thing in question.

If it be objected that 'pure non-being' in some sense 'exists' (such that we can intelligibly talk about 'it'), and that this is meant to betoken the primacy of existence, we would respond that on such an account, the term 'existence' becomes a concomitant of all distinct terms, and thus loses any essential meaning at all. If everything exists in some maximally broad sense of existence, even the non-existent, the term 'exists' becomes utterly dispensable. It is surely only possible to distinguish 'the existent' from 'the non-existent' because the existent is determinate, while the non-existent is not. Yet the determinate is only so because it is a unity; whatever multiplicity that it contains has become subsumed into a principle of unity allowing it to be picked out as a 'this' thing, that is, as 'this thing' - whether intelligible or sensible, 'universal' or particular - and not 'that' thing. Being is not thus an irreducible predicate, while unity is irreducible. Everything, even if it involves a multiplicity, participates in unity, is only knowable in terms of unity. 'Everything participates in being, even if it is non-being', however, yields a contradiction. It becomes impossible to distinguish being and non-being, whereas their opposition is meant to be a stark one, *lā wāsiṭata bayn al-wujūd wa al-ʿadam*, 'there is no intermediary between existence and non-existence.' Multiplicity, however, is not analogous to 'non-being', in being equivalent to 'non-unity', because 'unity' and 'multiplicity' are not always in strict opposition; every multiplicity is also a unity, just as all of the items that participate in the principle of unity to form a unity are, taken alone, themselves unities. '7 ones', that is, 7, to take one particularly unsubtle example, is still the determinate unity of 7, rather than of 8. The human body is the unity of the human body, despite its plethora of parts (each of which are also unities, like the heart and the brain); 'earth' remains a single world, despite containing all that the earth contains. Amongst unities, then, there are some that are multiplicities-within-unities, so that multiplicity, which is never completely devoid of a unifying principle, can nonetheless be intelligibly classed as a subset of unity. But how can non-being, in the sense of the indeterminate, be classed as a subset of 'being' construed as the determinate? The designator of 'indeterminate' is mentally determinate, certainly, but this hardly tells us anything about the indeterminate 'itself'. And if on the other hand, 'being' is not to be construed as the determinate, how are we to construe it, such that it does not reduce to unity, which unlike being, actually tells us, in the course of the epistemological and aetiological roles that it plays, something about what it is?

In fact, anything that is in any way determinate does exist, in so far as no more adequate construal of existence can be found than that existence = determinateness. Even *sharīk al-bārī* (the impossible individual separate from God, who nonetheless putatively participates in godhood) 'exists' as a mental form, but with no genuine reality at all, because far from constituting a principle of unity to anything at all, merely represents a weak form of combinatory being, formed by artificially affixing the concept of multiple individuals to the concept of God; its principle of unity is thus the very human mind that effects this affixation. On the opposite pole of our notion of the scale of being, is God Himself, the ultimate principle of unity of all things, who contains no real multiplicity within Himself. Ultimate 'unity' thus becomes the criterion for the 'real', rather than 'being'. Therefore,

> All beings, just insofar as they are beings, depend, in order to be, on unifying determination itself, which is not any one determinate 'this,' and so not a being, but rather that in virtue of which every being is one, is determinate, is a being … "The One itself" thus represents integration or identity as such as the condition for all being whatsoever. It is in this sense that the One is the source, or cause, of reality itself, that in virtue of which there are any beings, anything to be apprehended by thought.[75]

The real content of the term 'being' even in the Akbarian notion of 'Absolute Existence', turns out to be 'ultimate unity' (that is, absolutely simple unity, such that it can constitute the absolute principle of unity of all being, and itself requires no such principle), because the 'pure existence' of 'Absolute Existence' means that it is an 'existence' unconditioned by being determined by qualifications (*muṭlaq 'an al-qayd*), and this is precisely what 'beyond being' denotes in the Platonic tradition.[76] This becomes clear if we note that the Akbarian framework speaks of the Absolute in itself (rather than in terms of the participation of contingent being in Absolute Being) entirely in terms of a unity that excludes all determination. God is *muta'ayyin* in Himself (for He is Himself, and not the world), but this *ta'ayyun* does not represent anything analogous to the individuation of any finite being (since all of our examples of individuation involve the individuation of an essence or property that is distinct from the individuated thing itself, whereas there is nothing that is prior to, or with God). This is God as *al-aḥadiyya* (exclusive unity) the absolute principle of unity, which according to al-Qayṣarī is the essence of 'existence' (*ḥaqīqat al-wujūd*) in itself.[77] The 'first determination' (*al-ta'ayyun al-awwal*), which is *al-waḥda* (determinate unity) the unified principle of the emergence of multiplicity upon which the unfolding of creation depends, is evidently also accounted for in terms of unity, as the first finite determination of the infinite Divine plenitude (such that we might capture its metaprincipial intelligible unity in the term 'infinity-limit'), and, indeed, the most perfect such determination possible, namely *al-ḥaqīqa al-muḥammadiyya* ('the Muhammadan Reality'), blessings and peace be upon him. The second determination, *al-wāḥidiyya* (unified multiplicity) represents the actual distinct emergence of the specific principles of all subsequent multiplicity, namely, the Immutable Archetypes as images of the Divine Names. Even created reality is defined in terms of henological participation in the Akbarian tradition. As Mulla Fenari tells us, 'The world' is the very fact of all multiplicitous phenomena being rendered intelligible within a single principle of unity.

> The essence of 'the world' is the *intelligibility* of the unifying relation of the governing properties of multiplicity, in terms of their unity ... regardless of whether the aspect of unity dominates it, as in the spirits, or the governing properties of multiplicity, as in composite bodies.[78]

Granted, Thomists, certain prominent later *kalām* practitioners (especially those that drew the ire of Mustafa Sabri in the third volume of his *Mawqif al-'Aql*) and various forms of Avicennan, also say God is beyond knowable determinacy and description, despite affirming, in a not solely apophatic way, that God is 'Pure Being'. The question remains, however what positive meaning of 'being' can persist if a mode of determinacy that we can only grasp in limited, contingent beings be ruled out? Certainly, it is true that 'God exists', but we need not, and I think, should not, say 'God is being/existence', if 'being/existence' is taken to be in any way definitive of the essence of God.[79]

The One stands 'outside' of the world in which 'being and 'non-being' is the fundamental binary. Although true for what it is worth, it is not enough to say that His 'non-being' is impossible. When we take the trouble to say that something 'exists', the practical utility is to point out that it not amongst the (conceivable) 'things' which do not exist. Horses exist, we say, while in differing ways unicorns (or dodos) do not. Thus, while it may be intelligible in terms of the logical exigencies of a particular epistemological system, it is ultimately unintelligible for 'being itself' to be made equivalent to the Real in which there is no question of non-existence, that is, for it to be construed as somehow identical to the Divine Essence.

I do not suggest, of course, that we cease to utilize the terms 'being' or 'existence' (the ability to refer to determinateness considered in terms of the source of that determinateness, as 'being', is an indispensable convenience entailed by any metaphysical system I can conceive of); rather, I am merely pointing out that the most genuinely primary and therefore real dimensions of our metaphysical discourse and our discourse about God, are founded in notions of 'unity', rather than any vague notion of 'existence itself'; and this is taught, it seems clear, not only by the higher forms of philosophy, but moreover by the religion of *tawḥīd* or 'making one' itself. And after all, the sublime riches of the Beautiful Names that the religion of *tawḥīd* has bestowed upon us, leave us decisively free of any need to contrive our own 'master name', a coherent sense for which cannot even be found.

To sum up the results of this short excursus on unity and being, then: 'Unity' and 'the one over the many', are prior to 'being', both in the order of reality and in cognition, because they represent the prior conditions of being as 'determinateness'. 'Exists' in 'such-and-such exists', and 'such-and-such does not exist' are meaningful, but not truly primary, because their sense depends upon the explication of a henological account of the greater reality of the 'existent' over and against a similarly determinate 'non-existent thing' (in the case of possible 'non-existents' rather than pure nonexistence), in that the 'non-existent' does not serve as a principle of unity for other things that themselves serve as principles of unity, and is in itself contingent upon many principles of unity, whereas the 'existent' both serves as principle of unity, and exists in closer proximity to the One. While a one-many is intelligible, an existent-nothing is not; and it is 'unity', not 'being', that constitutes the fundamental principle out of which the transcendentals and other primary intelligible notions arise.

4.2.2 METAPRINCIPLES AND TRANSCENDENTALS IN NAFS AL-AMR

In returning to the matter at hand, namely, the rootedness of the transcendentals in reality, it would be valuable to clarify, from the outset, an eminently foreseeable source of doubt concerning the sheer *a priori* attainability of the entire endeavour, namely that since we must employ the intuition of unity and the one over the many (as well as the other transcendentals, primary principles of assent, and so on) before we *know* that they correspond to *nafs al-amr*, in any *formal* manner, our theory of *nafs al-amr* would seem to be discredited from the very outset, by the ignominious spectre of a 'Cartesian Circle' of some variety or another. Yet this is not, in fact, the case. For in the 'henological' intuitions, we directly experience the sole *grounds* of all *individuation*, and of all intelligible discourse, including that of any doubt that we may have about the *reality* of that most primary of intuitions; universal doubt is then outed as merely a participation in unity and thus a determination of 'existence' like all else – yet one that rather than being expansive, inclusive and open-ended onto all else, is merely limited, blind and closed onto itself.

The *real* (rather than merely conceptual) one over the many, that is the ultimate exemplary, intelligible reality (which we call its 'metaprinciple') rooting the particular *conceptual* appearances of say, 'identity' in individual minds and guaranteeing their application to diverse particulars, thereby roots these 'concepts' exemplarily as far more than mere concepts, but instead as the intelligible enabling-conditions constituting sensible being. The justification and grounds of validity, thus, of the application of these abstract concepts –that have no sensory referents–to sensory things and to other concepts, is that these concepts constitute, in their exemplary metaprincipial manifestations, the underlying principles and the grounds for the possibility of the appearance, as determinate being, of those very sensible referents; as Qayṣarī and Mulla Fenari and indeed al-Rāzī have shown us, the existence of the particular necessitates the ontological priority of the corresponding universal nature; moreover, even in intellection 'it is not possible to cognize an individual without [i.e. except in terms of] universality' (Qayṣarī, *Maṭlaʿ*, 69). The same, we contend, must be true of the intelligible principles – which include the transcendentals, but that far exceed in number and variety those usually counted as transcendentals – without which the sensible world would not be distinctly knowable. Indeed, the priority of the archetypal metaprinciples and the ectypal *umūr ʿāmma* (as well as other agents of intelligibility such as 'relation') that participate in them, both in terms of ontology and intellection, is even more fundamental than that of the exemplary forms of species, because the exemplary forms of species presuppose the metaprinciples, quite as inescapably as do any of their instantiations. The transcendentals and like notions represent the conditions of the intelligibility of the world determining the particular individuation-conditions of the spatiotemporal world; but the metaprinciples that constitute the 'one over the many', prior in reality to the transcendentals themselves, determine the individuation-conditions of intelligible degrees in the hierarchy of being that underlie the world of appearances.

Suffice it to be said here, that the *substrata* of the metaprinciples that underlie the transcendentals, are the *ḥaqāʾiq* or 'spiritual realities', known by the direct experience of *kashf*. The *Ḥaqīqa Muḥammadiyya*, for example, is the substratum of *infinity-limit*, which is also the principle of 'intelligibility' of all things. These *ḥaqāʾiq*, cognized in the light of purification (*taṣfiya*) and permission (*idhn*), leave their *āthār* or effects in their determination of the intelligible structure of being, a structure in which all subsequent being participates. From *infinity-limit* arises *generative-conjunction*, that is, *love* (the Akbarian *nikāḥ*) and the *one-many*, the substratum of which is *al-wujūd al-ʿāmm*; from the descent in the creative act, of the *plenitude* of *infinity*, arise *multiplicity* and *possibility*; from *limit* or '*bound*' which is a consequence of one aspect of the 'first determination' of the Reality of Muhammad, blessings and peace be upon him, arise *disjunction*, *distinction* (essence), *stability*, *individuation* and the subordinate (merely transcendental) *one*. *Causality* arises from the first *relation*, that of *priority-posteriority*, which itself emerges in accordance with the degrees of the primacy of 'one' in the subsequent *determinations* of 'infinity-limit', that is, 'the first determination', as *generative-conjunction* yielding *motion/act* and subsequently, *action* and *affection*.

But before we continue with intemperate haste too long down this heady road – for we make no claim to be able to provide an exhaustive account of the nature of the intelligible world, although we can nonetheless now aver that its existence is a demonstrated reality – let us return to examine the basic contention that superordinate 'enabling conditions' of intelligibility, such as the transcendentals, constitute real frameworks that exist prior to the emergence of any subordinate degree of being (in which the individuation-conditions of the domain in question – for example, the world of spatiotemporal particulars – presuppose the prior existence of these 'enabling conditions').

What, after all, of the classic Peripatetic (as well as majority-*kalām*) immanentist assumption? How is it that we know that these principles are prior, ontological *preconditions* of species and individuals? Could they not be merely perspectival abstractions from individuals, not rooted in anything beyond the individual? After all, we surely can only become acquainted with such concepts via our sensory acquaintance with individual things; abstract terms can be *true* of individuals without having to exist independently of the individuals. Why then should we think they have any reality beyond the mere manner in which we *mentally process* individuals, that is by calling them possible, essences, unities and so on?

Let us consider some reasons. Take a situation in which an object is seen from afar; perhaps the murky light, our distance from it, or its ambiguous shape ensure that we cannot make out its essence, *what* it is; it could be a number of things. However, we must be entirely certain that it is a *unity* subsuming a *multiplicity*; and this subsumption entails that it have *some form* of distinct *essence*, even if we are presently unable to distinguish it (and thus, the fact that it 'exists' in the broad sense), as well as an *identity* resultant of its special individuation; it must also be *possible* in its contextual relation to other things, yet *necessary* with respect to its identity; and must possess both active and affective *causal* relationships (and more broadly, stand in all manner of other types of relations to other things). It is impossible to negate these predicates of it, even though we had thought we knew nothing of it, except that it is a determinate thing, with which we have not yet become adequately acquainted to describe or distinguish from other determinate things. The same principle is true even of any *imagined* individual; we cannot coherently conceive of any possible 'existent' individual except under these conditions, and it is thus absurd to maintain that the conditions do not possess some form of priority to individuals; this is especially clear in the case of those that have not yet come into existence, when existence is taken to mean sensible individuation.

The immanentist might counter that these abstract predicates should simply be reduced to our mental processing of experience of *individuals*. Before we encountered such ambiguous or imaginary existents, we had encountered actual individuals, the essences of which we *were* directly acquainted with; this is where we have derived these abstract concepts from. Because all our previous *experience* has taught us that *we cognize* individuals as existents, essences, possibles, unities and so on, we naturally assume that any hypothetical thing must also be characterized by such predicates; but this does not mean that such predicates are *prior to*, or exist independently of particulars.

Yet this simply amounts to the unfounded presumption that an individual could in principle *exist* without participation in the transcendentals (if, perhaps, a different species of observer had different representational apparatuses to us, that is, ones not involving unity, existence, essence and so on), the absurdity of which is clearly demonstrated by the fact that this would imply the negation of the *individual* particular itself; it would entail the truth of 'this individual is not an essence alongside individuations', since these are two of the transcendentals (two which in different ways presuppose and imply the rest). Yet definitionally, an individual is the unified composite that is resultant of an essence alongside its individuations. It is only distinct because it participates in a unitary essence; it is only an individual, because of a principle that has rendered it a separate unity, from other participants in that essence. In some real manner, then, the transcendentals – not as concepts, but as principles or conditions of existence – are prior to individuals. If the principles that in the lowest level of their manifestation become the universal principles of *conception*, in fact constitute the necessary conditions that *any* individual from *any* species must instantiate, in order to exist, and if they apply equally to all individuals, they must be prior to any specific individual. For if this is not so, how is it that a new individual is able to *come into* those conditions? Would the immanentist say that it *creates* them when it comes into existence? Yet they were already 'there' – they have also conditioned all previous individuals. If each temporal individual participates in them, they must surely *already* exist, for if they are rooted in nothing beyond the individual, how can properties *that apply universally to all individu-*

als, be contingent on any given temporal individual? Nor yet can they be properties that arise solely from our mental apparatuses, without being rooted in anything beyond them. As Halfwassen affirms, drawing on an argument from *Enneads* VI.6:

> that which is presupposed by each intellective act from its very beginning cannot itself be the *product* of an intellective act which presupposes it. An intellective act originally positing unity would not be unitary before this position and would therefore be nothing, and thus not be a thought either. The One presupposed by every intellective act as a condition for taking place does therefore not rest upon the subjective positioning of Thought itself, but rather necessarily precedes all subjective unifying actions of Thought.[80]

These reductions of the transcendentals to extramental particulars are all impossible because of the contradictions they imply; and we can therefore conclude that the transcendentals constitute the pre-existing intelligible *framework* to which individuals must conform, not a framework instantiated solely by individuals, nor one somehow 'originating' in the mind.

There is also a more general reason, aside from arguments of this ilk, and which we have already alluded to somewhat, which explains why the *umūr ʿāmma* and other of the primary intelligible qualities must possess higher-order modes of existence in intelligible worlds prior to their determination at the level of the concepts in which we ordinarily perceive them; and this is the simple fact that they are likewise, as are all other existents, loci of manifestation of the Divine Names. Yet they represent a special category of the loci thereof – because akin to certain of the Names, they condition and determine, not a particular nature alone, but great multitudes of things, even when their proximate species-natures may be incompatible:

Mulla Fenari tells us

> that which is variously perceived in matter or outside of matter is the object of the science of the Divine Names and the universal realities, like knowledge, power, unity and multiplicity and others. These can exist both in incorporeal

entities and in corporeal substances. Yet in themselves, *they are independent of both*, for otherwise they could not exist in one or the other.[81]

In their exemplary forms *ante rem*, these broad classes of intelligible entity regulate, constitute and define the existences of possible entities, and in their conceptual realities, they become entified as the abstracted mental entities that necessarily attend those existences *in rebus*. Yet both are ultimately effusions from the Divine Names, shadows cast by those qualities, and providing both the metaphysical framework for individuated existence, and intelligibility for possible being.

The very *identity* special to each thing is only possible, for example, because there is His identity: 'the identity (*huwiyya*) of each thing is in reality a ray of His identity.'[82] 'Existence', too, possesses a meaning in its *abstracted* context – in which it is a mere perspectival being (*amr iʿtibārī*) – only in terms of the universal cognition of individuation, that is, in terms of *specific determinations of essences*. Prior, 'exemplary' realities nonetheless ground and guarantee the truth validity of this perspectival entity. *Al-Wujūd al-ʿĀmm* (general existence) for example, the infinite totality of the objects of God's knowledge in terms of their reception of the effusion from His Essence (that is, determinateness in terms of its source), constitutes the exemplary one over the many grounding both extramental and mental existences. As Qayṣarī tells us

> [God] possesses a unity, not that which is the opposite of multiplicity, yet that is the origin of the unity that *is* its opposite … the unity of the Names that has multiplicity as its opposite – [is a unity which is] *the shadow cast* by that original unity of the Essence … [likewise] general existence (*al-wujūd al-ʿāmm*), diffused upon the essences in the [Divine] Knowledge, is one of the shadows cast by [the Essence], by being 'restricted' by its being general (that is, general to a multiplicity), and likewise do mental existence and extramental particular existence constitute two shadows of that shadow, [that arise] because of the multiplication of qualifications (*quyūd*).[83]

The abstract principles, deep-rootedly prior, in their distinct, ontological forms, to the sensible particulars which are the sole substrata of such principles on the Peripatetic view – are necessarily prior to, and independent of, all particulars, possessing an influence that can variously be formative, constitutive, regulative and creative. The notion, then, common in Avicennan philosophy and later *kalām*, that abstract principles can only possess epistemologically defined modes of being, qua abstracted – and thus that they are in some sense reducible to a sensible substratum – and as directly cognized (*badīhī*), without the need for prior exemplary substrata – is indefensible, in the context of a fully developed theory of *nafs al-amr* and of the Akbarian critique of immanentism, as ultimately question begging.

Such principles, moreover, are not merely descriptive, nor causally inert (against, amongst other depictions, the 'standard' contemporary view of abstract objects that we have seen earlier); to the contrary, it is via their *conjunction* that material things are able to come into existence at all.

> Perspectival, non-existent entities can produce extramental effects, like ... 'conjunction' (*al-ijtimāʿ*) for the power of the individual soldiers and of rope, and for the formal configuration of a chair, house or wall; also of this ilk are ... the way in which the conjunction of prime matter and form – both intelligible (non-sensible) entities – produces the sensible nature of bodies ... It happens that the increasing multiplication of individuations, which necessitates the increasing multiplication of the characteristic properties of possibility (*al-imkān*), reaches a limit, at which point sensible multiplicity obtains;[84] 'conjunction' *is a locus of manifestation of the original unitive synthesis* (*al-jamʿ al-aḥadī*) by means of which manifestation and coming to be manifest occur ... and produces magnitude, via the secret of composition (*al-tarkīb*) by means of which the light of [the property of] unity mixes with the darkness of possibility (*ẓulmat al-imkān*) ... striking a balance between insufficiency and excess, in order that it might be able to enter into the scope of the perception of the weak senses of hearing and seeing.[85]

As we have already affirmed, it would be to depart from our strict objective to attempt to here provide, in so far as this is indeed possible, a *detailed* map of the world of uninstantiated relationships richly suggested by this account of the formation of the sensible world by the transcendentals, and prior to this, by their 'exemplary forms', which we have called their 'metaprinciples', and some intimations of which we have seen in the words of the Akbarian authors we have cited. This way of rooting, in *nafs al-amr*, the abstract apparatuses that render our world knowable, will naturally require considerable further study and elucidation.[86] We have mainly purposed to show that the fundamental tension requiring an identification of things as they are with a realm beyond particulars and minds, namely, that of the existence of true abstract propositions that possess no sensible referents and yet cannot derive their universal truth from their appearances in individual minds, is fully resolved, as also immunized against contemporary subjectivist challenges, in an account that identifies *nafs al-amr* with the Divine Knowledge, within an exemplarist ontology in which abstract predicates apply to particularized entities precisely because, in their prior, uninstantiated, metaprincipial forms, they are the very grounds conditioning the necessary frameworks that constitute the existence of those particularized entities. Such abstract truths appear within the particular (and largely sensory world) only because they mirror higher relationships between the exemplary forms underlying their terms, which ultimately reveal the interplay of the Divine Names.

Such realities can indeed only be known fully when the discursive intellect (*al-ʿaql min ḥaythu huwa mutafakkir*), namely reason, reaches the limit at which it must come to a halt, and the unbounded capacity for experience enjoyed by the receptive intellect (*al-ʿaql min ḥaythu huwa qābil*) begins; this account, certainly, employs and then surpasses 'reason', as usually understood. On the other hand, the immanentist account does not attain to genuine rationality at all, and any truly rational account must begin with the realization that the one over the many, as possessing genuine ontological priority to the individual, *is* itself an 'experience'.

These non-sensible predicates are real properties in *nafs al-amr* : ultimately real. They are the templates for individuation, that constitute the ontological grounds, and regulative and governing principles, determining the nature of the modes in which within each realm of manifestation, individual entities appear. 'Because it seems that way' is good enough for practical affairs; but in metaphysics, it is not sufficient merely to employ concepts because they come naturally to us; there must be some measure by which we confirm their correspondence to objective reality.

These intelligible principles are *real* entities, indeed the *ne plus ultra* of reality, for the uninstantiated is more closely identified with unity - our most objective intuition - than changing and disappearing particulars could ever be. Possessing their own form of non-sensible individuation, they are indeed immeasurably more 'real' than the sensible particular. Their abstracted forms are placed as it were as tokens, pointing to their subsumption by more fundamental realities. Each reveals a hierarchical order of signs, their instances as innate and abstracted entities constituting mere shadows of their exemplary origins, where their relationships mirror more sublime relationships ultimately rooted in the Divine Names. All is effusion from Him in conceptions, and in assents, true propositions are signs of the intelligible structure of a world of transcendent 'states of affairs'.

It being so, then, that abstract predicates are the most rooted of all the realities with which we are acquainted in this world of particulars and intelligible entities, it should be no surprise that when they appear appended to sensible realities, as in the method of traditional metaphysics and natural theology, they are capable of leading us transitively to higher realities. The transcendentals are such that simply to exist, an entity must be characterized by them; moreover, they possess an intrinsic subordinate and superordinate, hierarchical relation one to another which is reflected inversely in the logical order, and it is thus that they are capable of forming the basis of metaphysical science. In the order of being, they emanate from unity to multiplicity: in the order of logic, they lead back from multiplicity to unity. The traditional forms of natural theology are vindicated in the scheme made possible by the Akbarian identification of *nafs al-amr* alone; only thus are the abstract predicates of natural theology shown to mirror exemplary realities, in which the transitive relations of entailment obtaining between their conceptual instantiations are replicated, those of possible to necessary being, of multiplicity to unity, of the affective to the active, of the finite to the infinite, of the restricted to the unrestricted. Because such principles inform the being of particulars, metaphysical usage of the *conceptual* terms (of which they are a locus of manifestation) reflects genuine reality – for when we say that the world is contingent, on the Akbarian account, we know what the world truly is, and what contingent truly is; and the way is also opened to directly witness the qualities of the Infinite within the qualities of the finite; for the one over the many is not a concept, but an experience, it is the *presence of that which underlies*, it is an intuition of the Attributes of God.

This doctrine of *nafs al-amr*, then, is truly all-embracing. It is able to account for the ultimate nature of even impossible 'beings', and most fruitfully, of the modes of elemental ontological subsistence of the perspectival entities employed in the sciences. Or in other words, the ultimate states, uncovered by the henological ascent, that these entities possess with respect to their hierarchical degrees of actualization. And it thereby provides a truly integrated view, not merely of the ultimate ontological and henological statuses of the *objects* of our knowledge, but moreover our *modes* of knowing them. In short, that confers some real *reality*, as 'object', upon even our mode of knowing, and thereby safeguards philosophical speculation from the spectres of subjectivism and relativism, ever present dangers for the various forms of philosophy that only recognize the existence of natures in so far as they are already instantiated.

For this latter form of philosophy situates the fundamental reality of an essence in its individuals. It then demotes the principles and concepts that facilitate our intellection of those individuals to the status of entailments that arise from our mental processing of those individuals. Even if, on the most common interpretation of Avicenna, these concepts are validated by the perpetual intellective activity of the Agent Intellect, they do not seem thus to be necessarily rooted in the deepest ontological degree of reality. As 'Alā'uddīn suggested, the forms impressed in the Agent Intellect must themselves correspond to something. While it is true that Avicenna tells us God knows all things, because as their cause, He knows the manner in which the Intellects will give rise to them, how can the rich multiplicity of the sublunar world in any way 'correspond' to the higher intellects? Arguably, thus, scepticism as to the ultimate value of the intelligibles, and especially abstract objects, cannot be conclusively done away with on this Avicennan view.

It is significant, in any case, that two of the most eminent of all Aristotelians, Averroes and Aquinas no less, laid charges of Platonism against Avicenna's separate Agent Intellect.[87] That doctrine does indeed seem to attempt to fulfil the role of the Platonic Ideas – incorporeal 'forms' that provide the material world with its being and intelligibility – but within an overall system that fails to be as coherent as actual Platonism. In turn, the Platonic doctrine of distinct but timeless forms is rendered most coherent by situating these forms in the Divine knowledge, where they have arisen eternally as the images of the Divine Names.

It is for some of the early *kalām* theologians, who did not acknowledge that such 'objects' have any form of positive ontological status whatsoever, that the 'correspondence' to reality of non-existent and abstract entities seems most problematic. The group of especially earlier *kalām* theologians who denied the distinctness and subsistence of non-existent entities, as well as of forms of sciential subsistence (such as 'mental existence'), tell us that although God's knowledge is beginninglessly eternal, its 'pertaining' (*ta'alluq*) to temporally originated things is exactly its pertaining to their extramental particular existences. This is because before they exist, temporally originated things have (given the rejection of both sciential subsistence and the subsistence of non-existents) no ontological status whatsoever. Indeed, they are 'absolutely nothing' (*ma'dūm ṣirf*). God's knowledge of them must thus be of them as actual, extramental beings.

However, according to the later *kalām* theologians, this would 'entail that the Necessary Most High not know temporally originated things in beginningless eternity, for [on this early view], they have no form of existence [whatever] in beginningless eternity, such that their entities could be present to Him in beginningless eternity.'[88] Indeed, this dangerous doctrine might lead to their 'making the error that Abū Ḥusayn al-Baṣrī amongst the Mu'tazila made, namely [maintaining] that God knows temporally originated things only after they come into existence, not in beginningless eternity.'[89] Later *kalām* theologians, like Jurjānī, Dawānī and Gelenbevi, show considerable vehemence in refuting the notion that God's beginninglessly eternal knowledge of things pertains only to their temporally originated, extramental existences, for they deemed it starkly contradictory; their extramental existences 'are contingent upon their having been existentiated by God, which is in turn preceded by Divine volition, which is preceded by Divine knowledge.'[90] God's knowledge of their forms as extramental particulars is thus contingent on his knowledge of their beginninglessly eternal forms, which made the existentiation of the extramental particular forms possible. According to Dawānī, the early *kalām* position that while the Divine knowledge is beginninglessly eternal, its pertaining to its objects is temporally originated (he describes those upholding this view as 'externalist'[91] *kalām* theologians, 'neither nourishes, nor appeases hunger (*lā yusmin wa lā yughnī min jūw'*).' This is because 'as long as knowledge does not pertain to a thing, that thing is not an object of that knowledge, and [this position] leads to the denial of God's beginninglessly eternal knowledge of temporally originated things.'[92]

The Akbarian position, that the Immutable Archetypes arise as the beginninglessly eternal knowledge God has of the perspectival 'images' of His Names, is the only option able to ground all possible beings in the ultimate level of reality. On this view, since quiddities themselves are perspectival (albeit fixed and subsistent), the perspectival, 'non-existent' status of intelligible entities poses no difficulty. Every aspect of our knowledge in the world of normative experience is itself a 'locus of manifestation' (*maẓhar*) of a single effusion of being, which has diverse domains and degrees.

What is perhaps the most important solution to the question of the identity of *nafs al-amr* thus set forth in Qayṣarī's account of the Immutable Archetypes as the ultimate truthmaking domain, it would be natural for the reader, despite appreciating the beauty of Qayṣarī's position, to again ask how it is we can be sure of the truth of our judgements and thus of the validity of our knowledge, if its referent is a metaphysical domain, that of the Immutable Archetypes of God's knowledge, that seems to lie altogether beyond our possible experience? Although one answer to this crucial question is discernible if one reads carefully between the lines in Taşköprüzade's position (which is now close at hand) we will nonetheless attempt to make this plain in the briefest possible terms, before we read that venerable synthesis.

The first thing that must be noted is that the guarantor of this epistemology is an ontology; the distinct intelligibility of distinct essences across particulars of the same species (the 'one over the many') can only be accounted for if we are to infer the prior existence of an exemplary Form. These Forms in turn derive their reality from the infinite plenitude of God, Who although transcendently unlike His creation, is the origin and wellspring of the essences of all created beings.[93] This is because a necessary element of God's nature, as the Absolute, is to possess every possible perfection, and one of these is to have knowledge of infinite possible perspectival aspects of His own infinite Names.

Through His free creative act, God takes these objects of His knowledge out of their purely sciential state, into a state of 'independent', self-conscious subsistence, and they become manifest within numerous states and worlds, appearing finally in the 'physical' world. Now, we find ourselves here, with knowledge, the intelligible nature of which clearly marks it off from our notion of physicality. The affective (*infiʿālī*) nature of the knowledge – it is pressed upon us from without – requires that it must proceed from an ontological degree – a 'world' – that encompasses the one that is the object of our everyday experience, and that confers the forms upon it that make it intelligible at all. The question 'how do we know?' becomes inseparable from the fact of being; the fact and manner of our knowing is just one of the effects of the effusion that causes us both to find intelligible form in the world, and knowledge of it in individual experience. Asking 'how do we know?' as if cognition is a static phenomenon inherently separated from its objects, the world around it, is to frame the question fallaciously. Our knowledge in its ontological[94] and formal[95] contingency is inseparable from the intelligible forms of the world in their ontological and formal contingency, the latter being definable only in terms of the former. 'How do we know?' becomes equivalent to 'what is it to be?' With our *ordinary intellectual, psychological and sense faculties*, interfacing with a world of a similar multiplicity, we can achieve knowledge of the world in its relational, accidental aspects, and some of its essential aspects, as well as deducing the outlines of fundamental truths, such as the nature and objective validity of general metaphysical principles, the existence of exemplary Forms and the hierarchical structure of being, the nature of human freedom, the existence of God and revelation, and so on, and these qualify as instances of real knowledge of 'things as they are in themselves' (even be this only within a particular and restricted determination amidst knowledge's wider and more sublime scope), and this is precisely because these faculties reveal, because of the intrinsic intelligible structure within which we encounter them and within which they participate, their own prior principles, that must culminate in the Immutable Archetypes and the Divine Names via the henological ascent.

Yet knowledge of things as they are in themselves in the strictest sense of their original state as direct objects of God's knowledge, ontologically prior to their procession out through worlds of ever-increasing multiplicity and density, is nonetheless impossible with our ordinary rational and sense faculties.[96] This is confirmed by Ṣadr al-Dīn al-Qūnawī,

> Knowledge of the essences of things in their simplicity and detachedness in the Divine Sciential Presence (*al-ḥaḍra al-'ilmiyya*) is impossible, and this is because of the impossibility of our perceiving anything in terms of our own non-composite singularity ... we know nothing through our own detached essences, nor through our ipseity alone, but

only in so far as our individuated essences are characterized by existence, life, knowledge, and the removal of obstacles between us and the thing we desire to know such that that thing becomes susceptible to being known. This is the least that our knowledge depends upon, and it is a multiplicitous agglomeration, whereas the essences of things are in their detachedness singular and simple, and are cognized only by that which is also singular and simple ... thus is it that we know no more than the attributes and accidents of things in so far as they are attributes and concomitants of a particular thing, but [we do not know the things] in terms of their pure [detached] essences.[97]

Qayṣarī makes a similar point,

The forms of [the] quiddities in our minds are shadows cast by those sciential forms [in the Divine knowledge], which obtain within us ... via the manifestation of the light of Existence that is within us, and in accordance with the extent of the share from that [Sciential] Presence [that has been allotted to us]. This is why knowledge of the realities of things as they are in themselves is *difficult* except for one whose heart has been illuminated by the light of the Real ... for by the Real such a person perceives those sciential forms as they are in themselves; yet even then, in accordance with the nature of his ipseity he is veiled from this [to some degree], such that God's knowledge of [those realities] and the knowledge this perfect [man] has of them be distinguished. For the ultimate goal of the gnosis of the gnostics is their acknowledgement of their own powerlessness and deficiency, and their knowledge that all returns to Him, for He is the All-Knowing, the All-Aware.[98]

Only by breaking loose from the shackles of our normal intellectual and sense faculties, then, by becoming susceptible to illumination and an effusion from the world of Immutable Archetypes directly into our receptive intellects, through spiritual exercises, asceticism, Divine remembrance, and embodiment of the Sacred Law, can we overcome this intellectually debilitating multiplicity, and perceive things as they are in themselves. Although, of course, direct verification is substantially difficult, we can nonetheless be assured that our more humble modes of knowledge of the world and larger reality *do* correspond to *nafs al-amr* – even if this only amounts, in the grander scheme of things, to rather a small region thereof.

4.3 Taşköprüzade's Solution and Synthesis

Like his friend Ibn Bahā'uddīn, Taşköprüzade begins his 'critical verification' of the question of the identity of *nafs al-amr* with an allusion to the explicitly Akbarī doctrine of the *marātib al-ẓuhūr* of the Divine Attributes, in which created loci – including the infinite possible quiddities, some of which we go on to encounter in this world – reveal the manifold aspects of the Attributes, and arise from the endless possibilia of relations and perspectival aspects of Divine Self-knowledge.

> There is no doubt that in beginningless eternity (*al-azal*), God Most High knows His Essence and Attributes, and the loci of the manifestation of His attributes (*maẓāhir ṣifātihi*), amongst which are extramental essences (*al-ḥaqā'iq al-khārijiyya*), as well as their concomitant properties (*awṣāfihā al-lāzima*), and their perspectival modalities (*aḥwālihā al-i'tibāriyya*); the alternative would entail that His knowledge not encompass them in beginningless eternity, Transcendently Exalted be God above such a notion![99]

This accounts, then, for the ultimate ontological status of extramental essences – their timeless state in the Divine knowledge:

> All quiddities then, are with respect to themselves amongst the entailments and concomitants of His Attributes, and are not formed (*ghayr maj'ūla*) … because 'forming' is an effect of Divine Power contingent on knowledge, which is contingent on the object of knowledge. This is what they mean when they say 'quiddities are not formed.'[100]

Taşköprüzade alludes here to the doctrine that, considered strictly with respect to themselves, quiddities are not formed – that is, that quiddities possess an inherent timelessness 'prior' to their creation, in so far as the necessary all-encompassingness of God's knowledge entails His beginninglessly eternal knowledge of them as distinct. 'The degree of the knowledge of the Most High (*martabat 'ilmihi ta'ālā*) is prior to "forming" (*al-ja'l*, i.e. creation). In the degree of Divine knowledge, quiddities are distinct and multiple, without "forming" pertaining to them [at all].'[101]

In the purely logical terms in which the discussion is often framed,[102] it would be a contradiction for the *quiddity* of, for example, 'the sea' (not to be confused with its reality in extramental particulars, which is certainly created) to have been 'made to be the sea' because this implies that prior to being 'made,' *itself*, it (namely, the sea) was not the sea (such that in a certain hypothetical state it would be possible to say 'the sea is not the sea,' which is impossible).[103] This is because, *'prior'* to its having been 'made to be itself,' it would have had no reality at all in the knowledge of God (which would be a heretical statement across all of the schools of Islamic theology). Moreover, Taşköprüzade makes clear that the reason quiddities must not be *maj'ūla* is that 'making is an effect of Divine Power contingent on knowledge, which is contingent on the object of knowledge.'[104] Taşköprüzade continues:

> In that ontological degree (*fī tilka al-martaba*), quiddities are not fixed in particularized essences, such that the eternity of the world or the instantiation of non-existent entities be entailed, but fixedness in particularized essences (*al-thubūt fī al-a'yān*) only obtains after Divine Power brings them out of Divine Knowledge and into extramental particulars, through Divine Volition's causing their existence in extramental particulars to preponderate [over their non-existence]. Now, this preponderance is the reason that His knowledge (Exalted be He!) is active knowledge,[105] which calls for the subsistence of [some of] His objects of knowledge in particularized essences.[106]

Taşköprüzade has explicitly detailed the grounds for the *appearance* of distinct essences in extramental particulars, that is, as constituting 'our side' of the hierarchical order, and the ensuing discussion of the manner in which the human mind abstracts universal essences from extramental particulars thus takes on a dimension of especial depth and seriousness, when compared to treatments that are silent concerning the mystery of that appearance. In embarking upon this discussion, Taşköprüzade is unprecedented in attempting to resolve simultaneously both the ontological and the epistemological problems of *nafs al-amr*.

> By means of the power of differentiation that God has placed within the soul and has made an innate quality, the soul abstracts the quiddities that are established in the active Divine knowledge (*al-'ilm al-fi'lī*) from those extramental essences. This is called affective knowledge (*'ilman infi'ālīyyan*), in the sense that the soul *receives* these forms from them. 'Abstraction' is the following: When a particular obtains within the faculty of the soul [known as] the imagery (*al-khayāl*), it readies the soul for *a universal to effuse itself upon it*, that corresponds to the particular present in the imagination, such that from those particulars a quiddity obtains that corresponds to it, with its individuating characteristics removed. It may then analyse it into a concept shared by it and other than it, and into a concept specific to it, and it may extract accidental, shared [and] specific concepts from it, such that the forms of the realities of things as they are in themselves obtain in the mind, corresponding to the Active Knowledge – if the abstraction has been sound.[107]

The immanent forms of things are *received* from their transcendent forms; they are not *imposed* onto extramental realities by some putatively 'subjectivizing' cognitive apparatus. What is more, even the 'perspectival modalities' (*aḥwāl i'tibāriyya*), that is, the accidents that pertain to an essence in the event of their obtaining in the perspective (*i'tibār*) of a subject, as well as their concomitant properties (*awṣāfihā al-lāzima*), are rooted in the forms in the Divine knowledge, whence the nature that informs our knowledge emanates.

> And one may in diverse ways abstract from extramental particulars entities which do not have extramental referents, such that concepts that constitute some of the concomitants of the essences in extramental particulars, the like of such as are called first intelligibles, as well as second intelligibles,

and so on, obtain in the mind. These matters too are amongst the things that have fixity in the Active Knowledge, and their not emerging into existence in extramental particulars is simply because they obtain there in a subordinate, not a foundational aspect.[108]

Our *mode of knowing* is just as objectively rooted as our objects of knowledge are considered in themselves. The supposed chasm between subject and object has been thus significantly bridged. Our temporal *mode* of knowing essences also timelessly pertains to those essences, even in their ultimate modes of being, in themselves,

> The soul then passes judgement upon the quiddities and concepts that have obtained in the mind, with judgements befitting the characteristics of those quiddities and concepts, judgements that correspond to that which is in the Active Knowledge, if its characteristics and entailments have been given their due consideration correctly (*in ṣaḥḥat riʿāyat shuʾūnihā wa muqtaḍayātihā*). Then is it that the forms of realities as they are in themselves obtain in the mind, as well as the modalities attendant to them, in a manner that corresponds to reality; the soul is then revealed dressed in holy forms, and this is the ultimate goal of knowledge.[109]

God has set up the world in such a manner that a human subject's giving 'due consideration' to the characteristics and entailments (*riʿāyat shuʾūnihā wa muqtaḍayātihā*) of natures, entails the correspondence of his resultant knowledge to the Active Knowledge. This notwithstanding, due to the difficulty of positing God's knowledge as an *epistemological* '*nafs al-amr*' (due to the considerable ascetic hardships usually involved in 'checking' if one's judgements correspond to things in that ultimate degree of how they are in themselves) 'mental judgements' themselves may be considered tantamount to *nafs al-amr*, once the background of God's knowledge as ontological *nafs al-amr* has been demonstrated. Taşköprüzade's solution enables the more terrestrial, mundane identification of *nafs al-amr* with 'the mind' to be tenable, yet only on the condition that its ontological identity be first discerned. For as the guarantor of the truth of propositions, *nafs al-amr* must constitute *that thing that propositions ultimately point to.* Now, in the immediacy of normal human experience, propositions seem to signify either extramental realities – the things 'out there' in the world, or, purely intelligible realities in their mental existence, and indeed, extramental realities in so far as they *obtain* in the mind. In so far as *nafs al-amr* must needs be the object of direct, normative experience,[110] then, Taşköprüzade makes provision for the notion of the mind being a locus of things-in themselves, *if and only if* the necessary ontologically prior guarantor of the reality of propositions is first apprehended. True propositions can be validated by their correspondence to our soul as it appears 'dressed in holy forms', because those true representations of reality are themselves an effusion from levels of reality of which the mind is a mere locus, and of truths rooted in ultimate being, indeed in the very Names and Attributes of God. Taşköprüzade now offers a final encapsulation of his theory

> If you have understood this, then know that by *al-amr*,[111] the quiddities in their state of fixity in the three domains are meant: the Active Knowledge (*al-'ilm al-fi'lī*), the extramental particularized essence (*al-'ayn al-khārijī*), and affective knowledge (*al-'ilm al-infi'ālī*). By '*nafs*', their characteristics and entailments are meant. The meaning of a judgement corresponding to that which is in *nafs al-amr*, is that the [particular] characteristics and entailments of [a proposition's] subject and predicate be given due consideration when the conception of the relations between them obtains, and when the judgement of affirmation or negation is made. Now, it being the case that this 'due consideration' is given to the characteristics and entailments of things, at the moment in which the judgement takes place, *only within the third domain* [that is, the mind], *nafs al-amr* – in so far as it contains the correspondence of judgements to [those characteristics and entailments] – has been made tantamount to those mental judgements. For we have no way to match our judgements onto the judgements that obtain in the Active Knowledge ... even though our judgements do indeed correspond in themselves to the Active Knowledge.[112]

In Taşköprüzade's *tahqīq*, 'extramental particulars' turns out to be a valid locus of *nafs al-amr* only on the level of conceptions (*taṣawwurāt*), in so far as quiddities are abstracted from extramental particulars. On the level of propositions and judgements, however, the particular 'characteristics and entailments' of a given subject and predicate can only be arrived at mentally, in so far as they are brought into full relief by the apparatuses of our modes of intelligible representation. Thus, in order to be true, any judgement pertaining even to an extramental particular must correspond to the essence, obtaining in the mind, that constitutes the substrate of the correct subject-predicate relation describing the given extramental particular entity.[113] The largely 'physical' world of extramental particulars, then, is strictly speaking not part of *nafs al-amr* at all, because its intelligibility is contingent upon relational elements which although not *merely* mental, do depend upon mental loci of manifestation in order to become manifest as truths pertaining to extramental particulars.

While Taşköprüzade evidently does not utilize the methodology of henological ascent in his account of *nafs al-amr*, and moreover, invokes only a partial Akbarian framework (and is thus unable to suggest a path to knowledge of reality in any domain beyond the three he mentions above) he has nonetheless provided a truly ontological account of *nafs al-amr* that faced with the problem of the 'correspondence' of abstract entities in knowledge, succeeds in safeguarding objective truth. Moreover, he is able to do so within a reasonably sober, and still recognisably '*kalām*' framework.

4.4 Later Developments and Notes on the Subalternation of the Sciences

The type of groundwork provided by the contributions of thinkers like Ibn Bahā'uddīn and Taşköprüzade would be given ever-greater definition and detailing by a host of major philosophers and theologians of succeeding centuries, in the Ottoman and Mughal empires, who made significant contributions to *nafs al-amr* theory. Particularly pertinent to our theme are the words of the great seventeenth century Naqshbandī, Akbarī sage Ibrāhīm Kūrānī (1025–1101/1616–90):

> The quiddities of possible beings are non-existent entities (*ma'dūmāt*) which are of their own essences distinct in them-

selves (*mutamayyiza fī anfusihā tamayyuzan dhātiyyan*) and they subsist in *nafs al-amr*, which is the knowledge of God Most High.[114]

In another of his works, Kūrānī treats the famous Avicennan distinction between possible perspectival aspects of quiddities: those which are *bi sharṭ shay'* (restrictively conditioned) *lā bi sharṭ shay'*, (unconditioned) and *bi sharṭ lā* (negatively conditioned).[115] The first and second of these categories exist in extramental particulars, because the first refers to a quiddity from the perspective of its instantiation as a particular, and the second because it refers to the quiddity as it actually is in its various domains, without any restriction imposed by any qualifying perspective. The third however, the pure quiddity in itself, considered completely separately from its possible or actual instantiation in any individual or indeed anything at all, does not exist, not even really in the mind, for the mere fact of its obtaining in the mind constitutes a restriction that precludes its genuine subsistence as an utterly abstract, self-subsistent entity.

> Others say that [the quiddity in itself] exists, for the mind can intellect it in abstraction and free from its adjunct properties (*lawāḥiq*). There is no real difference [between the various opinions regarding its existence or non-existence] because those who negate its existence in the mind mean 'with regard to *nafs al-amr*', and those who affirm its existence mean 'with respect to supposition' (*bi ḥasab al-fard*), for the mind does not adjudge that it is free [of adjunct properties] until it has formed a conception of it. That which is abstracted from all adjunct properties does not exist except in a mental supposition, then, and not in *nafs al-amr*, and this is grounded in the [position stating] that *nafs al-amr* is confined to the mind and extramental particulars, which is the most widely held position (*al-mashhūr*).[116]

Kūrānī has convincingly explained why, for the majority of thinkers who confine *nafs al-amr* to the mind and extramental particulars, the negatively conditioned essence-itself cannot possibly exist anywhere. However, despite having first presented this distinction as quite irreproachable, and exhaustive of the question of the existence of these types of quiddity, he will now dismantle it completely in the light of metaphysical Sufism:

however, according to the results of our precise reckoning (*'alā mā ḥarrarnāhu*), that the actualization of *nafs al-amr* is more general than the mind and extramental particulars, quiddities separate from mental and extramental particular existences have, in the absence of any [mental] supposition, actualization in *nafs al-amr*. This is a consequence of that which has become evident, that the essences of non-existent possibles subsist in *nafs al-amr* – which is the knowledge of God – separately from extramental particular and umbral, representational (*ẓillī irtisāmī*) existences.[117]

The Akbarian notion of the eternal genesis and subsistence of essences in the Divine knowledge thus allows for the possibility of an essence existing prior to, and therefore without any reference to, extramental particular instantiation or mental representation, and thereby gives a new lease of ontological life to the much-maligned *māhiyya bi-sharṭ lā*.

An abundance of even later treatments of *nafs al-amr* developed the main lines of thought that we have outlined in this study. Two of the most notable happen to have been written by two of the most important and influential 'ulama of the past two hundred years: the Turk Ismail Gelenbevi (1143–1204/1730–90) and the Iraqi Abū Thanā' al-Ālūsī (1217–70/1803–54). In the commentary on Qur'an 2:20 in his monumental, 10,000-page magnum opus *Rūḥ al-Maʿānī*, Al-Ālūsī demonstrated the connection of the question of the subsistence of non-existent entities to the question of the real nature of *nafs al-amr*.

> The true position is that asserted by the gnostics [namely, that non-existent objects possess a form of subsistence in the Divine knowledge]. This is because a [distinct] conception of a possible non-existent entity (*al-maʿdūm al-mumkin*) can be formed, and one [particular non-existent entity] can be intended rather than another. Anything that this is true of is, separate from any mental supposition, distinct in itself; and all such [separate] things are subsistent and fixed, outside of our minds, and detached from individuated particulars. Such things are, then, nowhere other than in *nafs al-amr*, by which is intended the knowledge of the Real.[118]

In a beautiful passage, al-Ālūsī goes on to explicitly state that through God's knowing the infinite richness of His own essence, He also knows all of creation, that is, through seeing within Himself, in beginningless eternity, the possible 'images' of His Names and Attributes.[119]

Ismail Gelenbevi's treatment of transcendent form is similarly free of the reticence often associated with the great *kalām* textbooks. 'Know that every possible being ... has a beginninglessly eternal quiddity in *nafs al-amr*,'[120] he says in a short *taḥqīq* treatise. In another treatise he clarifies:

> God's Knowledge consists in His Essence's entailment of the perceptional forms of everything of which a conception can be formed, even be it a product of the imagination, like the fangs of a ghoul, or a sea of quicksilver... Plato held that those perceptional forms are self-existent, and this is why he adjudged that every universal, in abstraction from all accidents and individuating characteristics, exists extramentally in a [particular] world. Those self-existent perceptional forms are known as the 'Platonic Forms'. The majority of philosophers, however, were of the opinion that the forms of the sequence of possible beings are impressed in the Active Intellect, whereas since the forms of the Intellects [themselves] are not *temporally* prior to their extramental reality, they do not require a locus wherein to have their forms impressed; rather, [the philosophers] maintained that they are, in their extramental existence, sciential forms (*ṣuwar 'ilmiyya*) present, in their essences, to He Most High. Now, for the same reasons [underlying] the [theory] we have here critically verified,[121] Imām al-Rāzī said 'everything that we can form a conception of has an existence apart from us, either self-existent, as Plato says, or impressed in the Intellect whence proceeded the celestial sphere'[122] ... and, on the basis of the [theory] we have [here] established the truth of, light is shed on the intent of the critical verifiers, in their saying that every concept that can be formed, even two contraries that are conjunct in the mind, exists in *nafs al-amr*.[123]

The Syrian sage Ibrāhīm al-Madhārī (d. 1190/1776) of Ḥalab, (a student of the Akbarians 'Abd al-Ghanī al-Nabulsī (1050–1143/1641–1731), Abū

al-Mawāhib al-Ḥanbalī (1043–1126/1634–1714) and Ibrāhīm al-Kūrānī's
son Abū Ṭāhir al-Kūrānī (d. 1145/1733), amongst many others) wrote on
nafs al-amr in his remarkable *al-Lumʿa*, in which he attempted a bold
synthesis of Avicennan philosophy, Ashʿarī *kalām*, Akbarian metaphysics and, most surprisingly, the thought of Mīr Dāmād (d. 1041/1631). His
exposition of *nafs al-amr* is especially illuminating of the elegance of the
solution stating that *nafs al-amr* is God's knowledge, for His knowledge
encompasses not only the source-forms making human knowledge possible, but also human knowledge itself.

> [Quiddities] are distinct and possess a type of actualization
> and subsistence, beginninglessly eternally in the all-encom-
> passing Divine knowledge, which is *nafs al-amr*. For *nafs
> al-amr* is [the source] which all things are referrable to, *as
> well as the judgements pertaining to them*. Now, God, may He
> be glorified, is the First, and there is nothing before Him, and
> His knowledge is beginninglessly eternal and encompasses
> all objects of knowledge, *amongst which are the sciences and
> objects of knowledge of creatures*. [God's knowledge], then,
> must be [the phenomenon] known as *nafs al-amr*, that all
> things, and the judgements pertaining to them, are refer-
> rable to.[124]

Now, given the 'foundedness' that we have explored in this chapter, of
human knowledge and representation in *nafs al-amr* which is the Divine
knowledge, it would be logical to infer that the rootedness of the *sciences*
in the Divine knowledge also entails their rootedness in the Divine Names,
of which the objects of the Divine knowledge are images. For the sciences
are a branch of exemplary human reality[125] and yet the objects of science
pertain to all levels of created and uncreated being. This 'foundedness' of
the sciences in the Divine Names is elucidated by the Ottoman theologian
Said Nursi (1295–1379/1878–1960):

> A sublime reality corresponds to every perfection, science,
> craft and branch of knowledge; and every one of those realities
> is founded in one of the Divine Names, in that each particular
> science, art and branch of knowledge, as well as those perfec-
> tions and crafts, find their perfection and become a reality by

resting upon that Name, which has many veils, multifarious manifestations and diverse domains. Without [that Name], they are [no more than] defective shadows, fragmentary and incomplete ... For example: Geometry is a science, and its reality, outermost point and pinnacle is to attain to the name of God, of the Real, 'the Just,' (*al-'Adl*) and 'the Determiner,' (*al-Muqaddir*) and to witness the wise manifestations of that Name, in all its sublimity, in the mirror of geometry ... Philosophy, which researches the true nature of being, can only be true wisdom for man in [his] witnessing within things, and in their benefits and advantages, the supreme directing, nurturing manifestations of a Name of God, [namely] 'the Wise' (*al-Hakīm*), [and in his witnessing] their actualization of that [Name], and in their being founded in that Name. Otherwise [the 'wisdom' of philosophy] amounts to fallacies, idle talk and meaningless sophistry...[126]

Clearly, to be just and to determine, God must be 'the Wise', and the former two attributes are thus 'conditional' on the latter, in a manner that recalls the Akbarī account of the 'hierarchy' of the Divine Names and Attributes. Take Qayṣarī's words, for example,

The Attributes are divided into those which have complete, universal encompassment,[127] and those which do not, even though they may encompass the majority of entities ... now, these Attributes, even though they be the source of others, may also be conditional on one another *in their actualization*, for Knowledge is conditional on Life, and Power and Volition on both of them.[128]

And the words of Mulla Fenari, in distinguishing between the Essential Names (*asmā' al-dhāt*) and the Names of Divine Actions (*asmā' al-af'āl*),

The first of the degrees of the Essence, with respect to these Names,[129] is that of Divinity, which is like a shadow of the Presence of the Essence; and the Source-names of Divinity, the Living, the Knowing, He Who Wills, and the Almighty are like shadows of the Names of the Essence that we have

> referred to ... and know that the Supreme Name in the degree
> of actions is the Name 'the Almighty' ... for 'the Creator', and
> the 'Originator', and 'the Shaper', 'the Constricter' and 'the
> Expander' and the like of them are as if instruments of the
> Name 'the Almighty' ... likewise, 'the Kind' ... and 'the Loving'
> and the like are subordinate to the Name 'He Who Wills'.[130]

It must be pointed out that this conditionality and subordinateness obtains with respect to the sequence of our intellection, and of course does not at all imply any contingency in the Divine Essence – which is impossible. This is just as the hierarchy of the sciences themselves pertains to their sequence of intellection; physics, for example, is not truly intelligible except against the backdrop of metaphysics. Now, although we may not fully perceive the precise essence of this 'foundedness', it is clear that the hierarchical nature of the sciences must in some way ultimately be rooted in and necessitated by the hierarchical nature of the Divine Names and Attributes, for thence all proceeds.

Moreover, the transcendentals and the second intelligibles that also attend essences in their timeless state in *nafs al-amr*, must similarly be rooted in the Divine Names and Attributes. Are not these principles, which in various of their manifestations inform, constitute and attend all existents, and which are then extracted therefrom in human intellection, themselves rooted in the ultimate degree of the metaphysical hierarchy? Is 'possibility' not a symbol of the infinite plenitude of God's power, 'unity' a distant image of God's true Oneness, 'quiddity' an echo of God's distinct Essence, and the varieties of 'causality' loci of manifestation of aspects of the Names of Divine Actions and of His Power and Volition? Reason and our highest traditions of metaphysics assure us that they are so. And our belief that the intelligible concepts that define our intellective apparatuses represent the world as it is, thus finds justification in our discovery that in a higher form, these 'concepts' (really intelligible principles) already pertained to the world prior to its individuation. The light-shedding that abstract human 'perspectives' offer, therefore arises from the intrinsic intelligibility of their source-forms in the Divine Names. Moreover, reason's discernment of the hierarchical order that obtains amongst these 'concepts', genuinely reveals the intelligible structure of the world, and thus, of things as they are.

Conclusion

We began this study by asking if traditional doctrines stating the objectivity of 'truths' about the nature and attributes of physical and especially of metaphysical being can be justified in an age in which methodological scepticism and relativism are ubiquitous. Yet in doing so we set ourselves no easy task. Even at the best of times, civilizationally speaking, answering the question of the possibility and nature of objective truth has been something of a philosophical holy grail. The desire to discern whether or not our apparently mind-dependent cognitions and 'knowledge' genuinely mirror a fully mind-independent world often seems, especially to the modern mind, an aspiration that to be realized simply demands that we cease to be ourselves. Is it not a contradiction, after all, to try to escape completely from our own subjectivity, even regarding 'truths' about the world of ordinary sense-perception? And is not the notion of ascertaining 'objective' truths about a 'metaphysical' realm (that unlike the objects of sense, we do not even *appear* to have direct access to) even more far-fetched?

The inability of any form of philosophy to provide genuine warrant for substantive notions of objective truth in metaphysics is one of the cherished anti-traditional doctrines upon which many aspects of dominant modern Weltanschauungen of scientism and subjectivist individualism are founded and justified. It is for this reason that in this study, we have contended that any putative 'renewal' of Islamic theology for our times must begin with a rigorous defence of the objectivity and scientific status of the most fundamental elements of general metaphysics, upon the validity of which the authority of the results of natural theology rises or falls. This entails systematic investigations of the ontological groundedness of the components of 'universal science', upon which any possible field of human knowledge capable of ultimate justification must derive its most basic first principles, including being, essence, individuation, unity and multiplicity, modal operators and their ontological bases, and causality;

namely, the questions traditionally treated in the *umūr ʿamma* components of advanced works of post-Rāzian *kalām*, (although further explorations of the Categories and other general metaphysical topics are also essential).

True statements about these non-empirical entities have no referents in extramental particulars (*al-khārij*), yet they represent the most fundamental ingredients of all human knowledge, and of the most basic truths that pertain universality to almost everything, concerning causality, essence, necessity, universal properties *qua* universals, the figures and moods of the syllogism, the principle of non-contradiction and so on. What constitutes the guarantee of their truth?

As we have seen in this study, true statements that do not possess empirical or individuated-particular truthmakers are instead true by virtue of corresponding to *nafs al-amr* or 'things as they are' (of course, to be more precise, even true statements about extramental particulars are true by virtue of correspondence to *nafs al-amr* rather than correspondence to extramental particulars). Although this realm of objective truth was widely invoked in many, even non-philosophical disciplines in the later Islamic sciences, its ontological identity was typically passed over in silence except in the most advanced of *kalām*, *falsafa* and metaphysical Sufi texts from the 13th and 14th centuries onwards. It was in this age that the previously widespread, ostensibly common-sense assumption that *nafs al-amr* simply constitutes the aggregate of extramental particulars and minds began to be widely challenged, first and in widely differing ways by Muḥyī al-Dīn Ibn ʿArabī, Fakhr al-Dīn al-Rāzī and Naṣīr al-Dīn al-Ṭūsī, in what was a major breakthrough for metaphysics. Ibn ʿArabī was the first to suggest that only the sciential aspect of Absolute Being – the knowledge of God – can truly constitute fully 'objective' reality; al-Rāzī, and al-Ṭūsī building on much that was implied in the former's work, demonstrated that *nafs al-amr* can neither be the aggregate of individuated particular entities (because they provide no ontological grounding for abstract, intelligible entities – which constitute a broader category then mere *abstracted* entities), nor the aggregate of minds (because the fact of obtaining in a mind is no guarantor of truth, hence the mentalness, yet falsity of the like of $1 + 1 = 3$) nor the combination of both (because many abstract truths do not correspond to extramental particulars and the latter can thus provide no justification of those truths, despite Ṣadr al-Sharīʿa's later attempt to reduce intelligibles to aspects of extramental particulars). This establishes the existence of a 'third realm', which al-Rāzī identified with the Platonic Forms and the inveterate Avicennan al-Ṭūsī identified with the Agent Intellect. While Rāzī and Ṭūsī's affirmation of the *existence* of this 'third realm' was appreciated almost across the board, Rāzī's *identification* was not widely accepted, and as we have seen Ṭūsī's was rejected almost universally, including by his student al-Ḥillī, as well as by Jurjānī, Taftāzānī, al-Qūshjī, 'Alā'uddīn al-Ṭūsī, Taşköprüzade, Mīr Zāhid and many other prominent figures working in the *'aqliyyāt* in the formative period of the post-Razian *kalām*, as well as in its subsequent periods of Ottoman and Mughal vigour.

The theory around which a later *taḥqīq* consensus would be finally built instead came in the work of the Ottoman philosopher and mystic Dawūd al-Qayṣarī, who identified things as they are with the Immutable Archetypes, the timeless, infinite possible images of God's Names and Attributes that constitute the objects of His beginninglessly eternal knowledge. Instead of chiefly identifying objective reality with *al-khārij* or individuated extramental particulars, in which 'through a glass darkly', as it were, God must be proved into existence by human beings applying their reason to impressions of a world of somewhat coarse materiality, Qayṣarī built on the work of Ṣadr al-Dīn al-Qūnawī in laying the metaphysical foundations for the doctrine of Absolute Existence (*al-wujūd al-muṭlaq*) identified with God, of Whose Names and Attributes uninstantiated essences, and subsequently individuals, are perspectival determinations and limitations. Qayṣarī's contention is grounded in a demonstration that Peripatetic immanentism is self-contradictory; the notion that essences can exist only *in rebus*, in their individuated instantiations, falls victim to logical inconsistency. This is because the individual instance *requires* the uninstantiated essence in order to come into existence as an individual *of* that particular species, to be an individual *of* that universal, whereas the original immanentist claim is that the essence can only exist through its individuals. As Qayṣarī has told us, 'the posterior cannot be the cause of the actualization (*taḥaqquq*) of that which is prior.' Genuine logical consistency is thus committed to the *ante rem* existences of essences, and an exemplarist ontology is affirmed, which in later Islamic thought finds its most precise and powerful schemata in the school of Ibn 'Arabī. Truth is a purely metaphysical phenomenon and the intelligibles must be prior to the sensibles, exactly so as to provide the grounds that would ensure that when the latter become intelligible, it is not because a purely subjective 'intelligibility' has been imposed by human perceptional apparatuses. Knowing and being are intimately intertwined.

The most direct window on the priority of the intelligible realm to the sensible is exactly that the world is not intelligible to human beings except via the superimposition of 'perspectival', non-sensible and yet objective concepts (*i'tibāriyyāt ḥaqīqiyya* rather than *fardiyya*) onto the world. Armies, countries and the very cosmos do not strictly speaking exist as extramental particulars because of the perspectival, purely intelligible and non-individuatable elements which constitute them (such as mentally particularized relationality, and perspectival aggregates), but they do exist in *nafs al-amr*. Other types of objects, such as blindness and darkness, *subsist in* extramental particulars, and houses, ships and clothing *exist as* extramental particulars, yet both categories are entirely informed by and depend upon elements that are *objective*, despite being fundamentally mental. As our study has argued, the mere existence of inescapably 'perspectival' aspects of quiddities and intellection uncovers the fact that human perspectives are objective, '*nafs al-amrī*' elements of the world – indeed, that they are indispensable mental elements without which the world would not be intelligible to human beings. Accurate human representation of the world is a part of the world quite as objective as the rest of the world, as is the human contribution to the world's intelligibility. *Nafs al-amr*, or 'objective reality' is partially thus a human reality, though not a 'subjective' human reality.

In this short study, then, we have presented numerous theories concerning the nature and grounds of objective truth, from diverse Islamic philosophical, theological and metaphysical Sufi traditions. We have argued that a proper treatment of objective truth must take place in the context of an ontology adequate to the task of fully accounting for the appearance of that phenomenon. Supplementing our own arguments with those of scholar-sages from different schools of philosophical thought, one of our central motifs has been the insufficiency of the ordinary realms of our experience, the mind and the physical world, to explain by themselves how 'science', in the broad, traditional sense of 'certain human knowledge' is possible.

Human knowledge of the world and existence is only able to obtain because of representational apparatuses of abstract, universal concepts and principles, the fundamental nature of which *appears* to be to *supervene upon the extramental particular world* in the event that a mind perceives these extramental and particular objects. Our study has shown that although *epistemologically*, this abstractive view is attractive and seems to accord with experience, it cannot solve the *ontological*, and even more aptly *henological* questions concerning the ultimate origins and validity of these apparatuses. If they originate purely in the human mind, subjectivism is entailed. If it is the physical world that has originated them, a self-refuting epiphenomenalism is implied that the majority of even contemporary materialists find difficult to take fully seriously.

The solution we have proposed in this study is a view about the phenomenon of knowledge maintained by ancient and venerable traditions of thought that have never ceased to be upheld and nuanced, right up to the present day. On this view, *it is in fact the 'physical' world of extramental particulars that supervenes upon the intelligible world* of which abstract intellectual principles and concepts are one set of manifestations that inescapably invade and inform our physical world. Drawing on principles from the Platonic and Akbarian traditions, we have argued that the awareness we have of abstract objects, first principles of both conception and assent, universal quiddities and uninstantiated essences 'in themselves' amounts to no less than the intuition, albeit filtered through the world of ordinary experience, of the different 'metaprincipial' forms that these entities take in higher realms of being. It is through an effusion from these higher realms, their 'overflowing', that such purely intelligible realities have appeared in our lower world at all. In the language of our study, thus, the realm of extramental particulars (*al-khārij*) is *inside* the realm of things as they are in themselves (*nafs al-amr*). In this metaphysical context, the distinction between *al-khārij* and *nafs al-amr* has appeared in the *logical* realm in terms of *nafs al-amr*'s being simultaneously inclusive of and independent of extramental particulars (as illustrated by al-Jurjānī in this study), *exactly because of the actual existence* of first principles and intelligible realities that *govern* extramental particulars, whilst not being *dependent* upon them. It is the human intellect that constitutes a metaphysical isthmus between the limited, physical, individuated world of particulars, and the unlimited, incorporeal, uninstantiated world of timeless truths. The objectivity and applicability of our abstract concepts and principles and their indispensability to the intelligibility of the world entails their priority to the minds that merely constitute some of their loci; moreover, it suggests that the extramental particular, 'physical' world is informed by, and indeed constitutes a part of, an intelligible realm of much greater scope than itself: *nafs al-amr.*

Intelligibles then, are in no way reducible to extramental particulars. Yet we have learned that even intelligible realities must themselves 'correspond' to something, something that has bestowed upon them their distinct natures, and indeed, their intelligibility. All reality, universal and particular, intelligible, abstract, 'concrete', instantiated and uninstantiated, is rooted in the Divine knowledge that is an infinite reflection and image of the infinite Divine Names. All things, then, are truly grounded in the Real, each possesses a 'face onto God.' Another remarkable truth bestowed upon us by the school of Ibn 'Arabī, moreover, is that intellective consciousness, *is the very meaning* of created being. The meaning of creation is God's bestowal of actual self-consciousness upon the distinct entities in His knowledge, which are themselves perspectival aspects, 'images' of His Names and Attributes. Otherwise, as al-Shaʿrānī asked in Chapter 4, given that the entire world already exists in the knowledge of the Real, what can it have gained by appearing as the observed world?

This softening of the distinction between knowing and being has extremely profound implications for the nature of truth and especially for the correspondence to *nafs al-amr* of the propositions that human beings give vent to in this sublunary world. On this view, the very representational apparatuses of abstract, universal concepts and principles, and even non-existent 'entities', constitute the outermost tips of a single effusion of intelligible being. The question is no longer 'how we know', for if we are able to perceive that we know anything at all, the object to which that perception pertains must have some share in being, however fragmented or distorted it may be, and however distant from its source. It is the natural order of things that henology and ontology should have primacy over epistemology. The correct question, instead, is what it is that the limited beings that constitute the proximate objects of our experience derive their being from; and as Qayṣarī and Mulla Fenari have shown us in this study, the intelligibility of essences across particulars of the same species can only be genuinely accounted for by the prior existence of timeless exemplary forms.

Ultimately, then, we find that all is rooted within, and proceeds from, the Absolute fount of all particularized existence. The less muddied the human receptacle of knowledge, by egoistic restrictions and distortions man has himself inflicted upon his own faculty of cognition, the closer man will *be* to his source, and therefore, the *truer* man's knowledge. The question 'how do we know?' becomes inseparable from the fact of being. That is, 'how do we *know*?' becomes equivalent to 'what is it *to be*?' Man's spiritual ascension through the degrees of being is thus identical to his ascension through ever greater realities of understanding, and his drawing near to the Real whence all being and truth proceeds.

By rooting the apparatuses of demonstrative metaphysics in the very fountainhead of being where the particular is a branch of the purely intelligible, the Akbarian doctrine is uniquely able to assure the modern mind that metaphysical principles arise from beyond, and apply beyond, the world of subjective phenomena, thus justifying the serious practice of traditional natural theology, understood to be subordinated to an even higher form of 'Divine science', the Akbarian *'ilm al-taḥqīq*.[1]

Every age has its own ideas about what constitutes a plausible picture of reality, and conversely, what is incurably far-fetched. The philosophies dominant in our age are not usually well disposed to any ontology showing itself insufficiently hesitant about affirming a reality not somehow 'relative' in its description, and yet (paradoxically) ultimately 'physical' in its nature. The philosophical zeitgeist of the globalized twenty-first century views with undisguised scorn the notion that some Platonic, 'Ideal' reality underlies our physical reality. Let us look, for example, (with a view to helping us remember just how much is urgently at stake in the question of *nafs al-amr*), at the new 'certainties' that have paradoxically replaced belief in objective reality, in the words of a passionate advocate of the 'absolute' relativity of our new world,

> our modern experience is that there isn't any objective, fixed reality out there ... We now live wholly inside our own history, our language, and the flux of cultural change. We find that our world isn't made of Being anymore, but of symbols and of conflicting arguments. (...) Let us now by contrast briefly evoke the traditional religious and philosophic outlook of medieval Christianity. It was Platonic, making a sharp contrast between this changing and corruptible material world below and the eternal controlling intelligible world above. It was pre-critical, so that people made no very clear distinction between culture and nature. They blithely supposed that their own cultural conceptions were part of the natural

order of things. (...) Now consider how completely we have reversed the traditional outlook of Christian Platonism. The world above and all the absolutes are gone. The whole of our life and all of our standards are now inside language and culture. (...) Just as, indeed, the whole of the former world above is now resolved down into the life of this world - so also God is now in each of us. (...) Realists think our religious language tells of beings, events and forces that belong to a higher world, an invisible second world beyond this world of ours. But I believe that there is only one world and it is this world, the world we made, the human life-world, the world of language. To think of language as replicating the structure of some extra-linguistic reality, some world beyond the world of our language, is I believe a mistaken way of thinking of language *anyway*.[2] (...) There is only one world, and it is *this* world ... it doesn't depend in any way on anything higher.[3]

Few, perhaps, would wish to *formally* subscribe to this starkly relativistic view of the world (directly inspired by the doctrines of Nietzsche that we saw in the preface), preferring instead to at least suspend judgement on the rumoured failures of realism. Yet it is nonetheless undoubtedly the case that many elements of this absurd picture of 'unreality' have become normative sentiments, which the postmodern Weltanschauung is constantly to be heard pronouncing, and increasingly even in our Muslim countries.

Of course, today many philosophers do not give any serious credence to even the notion of 'truth' as correspondence to an extramental state of affairs. The fundamental claim uniting various incarnations of the anti-metaphysical deflationary theory of truth defended most influentially by W. V. Quine (and also known, somewhat risibly, as the 'no-truth' theory), is that the so-called 'truth' of a proposition is *identical to its assertion*. Truth is a fundamentally empty concept that does not involve a 'correspondence' to any reality beyond the proposition itself.

The ontological 'grounds' (according to the general naturalistic picture) of this 'untruth', are neural impulses in the human brain that give rise to the unpremeditated 'epiphenomenon' of consciousness. Completing this picture is the view that things have no 'essential' properties, and that there are thus no 'essences'; our 'knowledge' of a thing is determined purely by the ultimately subjective *description* we give of it, if there is indeed any 'it' left at all. Powerful criticisms on analytic philosophy's own terms, by Saul Kripke and others notwithstanding, this overall view of the components of truth or no-truth today remains highly fashionable, perhaps even the 'standard' view.

Yet all this need not overly concern us. We must not be tempted to refute either naturalistic views or anti-realist views 'on their own terms', because both approaches are at base fundamentally unintelligible. Both entail a rejection of any substantial notion of metaphysics, as well as of the reality of Divine revelation, a rejection grounded not in a carefully argued alternative view of the world, but in a doctrinaire spurning of a half-understood past, and in the intellectual exigencies of a social fashion that must scoff, *a priori*, at the notion of any substantial reality beyond a socially-constructed individual, and the 'real physical stuff' of which he is thought to be made. The historical question of how these advanced stages of degeneracy could have been arrived at has not been the chief issue under consideration in this study. Rather, we have wished primarily to uncover some of the real theoretical underpinnings of exemplarist, realist and objectivist norms in *'ilm al-kalām, falsafa* and *'ilm al-taḥqīq,* which have only substantially vanished from sight in the last one hundred years or so. We need not uphold these norms as part of a pious reaction to the stunning prevalence of relativisms and scientisms, and so on, in our contemporary world. Instead, we should uphold them simply because they are the results yielded by the demonstrations of our most powerful forms of metaphysics, of our universal science.

What have a thousand years of Islamic philosophical traditions said about truth, its mode of correspondence to reality, about the ontological grounds of truth, and the nature of real essences? Our broadly 'Islamic' philosophical tradition represents, arguably alongside the Platonic (including the so-called Neoplatonic) school and some of the philosophies of the European High Middle Ages, the most powerful and sophisticated set of philosophical principles and tools in human history. It has been our view that the profound and nuanced views on the nature of truth existing in the Islamic tradition should be understood, maintained and defended first without reference to the flailing, floundering confusions of Modern philosophy (with notable exceptions made, only for some of its most pivotal figures, such as Kant). One had surely better determine one's own position before attempting to exhaustively refute those of others. Later, one may be required to employ one's own principles in order to correct specific errors encountered in the vast proliferation of disjointed, modern systems of thought. Then, one will be well-equipped; when such principles have been understood in their full profundity and on their own terms, the unsound elements in other schools of thought become revealed, in reason's inherent unity, as merely so many branches of hardy, deep and spreading roots, only decayed and twisted because of their distance from their source.

Improper schooling in the metaphysical tradition – an integral part of which must needs involve a robust theory of objective reality or *nafs al-amr* – leads inevitably to some of the fundamental tenets of the primary philosophies that underpin modernity being accepted, tenets which have arisen from a godless view of the world, and that when blindly adopted in 'Muslim' societies have led directly to the sometimes absurd and brutal chaos that is the contemporary reality of many of these societies, where basic respect for the dignity, integrity and interrelatedness of the human and natural orders has often been replaced by a blind worship of Western technology and notions of necessary progress, as well as by views of nature and even of fellow human beings as possessing only instrumental value. It is the holism and integrative synthesis that constituted the hallmark of the developed incarnations of the Islamic sciences until very recently, especially in the Mughal and Ottoman worlds, that is perhaps the only credible solution to this profound disharmony and confusion, so characteristic of our times. This notion of synthesis might be best exemplified by the High Kalam of the later Rāzī, and of Mulla Fenari, Jurjānī, Ibn Kemal, Taşköprüzade, Ibn Bahā'uddīn, Dawānī, Siyalkoti, Mīr Zāhid, Gelenbevi, al-Madhārī, al-Ālūsī and 'Abd al-Karīm al-Mudarris, a *kalām* open to the data of intuition and mystical experience, as well as to the results of the Avicennan philosophers, while preserving *kalām* as a distinct science whose specific role it is to serve the revelation in its most important capacity, namely that of being the truth. In our times, the epistemological alternatives to this integrated *kalām* seem to be variations on esotericism and fideism, both of which are products of Western philosophical scepticism. There are also some who would like a simpler *kalām* theology, devoid, as much as possible, of philosophy and metaphysics, to do the job. However, it simply cannot, for as the intensity of the sceptical challenge increases, so must the sophistication of the response.

Chief amongst the ubiquitous neo-manifestations of Protagoras' 'man is the measure of all things' is the notion of the relativity of the ordering of the sciences. The sciences, on this picture, are not so much a mirror of being and nature, as they are contrived conglomerations of man's subjective pictures, with which he tries to build 'models' – ultimately pictures of himself – that, in the context of contemporary, broadly post-Kantian sentiments, in fact only serve to further cement his distance from unattainable things-in-themselves. Hence, in one omnipresent contemporary manifestation, physics can serve as the de facto 'highest science' that it has become today, ultimately able to pass judgement upon all the others, including philosophy and theology, simply because of the empirical-bias of a naturalist materialism that has permeated the mainstream public consciousness worldwide, and an utter incomprehension of the actual, extremely limited subject matter of physics; or, indeed, of the real nature of the questions at stake, which physics is inherently unqualified to treat.

Similarly, and in terms of the problematics of this study, if objective reality or *nafs al-amr* is merely extramental particulars or the mind, structures of subalternation and subordination are ultimately quite subjective, and merely reflect a pragmatic arrangement, or even a dogmatic and baseless prescription, in danger of suffocating scientific methodology by making, for example, the natural sciences needlessly subject to metaphysics. In which case, what is there to stop us from casting off our ancient tradition in its entirety? Nominalist, quasi-subjectivist theological doctrines, downplaying the power of pure reason to know much more than its subjective impressions, developed perhaps to counteract an overconfidence in the eternal concreteness of the foundations of a Neoplatonized Islamic Peripatetic philosophy; but in times in which we are faced with an intellectual establishment that suffers from both a pronounced lack of confidence in pure reason and the nonrelative nature of truth, and from a lack of belief in God, these potential elements of our theological tradition should perhaps not be so emphasized.

For if we can instead uncover truth at the root of all things, in the self-consciousness of the creation as they gaze upon the source Names and Attributes of the Absolute, the hierarchy of the sciences – that facilitates the miracle of the intelligibility of the world – is revealed as a mirror, granted us by God, of the very nature of reality. ❧

Notes

PREFACE TO THE SERIES

1. Scientific knowledge in this instance does not refer to the natural sciences
    but to a body of knowledge that is ordered in line with an external hierar-
    chy, its place in the division of the sciences, and an internal hierarchy, the
    architectural composition of its subject matter and scope of interest in line
    with ordering principles.

FOREWORD

1. J. Hollingdale, ed and trans. *A Nietzsche Reader* (London: Penguin Books,
    1977), 56.
2. Ibid., 69.

CHAPTER 1. *NAFS AL-AMR* AND THE POSSIBILITY OF OBJECTIVE TRUTH

1. Tahānawī, *Kashshāf iṣṭilāḥāt al-funūn wa al-ʿulūm*, ed. Rafīq ʿAjam and
    ʿAlī Farīd Daḥrūj (Beirut: Maktabat Lubnan, 1416/1996), sub *nafs al-amr*.
    Certain problematic aspects of this definition will be discussed below. All
    translations in this study are the present author's, unless otherwise stated.
2. The Avicennan Naṣīr al-Dīn al-Ṭūsī (597–673/1201–74) and the Akbarian
    Dāwūd al-Qayṣarī (d. 751/1350). The latter position became standard in the
    Akbarian school, and was deemed the true position by numerous prominent
    kalām theologians (see Chapter 4). Al-Ṭūsī's theory fared less well, as we
    will discover.
3. This is implied by the most important architect of later Islamic philosophy
    Avicenna (370–427/980–1037). As we will see in this study, Avicenna's views
    on the matter may have influenced the more developed doctrine of the great
    kalām theologian Saʿd al-Dīn al-Taftāzānī (722–92/1322–90).
4. This was the 'standard' view until the time of al-Ṭūsī. See the quote from
    al-Ḥillī (648–726/1250–1325) in Section 2.2.
5. Although there is much crossover here with the range of philosophical is-
    sues raised in contemporary analytic philosophy by the study of 'abstract
    objects', the main problematics of which were chiefly defined by Quine, it

should be noted that our starting point in this study is substantially different. This is primarily because in contemporary analytic treatments the distinction between abstract and concrete objects is most often struck in a context of ontological ambiguity that makes the crude construal of 'abstract' and 'concrete' as involving a simple, dichotomous binary inevitable. On this broad account, the abstract exists outside of time and space, the concrete within, the abstract is causally inert, and the concrete (at least potentially) causally active. 'According to the standard definition, an object is abstract if and only if it has no spatial location and has no causal relations (abstract objects do not make things happen and there is no way to act upon them)' (Matteo Plebani, 'Recent Debates over the Existence of Abstract Objects: An Overview' in José L. Falguera and Concha Martínez-Vidal, *Abstract Objects: For and Against* (Cham: Springer, 2020), 2. Edward Zalta and others have nonetheless provided nuanced and philosophically interesting expositions, despite situating themselves firmly within the analytic 'tradition'. Zalta, for example, makes the distinction between the 'exemplification' of properties in concrete objects, and the 'encoding' (and only occasional exemplification) of properties in abstract objects, and also provides for the possibility that certain abstract objects possess correlates in the 'actual' world (see his *Abstract Objects: An Introduction to Axiomatic Metaphysics* Dordrecht: D. Reidel, 1983) and his *Intensional Logic and the Metaphysics of Intentionality* (Cambridge, MA: The MIT Press, 1988). However, almost without exception, contemporary 'analytic' treatments of the status of abstract objects lack adequate accounts of the ontological status of such properties and their various modes of being in terms of demonstrative epistemologies rooted in broader, realist metaphysical frameworks, that culminate in an ontologically explanatory and ultimate first principle. In common with most post-Kantian philosophy, then, they are as it were 'suspended between heaven and earth' without any binding foundation in either metaphysics or epistemology. It is our view that the tensions intrinsic to the question of the ontological status of 'intelligible' entities in pre-modern, broadly Platonic-Aristotelian thought (embracing primary intelligibles that *do* possess extramental referents, secondary intelligibles that *do not* possess extramental referents, logical and metaphysical first principles and so on) are largely given more credible treatments within these traditional forms of philosophy (that do not suffer from such metaphysical deprivations), specifically in terms of a synthesis of the Platonic view that intelligible entities underlie, and exist separately from particulars, and that such entities are *not* causally inert, with the Aristotelian modification of Platonism, in which 'objects' only perceptible by the mind (and that have no strictly *sensible* referents), such as substantial forms, nonetheless exist within, and inform, sensible particulars.

6. A demonstration of soundness which, we argue, cannot be achieved from *within,* in a didactic, linear form of theology that operates chiefly without reference to metaphysical principles; moreover, we contend that this type of theology is incapable of adequately responding to the deepest challenges of modern philosophy. Moreover, we have come to the conclusion that with notable exceptions, the pre-Razian *kalām* largely falls into this category, although it is also the case that certain forms of largely ametaphysical *kalām* continued to be practised and developed after Fakhr al-Dīn al-Rāzī (543–606/1148–1209).

7. By 'metaphysics' we do not refer here to the *conclusions* of some of the main proponents of traditional metaphysics like Avicenna, for example that of the past eternity of the world. Many of their results, from the division of metaphysics sometimes known as 'special metaphysics' are rightly rejected by *kalām* theologians. However, this rejection did not prevent them from drawing heavily on Avicenna and other metaphysicians in the context of the other fundamental division of metaphysics, known variously as 'general metaphysics' or 'general ontology', the systematic analysis of the nature of metaphysical principles, intelligible structures and concepts such as existence, causality, unity and multiplicity, quiddity, individuation, necessity and possibility (that is, the 'transcendentals' or *umūr ʿāmma*), as well as the Ten Categories of substance, quality, quantity and so on. They do not hide this debt; Avicenna is cited by name, often with unambiguous approval and adoption of his positions, on hundreds of occasions throughout orthodox Sunni works like al-Sayyid al-Sharīf al-Jurjānī's (750–817/1349–1414) *Sharḥ al-Mawāqif* and Taftāzānī's *Sharḥ al-Maqāṣid*. Indeed, it is demonstrable that in the later (post-Rāzian) *kalām* tradition, the views of the post-Avicennan tradition on such matters are preferred to those of the early *kalām* theologians, as well as to those of Rāzī himself, in the clear majority of instances (the division of metaphysics into special and general metaphysics is Christian Wolff's (1679–1754) innovation, and is problematic if construed as a genuinely fundamental division of metaphysics, but nonetheless useful, in this context, in so far as it indicates the distinction between *general* metaphysical principles capable of application in a great diversity of ways, and the potentially mistaken, *special* application of these principles, so as to entail conclusions that may conflict with orthodox Sunni creed). Amongst contemporary scholars focusing specifically on the post-Rāzian *ʿaqliyyāt*, it is our view that the work of Karim Lahham, Robert Wisnovsky, Peter Adamson, Wahid Amin, Muhammad Sami, Ömer Türker, Tony Street and Mustafa Styer particularly stands out, amongst that of some others, for the high quality of its *philosophical,* rather than merely exegetical or historiographical analysis.

8. Namely that of W.V. Quine (1908–2000), who developed the philosophy of the Vienna Circle into his own nominalist, deflationist, behaviourist and

scienticist 'anti-system', and who celebrated what he viewed as one of the main achievements of empiricism after 1800, namely, 'naturalism: abandonment of the goal of a first philosophy prior to natural science'. W.V. Quine, *Theories and Things* (Cambridge, MA: Belknap Press, 1986), 67. He is widely revered as one of the most influential philosophers of the twentieth century.

9. The fact that these last two modes of dealing with philosophical and theological questions will be shown to have overlapped significantly from the early fourteenth century onwards, may come as a surprise to some. Yet both modes were naturally informed by Avicenna's metaphysical synthesis, which played a great part in the shaping of the *umūr al-ʿāmma* components (the 'transcendentals' – for discussion of this choice of translation of *umūr ʿamma*, see note below) – standard from the fourteenth century – of advanced works of *kalām* such as Naṣīr al-Dīn al-Ṭūsī's *al-Tajrīd*, Saʿd al-Dīn al-Taftāzānī's *Sharḥ al-Maqāṣid*, and al-Sayyid al-Sharīf al-Jurjānī's *Sharḥ al-Mawāqif.* These books may be the three single most influential metaphysical *kalām* 'textbooks' of the last six hundred years of Islamic civilization, each providing thorough, post-Rāzian treatments (by which we mean treatments that take into account and resolve Rāzī's sceptical reformulations of the broadly Avicennan metaphysical tradition) of existence (*al-wujūd*), essence (*al-māhiyya*), unity (*al-waḥda*), multiplicity (*al-kathra*), individuation (*al-taʿayyun*) and non-existent entities (*al-maʿdūmāt*) as well as the justification of necessary knowledge (*ithbāt al-ʿulūm al-ḍarūriyya*) and many other metaphysical and epistemological questions. The *Tajrīd* and the *Sharḥ al-Mawāqif* were taught to advanced students throughout the Ottoman Empire, for almost as long as that political entity was in existence. See Mustafa Sanal, 'Osmanli Devleti'nde Medreselere Ders Programlari, Öğertim Metodu, Ölçme ve Değerlendirme, Öğretimde Ihtisaslaşma Bakimindan Genel Bir Bakış', Sosyal Bilimler Enstitüsü Dergisi Sayı 14 (2003): 149-168. *Sharḥ al-Maqāṣid* continued to be taught in al-Azhar until 1911 (See note below). Because these texts were the subjects of vast commentary traditions, especially in the cases of *Sharḥ al-Mawāqif* and the *Tajrīd*, they constitute some of our most important starting points for understanding later traditions of Islamic thought.

10. See Section 2.2 for some history of the term as a metaphysical concept.

11. To see this 'metaphysical' Sufism – broadly the Ottoman, Persian and Indian schools of the followers of Ibn ʿArabī – formally conceived as a distinct science (referred to as *ʿilm al-taḥqīq* and *ʿilm al-ḥaqāʾiq*) see Mulla Fenari, *Miṣbāḥ al-uns*, ed. Muḥammad Khawajavi (Tehran: Intisharat-i Mawla, 1995), 39-44.

12. That is, as the term used to define a proposition's 'truth' as 'correspondence to *nafs al-amr*' while leaving the actual nature of *nafs al-amr* undetermined.

13. This is largely echoed by the first part of Tahānawī's definition, which we have already seen above.

14. Burhān al-Dīn Abū-l-Ḥasan Ibrāhīm ibn ʿUmar al-Biqāʿī, *Naẓm al-Durar fī Tanāsub al-Āyāt wal-Suwar* (Cairo: Dār al-Kitāb al-Islāmī, n.d). In the realm of Qurʾanic exegesis, the reader might compare Biqāʿī's treatment of *nafs al-amr* with the magisterial synthesis of Avicennism, *kalām* and the school of Ibn ʿArabī achieved by Abū Thanāʾ al-Ālūsī (1217–70/1803–54), when he discusses the meaning of *nafs al-amr* in his *Rūḥ al-Maʿānī* (for Ālūsī's treatment of *nafs al-amr* therein, see Section 4.4).

15. Ibn Bahāʾuddīn, *al-Qawl al-faṣl, Sharḥ al-Fiqh al-Akbar li al-Imām al-Aʿẓam Abī Ḥanīfa*, ed. Dr. Rafīq al-ʿAjam (Beirut: Dār al-Muntakhab al-ʿArabī, 1998), 39. We will discuss Ibn Bahāʾuddīn's Akbarian views on *nafs al-amr* in Section 3.3.

16. 'Non-existent' as extramental particulars, that is, but nonetheless distinct. This distinction informs some of the most important themes of this paper as a whole, and will become fully clear to the reader, it is to be hoped, in the fullness of the paper.

17. This 'overlapping', which can be expressed logically in terms of relational predicative scope, is discussed in Section 2.3.

18. Najm al-Dīn al-Kātibī and Mubārakshāh (commentary), *Sharḥ Ḥikmat al-ʿAyn*, with the supercommentary of al-Sayyid al-Sharīf al-Jurjānī (Kazan: Maṭbaʿat Sharīf Jān wa Ḥasan Jān, 1319/1901), 43.

19. Ibid., 33.

20. For the 'pervasive myth' (apparently concocted by Aristotle himself) that in his doctrine of Forms Plato is affirming the transcendent existence of *universals*, see Lloyd Gerson's landmark study, which argues for the governing role of Platonism with respect to all subsequent forms of genuine philosophy, *Platonism and Naturalism: The Possibility of Philosophy* (Ithaca: Cornell University Press, 2020), 79-82.

21. For an exemplarily engaging and thorough account of Aristotle's doctrine of substance that argues decisively for this interpretation, see Frank A. Lewis, *How Aristotle Gets by in Metaphysics Zeta* (Oxford: Oxford University Press, 2013).

22. See Amos Bertolacci, *The Reception of Aristotle's Metaphysics in Avicenna's Kitāb al-Shifāʾ: A Milestone of Western Metaphysical Thought* (Leiden: Brill, 2006), 454.

23. Ibn Bahāʾuddīn, *al-Qawl al-faṣl*, 143. This opposite, Platonic and Akbarian view (and our own favoured position), in which uninstantiated essences exist as the ontologically prior preconditions of their participating instantiations, will be discussed in more detail chiefly in Chapter 4.

24. ʿAbd al-Nabiyy ibn ʿAbd al-Rasūl Aḥmadnagarī, *Dustūr al-ʿUlamāʾ* (many editions) sub *al-khārij*. See also Tahānawī *Kashshāf* sub *al-ʿayn*.

25. *Dustūr al-ʿUlamāʾ* sub *al-khārij*, Taftāzānī, *Sharḥ al-Maqāṣid*, vol. 1 (Istanbul: Maṭbaʿat al-Ḥāj Muḥarram Efendi, 1305/1888), 95.

26. Ibrāhīm b. Muḥammad ibn Aḥmad al-Bājūrī, *Ḥāshiyat Ibn Qasim*, vol. 2, ed. Muḥammad Ṣāliḥ Nuwaydir (Amman: Dār al-Nūr al-Mubīn li al-Nashr wa al-Tawzī', 2015), 1127.

27. This is Arberry's translation.

28. Ibn Kathīr, *Tafsīr al-Qur'ān al-'Aẓīm*, ed. Muṣṭafā al-Sayyid Muḥammad (Giza: Mu'assasat Qurṭuba, 1421/2000), sub Qur'an 2:188.

29. 'Abd al-Razzāq al-Kāshānī, *Tafsīr*, published as *Tafsīr Ibn 'Arabī*, ed. al-Shaykh 'Abd al-Wārith Muḥammad 'Alī (Beirut: Dār al-Kutub al-'Ilmiyya, 1427/2006), sub Qur'an 12:4.

30. Contrary to the pronouncements of a now very jaded narrative, that teaches the dominance of a strict dichotomy between esoteric and exoteric *'ulamā'* throughout Islamic history, the notion that this prostration of celestial bodies took place in *'ālam al-mithāl*, is not the sole preserve of so-called 'esoteric' works, but is echoed in, for example, the 'exoteric' exegesis (see e.g. sub Qur'an 12:6) of the great jurist and *şeyhülislam* appointed by Sulaymān the Magnificent, Abū Su'ūd al-'Imādī (896-982/1490-1574), his *Irshād al-'aql al-salīm* (Beirut: Dār Iḥyā' al-Turāth al-'Arabī, 1411/1990).

31. These concepts will be explained more fully in Chapter 4.

32. We will use 'extramental particulars' here to correspond to the Akbārian *'ālam al-mulk* or 'the world of the Dominion' (roughly, the world of ordinary sense experience). See Chapter 4.

33. As Kāshānī's disciple Dawūd al-Qayṣarī says in his famous *Prolegomena*, 'everything that has existence in the sensible world has existence in the world of imaginal representations, but the converse is not true'. See *Maṭla' Khuṣūṣ al-Kalim fī Ma'ānī Fuṣūṣ al-Ḥikam*, ed. Shaykh 'Āṣim Ibrāhīm al-Kayyālī (Beirut: Dār al-Kutub al-'Ilmiyya, 1433/2012), 81. For a more general account of the subordinacy of the sensible world to the world of imaginal representations, see ibid. 73-82.

34. For an agreeably thorough contemporary account of the Aristotelian roots of the concept of a 'universal science', see T.H. Irwin, *Aristotle's First Principles* (Oxford: Clarendon Press, 1998). For the even deeper Platonic roots, see Hans Joachim Krämer, *Plato and the Foundations of Metaphysics: A Work on the Theory of the Principles and Unwritten Doctrines of Plato With a Collection of the Fundamental Documents*, ed. and trans. John R. Catan (Albany, NY: State University of New York Press, 1990), 77-91 and especially 83-89 (see also our exposition of the ontological foundations of the transcendentals with Platonic-Akbarian correctives, in Chapter 4). For Avicenna's own exposition of his conception of universal science, upon which later Islamic conceptions are largely based, see Avicenna's *al-Shifā'*, at *al-Ilāhiyyāt* I, ed. Sa'īd Zāyid and George Anawati (Cairo: al-Hay'a al-'Āmma li Shu'ūn al-Maṭābi' al-Amīriyya, 1380/1960), 3-28. For two important later *kalām* expositions that identify many of the attributes of the concept of a universal science with *kalām*, see Taftāzānī, *Sharḥ al-Maqāṣid*, vol. 1, 5-15,

al-Sayyid al-Sharīf al-Jurjānī, *Sharḥ al-Mawāqif*, with the commentaries of Abd al-Ḥakīm Siyalkoti and Ḥasan Çelebi, ed. al-Sayyid Muḥammad Badr al-Dīn al-Naʿsānī (Cairo: Maṭbaʿat al-Saʿāda, 1325/1907), 32-61. See also Tahānawī *Kashshāf* sub *al-ʿilm al-ilāhī* for a good overview.

35. If it be objected that 'metaphysics', as a branch of modern philosophy, is alive and well, it should be emphasized that the operational reality of modern academic metaphysics is so marred by its having adopted – quite without justification – a universal and dogmatically 'unresolveable' scepticism as to the nature and validity of first principles, that it is unable to make any real progress, nor indeed even approach being adequate to the role, detailed above, of traditional metaphysics.

36. Prominent exceptions in the relatively recent Islamic intellectual world, in which this absence of first principles is less pronounced, include *şeyhülislam* Mustafa Sabri (1286-1373/1869-1954) in his *Mawqif al-ʿAql wa al-ʿIlm wa al-ʿĀlam Min Rabb al-ʿĀlamīn wa ʿIbādihi al-Mursalīn*, (Beirut: Dār Iḥyāʾ al-Turāth, 1950), see e.g. vol. 2, 326-341; and Ismail Hakki Izmirli (1286-1365/1869-1946), in his *Yeni Ilmi Kalam*, (Istanbul: Awqāf Islāmiyya Matbaasi, 1339/1921), particularly vol. 1, 217-246. The loss of first principles was also a key feature of the broadly 'neoscholastic' diagnosis of modern philosophical infirmity. See for example, Reginald Garrigou-Lagrange *Reality*, trans. Patrick Cummins (Bradford: Ex Fontibus, 2015), 27-31 and 316-323, Etienne Gilson, *The Unity of Philosophical Experience*, Charles Scribner's Sons, 1937, reprinted (San Francisco, CA: Ignatius Press, 1999), 248-257. For a basic overview of neoscholasticism seen from the outside, see P.J Fitzpatrick, 'Neoscholasticism' in N. Kretzmann, A. Kenny and J. Pinborg, eds., *The Cambridge History of Later Medieval Philosophy* (Cambridge: Cambridge University Press, 1982), 838-852.

37. This was not taken to imply, not in the Islamic world nor in medieval Europe, that first philosophy was an *essentially* higher science than the sacred sciences of revelation. Rather, the principles of first philosophy merely constitute the (albeit ontologically grounded) *epistemological* preconditions for *any* form of science. The *object* of an (epistemologically) subordinate science, however, may be immeasurably superior to that of the (epistemologically) 'highest' science. The science of Qurʾanic exegesis, for example, studies the Divinely revealed scripture, which is a manifestation of one of the attributes (Divine Speech) of God; however, *procedurally*, exegesis presupposes the foundations and assumptions laid by *kalām* with its metaphysical underpinnings. For a discussion that briefly touches on some of these points, and shows how Qurʾanic exegesis and *kalām* can both claim to be, from different perspectives, 'the highest science', see Ālūsī's own introduction to his *Rūḥ al-Maʿānī*. Abū Thanāʾ Shihāb al-Dīn al-Ālūsī, *Rūḥ al-Maʿānī*, vol. 1, ed. al-Sayyid Muḥammad Sayyid and Sayyid ʿImrān (Cairo: Dār al-Ḥadīth, 1426/2005), 25.

38. The signing into law, by the Committee of Union and Progress, of the Ottoman 'Reform of the Medreses' bill in 1914 put the survival of the traditional Islamic sciences in great danger. Students were now to study Western natural sciences and sociology, and the traditional subjects were vastly truncated. See Amit Bein, *Ottoman Ulema, Turkish Republic: Agents of Change and Guardians of Tradition* (Stanford, CA: Stanford University Press, 2011), 56-64. The reforms were not to last long, however, before an event took place even more disastrous for the survival of the traditional curriculum: the dissolution of the Ottoman state itself (1922). A similar decline occurred in post-Mughal India, especially with the disintegration of Farangi Mahall. See Francis Robinson, *The Ulama of Farangi Mahall and Islamic Culture in South Asia* (London: C Hurst and Co. Publishers, 2001), and the rise of Deobandism, a phenomenon whose scholastic reforms were largely opposed by the traditionalist scholars of India. For example, explaining the remarkable intellectual power and openness that the traditional *'aqliyyāt* curriculum provided students, one of the last of these prominent traditional scholars, 'Abd al-Bārī Farangi Mahall (1295-1344/1878-1926), said 'would you rather have it that students became like sheep, like the alumni of Deoband, or people whose knowledge is superficial, like those from the Nadwa since Shibli's death, or those who belong to the Ahl-i Hadiths in Delhi?' (ibid. 167). At al-Azhar as elsewhere, the 'intellectual' sciences (*'aqliyyāt*) were certainly the most sharply affected by the almost universal waning of the Islamic sciences throughout the Sunni world at the beginning of the twentieth century. The 1911 reforms of the Azhari curriculum signalled the end of study of advanced philosophical works of metaphysical *kalām* like Sa'd al-Din al-Taftazani's *Sharḥ al-Maqāṣid*, and their replacement by far more basic books, like *Jawharat al-Tawḥīd*, *al-Kharīda* and *Umm al-Barāhīn*. See Ṣāliḥ Mūsā Sharaf's preface to Sa'd al-Dīn al-Taftāzānī, *Sharḥ al-Maqāṣid*, vol. 1, ed. 'Abd al-Raḥmān 'Umayra (Beirut: 'Ālam al-Kutub, 1419/1998), 13. For certain aspects of upheavals in the Azhar during the nineteenth century, see J. Heyworth-Dunne, *An Introduction to the History of Education in Modern Egypt*, (London: Luzac & Co., 1938), 395-405, and Indira Falk Gesink, *Islamic Reform and Conservatism: Al-Azhar and the Evolution of Modern Sunni Islam* (London: Tauris Academic Studies, 2010).

39. That is, whether it is limited to the world of extramental particulars, or, contrarily, that it is not limited to extramental particulars but encompasses a vast domain of distinct intelligible realities that is prior to extramental particulars, and of which the world of extramental particulars constitutes a mere restricting particularization.

40. Of course, 'foundationalist' theories are very numerous today; here I intend to use the term in its broadest sense, as a theory that in some capacity invokes an epistemic regress argument like that initiated by Aristotle in *Posterior Analytics*, I.3.

41. That is, that we perceive ourselves to be equipped, by nature as human beings, with first principles and innate concepts which we cannot rid ourselves of, and which all of the further knowledge we acquire, whether it is empirical or theoretical, seems in some sense to presuppose and be rooted in.

42. And moreover, the abstractive cognitions of the objects of sense, as they can only be the object of discussion post intelligible representation. For a concise, incisive late summation of *tahqīq* positions on abstraction, including the cognitive synthesis of sense and intelligible, see ‘Abd al-Rahmān Shirbīnī's (d. 1345/1926) *taqrīr* in al-Bannānī, *Hāshiyat al-‘allāma al-Bannānī ‘alā sharh al-Jalāl Shams al-Dīn Muhammad ibn Ahmad al-Mahallī ‘alā matn Jam‘ al-jawāmi‘ li al-imām Tāj al-Dīn ‘Abd al-Wahhāb ibn al-Subkī*, with Shaykh al-Islām ‘Abd al-Rahmān al-Shirbīnī's *Taqrīr*, vol. 1, (Cairo, 1285/1868, Repr. Beirut: Dār al-Fikr, 1402/1982), 142-43.

43. That is, consisting in innate necessary concepts, the intuition of the one over the many, abstractive representation, first and second intelligibles, and so on.

44. Indeed, we are keenly aware that at the most hostile extreme of criticism, our approach and results may be dismissed as merely so much philosophical and exegetical fantasy. Presumably, those in possession of these feelings will also be able to infer the fact that we are likewise inclined to hold a similar opinion of their own approaches. In light of this, we implore all who engage with this work to do so in accordance with the *ādāb* of *al-bahth wa'l munāzara*. Purely rhetorical dismissals and affective outrage at a perceived excess of ‘mysticism’ and exemplarism (or indeed, of naturalism and nominalism) scarcely befit either party in a rational debate, and we invite those who wish to investigate the truth or otherwise of the conclusions of this study to engage, in the pursuit of truth, on the terms set in the pages that follow, namely those of metaphysical principle and logic, by actually engaging its arguments. The problem of the possibility of objective truth depicted in this study is not one, I believe, that can be solved by any properly nominalist or epistemologically ‘naturalist’ approach, nor indeed, even by a realist methodology that insists upon maintaining a broadly immanentist account of the apparatuses of our cognition. I would be fascinated to encounter a philosopher who, genuinely understanding the problem, is nonetheless able to provide a solution that need not depart from the bounds set by the methodological approaches just mentioned.

45. Muhyī al-Dīn Ibn ‘Arabī, *al-Futūhāt al-Makkiyya,* vol. 1 (Cairo: Dār al-Kutub al-‘Arabiyya al-Kubrā, 1329/1911), 41.

46. Ibid., vol. 1., 288.

47. Ibid.

48. Ibid., vol. 1. 288-290 The paragraphs we have written directly before and after this excerpt from the *Futūhāt* are partial summaries and paraphrases of the Greatest Master's larger argument at 290.

49. 'Metaphysical' in the narrower sense of the 'first philosophy' of post-Avi-cennan *ḥikma* and *kalām*.

50. Shams al-Dīn al-Anbābī's *Taqrīr* on Ibrahim al-Bājūrī, *Ḥāshiya ʿalā Matn al-Sullam* (Cairo: Būlāq, 1297/1879), 21.

51. Ḥasan Çelebi in al-Sayyid al-Sharīf al-Jurjānī, *Sharḥ al-Mawāqif*, with the commentaries of Abd al-Ḥakīm Siyalkoti and Ḥasan Çelebi, vol. 1, 35.

52. Qāḍī Mīr Ḥusayn Maybudi (commentator) and Athīr al-Dīn al-Abharī, *Hidāyat al-Ḥikma* (Istanbul: Dār al-Ṭibāʿa al-ʿĀmira), 1262/1846, 3.

53. Ibid., 3.

54. Ṣadr al-Dīn al-Qūnawī, *Miftāḥ al-Ghayb*, in Ṣadr al-Dīn al-Qūnawī and Mulla Fenari, *Miftāḥ al-Ghayb wa-sharḥuhu Miṣbāḥ al-uns*, ed. Muḥammad Khawājavi (Tehran: Intisharat-i Mawla, 1415/1995), 9.

55. See Chapter 4 below.

56. Qāḍī Mīr Ḥusayn Maybudi (commentator) and Athīr al-Dīn al-Abharī, *Hidāyat al-Ḥikma*, 104. Qāḍī Ḥusayn was executed by the early Safavid regime for his 'ardent Sunnism'. See Alexandra Dunietz, *The Cosmic Perils of Qadi Ḥusayn Maybudī in Fifteenth-Century Iran* (Leiden: Brill, 2016), 163.

57. Taşköprüzade straightforwardly tells us that the 'experiential philosophy' (*al-ḥikma al-dhawqiyya*), the most prominent later representatives of which he lists as Mulla Fenari (751–834/1350–1431), Jalāl al-Dīn al-Dawwānī (830–907/1427–1501), 'and their leaders, Ṣadr al-Dīn al-Qūnawī and Quṭb al-Dīn al-Shīrāzī' (for more on whom, see Chapter 4), relies on 'the way of purification' rather than 'the way of speculative thinking.' However, and most significantly, there is a level of speculative thought that shares a border with the way of purification, and which has a similar definition, namely the 'way of experience', which is called 'experiential philosophy' (*al-ḥikma al-dhawqiyya*). See Taşköprüzade, *Miftāḥ al-saʿāda fī mawḍūʿāt al-ʿulūm*, vol. 1 (Beirut: Dār al-Kutub al-ʿIlmiyya, 1405/1985), 289. See also the present author's *The Mystical Synthesis of Ibn Bahāʾuddīn: An Akbarian* Kalām *Theologian in 16th Century Istanbul* (Tabah, forthcoming 2021).

CHAPTER 2. THE STUDY OF THINGS AS THEY ARE IN THEMSELVES: HISTORY AND METHOD

1. See for example, Ismail Gelenbevi, *Sharḥ Isāghūjī*, ed. ʿAbdullah Hacdınmız (Istanbul: al-Maktaba al-Hanafiyya nd.), 84-85, Mulla Fenari, *al-Fawāʾid al-Fanāriyya*, ed. Ibrahim al-Hurānī and Muḥammad Diyarbakri (Istanbul: Haşimi Yayinevi, 2012), 45-46, and Saʿd al-Dīn Masʿūd b. ʿUmar al-Taftāzānī, *Tahdhīb al-manṭiq,* with the commentary of ʿUbaydullāh al-Khabīṣī and the supercommentaries of Muḥammad b. ʿArafa al-Dusūqī and Ḥasan al-ʿAṭṭār, ed. Aḥmad Saʿd ʿAli (Cairo: Matbaʿat Muṣṭafā al-Bābī al-Ḥalabī wa Awlādihi, 1355/1936), 225-227.

2. One of the most widely read of introductory logic texts, the great astrono-
    mer, philosopher and mathematician Athīr al-Dīn al-Abharī's (d. 663/1265)
    Īsāghūjī.

3. Mulla Fenari, *Al-Fawā'id al-Fanāriyya*, 45.

4. Abū ʿAlī Ibn Sīnā, *al-Ishārāt wa al-Tanbīhāt* with the commentary of Naṣīr
    al-Dīn al-Ṭūsī, vol. 1, ed. Sulaymān Dunyā (Cairo: Dār al-Maʿārif, 1983), 222.

5. Along with simply *al-Shaykh*, this is Avicenna's honorific title in later Is-
    lamic intellectual history, including the great works of post-Rāzian *kalām*.

6. Ibid., vol.1, 226.

7. Ibid.

8. The *Tajrīd* is of course fundamentally a *kalām* text, but with a very rich
    and influential *umūr al-ʿāmma* component. Its influence is attested to, in
    the Sunni world, by the tens of original commentaries written on it by
    Ottoman ʿulama - for mention of which see Taşköprüzade's *al-Shaqā'iq
    al-Nuʿmāniyya* (Beirut: Dār al-Kutub al-ʿArabī, 1975), *passim*. The most
    prominent amongst these was probably al-Qūshjī's commentary, which
    attracted famous supercommentaries from al-Dawānī. Al-Sayyid al-Sharīf
    al-Jurjānī's supercommentaries on Shams al-Dīn al-Iṣfahānī's commentary
    on the *Tajrīd* were a central part of the Ottoman curriculum. See Cahid
    Baltacı, *XV-XVI Yüzyıllarda Osmanli Medreseleri*, Marmara Ilahiyat Fakul-
    tesi Vakfi Yayinlari, 2005, vol.1, 73-89.

9. That is, with other extramental particulars, such that both subject and
    predicate have referents in extramental particulars, like 'some leaves are
    green.'

10. Naṣīr al-Dīn al-Ṭūsī and Shams al-Dīn al-Iṣfahānī (commentary), *Tasdīd
    al-Qawāʿid fī Sharḥ Tajrīd al-ʿAqā'id*, vol. 1, ed. Khālid ibn Hammād al-
    ʿAdwānī (Kuwait: Dār al-Ḍiyā', 1433/2012), 321.

11. The first possibility being represented by e.g. 'man is an essence' and the
    second by e.g. 'the species is a universal.'

12. Because if we are to identify *nafs al-amr* with the human mind, proposi-
    tions that merely *correspond to the mind* would by definition be true.

13. Ibid. 322-323.

14. For our purposes, after the thought of both of the intellectual poles of the
    Islamic tradition – Ibn Sīnā (370–427/980–1037) and Ibn ʿArabī – had been
    fully integrated into the normative language of that tradition (and not
    precluding their integration into the Islamic sciences in isolation from
    one another); that is, from the fourteenth century onwards, in the works of
    thinkers like Dāwūd al-Qayṣarī, Mulla Fenari, al-Sayyid al-Sharīf al-Jurjānī,
    Ibn Kemal, Taşköprüzade, Ibn Bahā'uddīn and others, who in their work
    incorporated both the theories of Fakhr al-Dīn al-Rāzī's critical Avicen-
    nism, and Ṣadr al-Dīn al-Qūnawī's philosophical Akbarianism (see Chapter
    4). This is contrary to the strongly held views of certain academics, such as
    Dimitri Gutas, who has recently felt moved to brand later Islamic thought

'paraphilosophy' in his article, 'Avicenna and After: The Development of Paraphilosophy. A History of Science Approach' in *Islamic Philosophy from the 12th to the 14th Century*, ed. Abdelkader Al Ghouz (Göttingen: Bonn University Press, 2018). In this article, Gutas departs from his usual scholarly modus of somewhat unphilosophical but historiographically and codicologically careful Avicenna exegesis, in order to offer a series of startlingly anachronistic pronouncements on what it is that constitutes 'real' science (essentially, an experimental, empirically biased, near positivist conception thereof, that had no real application before the early-modern period), as well as the naturalist assumption that Christianity and Islam constitute 'mythological approaches to reality', inherently opposed to (Gutas') 'science', a claim which he endlessly repeats in his article (see for example, pp. 26, 28, 31). One marvels at the dogmatic and simplistic narrative of 'scientific' modernity that is uncritically rehearsed in countless passages in Gutas' article: 'Briefly, traditional beliefs and religion can be understood as the account of reality provided in a mythological narrative endorsed by a society at large. This mythological narrative is generally considered sacrosanct and, in monotheistic religions, immutable and unnegotiable. But scientific research discovers ways in which reality works that are inconsistent with this narrative' (29); 'If science/philosophy is the open-ended rational investigation into reality, which all who possess reason, as all humans do, can follow, then it can be easily seen that asserting one's superior knowledge through some unspecified and mysterious "inspiration" etc. negates the entire scientific enterprise ...' For Gutas, the acknowledgement of this source of knowledge in some genres of later thought, justifies what he calls 'the Islamic *myth* of prophecy through waḥy.' (39). It seems that for Gutas, then, the *sine qua non* of 'open-minded' rational 'science', is the requirement that one must be dogmatically closed-minded about the possibility of revelation and mystical cognition. The post-Rāzian philosophical tradition had 'primarily theological aims, in that its principal intention was to argue in favour of Islamic doctrine in philosophical terms, but it was different from the traditional theology, *kalām*, it was not theology in that sense. It has been broadly recognized, as Gerhard Endress aptly put it, that philosophy after Avicenna was "reduced to an instrument of religious hermeneutic" (42); ... 'it violated all the basic principles of what historically had meant to do science (sic), which was the open-ended rational investigation of all reality. It was not open-ended, in that it strove to argue for one pre-determined thesis, the Islamic *mythological* narrative; it was not completely rational, in that it admitted selectively supra-rational modes of acquisition of knowledge; and it was not an investigation of all reality in that it narrowed the discussion to certain subjects, those of interest to religious doctrine ...' It is 'clandestine theologizing that simulates and presents itself as philosophy'. He goes on to brand later *kalām* 'paraphilosophy' and understands the term to mean, 'doing what appears to be philosophy/science in order to divert attention from, subvert, and substitute for philosophy/science, and as a result avoid doing philosophy/ science.' (43). By the time Gutas attempts to justify his position with examples, he has proceeded from the sublimely imaginative to the ridiculous, characterizing the work of Ibn Kemal on the theological *possibility* of the eternity of the world, an exemplar of sophisticated philosophical analysis and impartiality that would be notable in any age, as lacking 'any discernible criteria for evaluation. The arguments were just arguments, and the step from these conclusions to the position challenging the *mythological narrative* was not (or was not even intended to be) taken' (54). It is deeply troubling to find that in our time a so-called 'expert' on Arabic philosophy is to be found, at the culmination of his career, repeating tired nineteenth-century tropes dismissing the possibility that genuine philosophical activity could ever take place in a theological context (rather akin to Bertrand Russell's famous pronouncements about Aquinas not being a 'real philosopher'. Of course, this view is no longer viewed as remotely respectable). Far from constituting a profound diagnosis resultant of deep knowledge, or a startling *exposé*, Gutas (and Eichner, whose hasty, and easily invalidated conclusions he also cites from her *The Post-Avicennian Philosophical Tradition and Islamic Orthodoxy: Philosophical and Theological Summae in Context* (Halle: Habilitationsschrift, 2009), 420), simply repeats what the later *kalām* theologians *explicitly state*, namely that their philosophical engagement takes place in the context of the analysis of the data of revelation and the evaluation of the truth of the items of creed (just as Aquinas similarly acknowledges in his own work). Yet this in no way detracts from their serious and impartial engagement with the whole array of general metaphysical, physical and logical debates in the pursuit of truth. All philosophers cannot but have presuppositions of some sort or other; another of Gutas' mistaken assumptions about 'science' is its putative methodological 'neutrality'. How does Gutas square his claim about 'doing what appears to be philosophy/science ... in order to avoid doing philosophy/science' with the impassioned debates on the most abstract questions of general metaphysics and the Categories, found all throughout the later traditions of Islamic philosophy, in which the concerns are not only extremely distant from any pertinence to the items of creed, but the disputants moreover end up arriving at starkly opposed results? Or for that matter, the exonerations of Avicenna, *against* al-Ghazālī, based on a more careful, '*taḥqīq*' reading of Avicenna's *philosophy*, in thinkers like Hocazade, Dawānī, and Ibn Kemal?

15. Plato, *Sophist* in *Plato: Complete Works*, ed. John Cooper (Indianapolis, IN: Hackett Publishing, 1997), 263b

16. Aristotle, *Metaphysics*, in *The Complete Works of Aristotle: The Revised Oxford Translation*, ed. Jonathan Barnes (Princeton, NJ: Princeton University

Press, 1984), IV.6, 1011b25. Of course, despite its apparent simplicity, Aristotle's definition conceals highly significant assumptions – for example, that there are real essences in the world distinct from one another ('that which is'), and that human beings are able to objectively grasp them ('saying of that which is that it is').

17. See Van Den Bergh's note in Averroes, *The Incoherence of the Incoherence*, trans. Simon Van Den Bergh (London: Luzak, 1954), reprinted in one volume 1987, on page 46 of the notes (which have a pagination distinct from the rest of the book).

18. '... statements are true according to how the actual things are.'

19. 'Imagination is different from assertion or denial; for what is true or false involves a synthesis of thoughts.'

20. 'The terms "being" and "non-being" are employed firstly with reference to the Categories, and secondly with reference to the potency or actuality of these or their non-potency or non-actuality, and thirdly in the sense of true and false.'

21. See Paolo Crivelli, *Aristotle On Truth* (Cambridge: Cambridge University Press, 2004), 6.

22. In his classic *Recollection and Experience: Plato's Theory of Learning and its Successors*, (Cambridge: Cambridge University Press, 1995), Dominic Scott has argued persuasively, against Ackrill and Bostock, that the Theory of Recollection was not intended to account for our knowledge of sense particulars or our basic concept formation, but constitutes rather a theory of our acquisition of knowledge of the Forms, which are not accessible to sense perception, and are distinct from their deficient particular instances.

23. See Gerson, *Platonism and Naturalism*, 120-193, for an incisive correction of the mistaken notion that 'the Good' is a Form amongst the other Forms, or that its identification with the One is merely a later 'Neoplatonist' innovation. Indeed, in his trilogy on the nature of the Platonist tradition, of which the above-mentioned book is the final instalment, Gerson argues decisively against an earlier generation of Plato scholars, who following in the footsteps of Schleiermacher, had held that Plato himself espoused no single philosophical system, and moreover claimed that Neoplatonism (contrary to the claims of the Neoplatonists themselves) was not fundamentally continuous with the actual philosophy of Plato. Some of Gerson's conclusions, which are quickly shaping the scholarly consensus, were anticipated in the work of J.N. Findlay in his pivotal article 'The Three Hypostases of Platonism', in *The Review of Metaphysics* 28, no. 4, (1975), 660–68), amongst other works.

24. Paul Vincent Spade, trans., *Five Texts on the Mediaeval Problem of Universals* (Indianapolis, IN: Hackett, 1994), 25. The emphasis is mine.

25. Plotinus, *Ennead IV.8 On the Descent of the Soul into Bodies*, trans. Barrie Fleet (Las Vegas, NV: Parmenides Publishing, 2012), 65. For more on Ploti-

nus' account of truth and reality, see my forthcoming article 'The Henology of Nature in Plotinus and Kant.'

26. Joseph Owens, 'Faith, Ideas, Illumination and Experience', in *The Cambridge History of Later Medieval Philosophy*, 442.

27. Augustine, *Confessions*, trans. Henry Chadwick (Oxford: Oxford University Press, 1991), XII.xxv.35.

28. Augustine, *The City of God Against the Pagans*, trans. R.W. Dyson (Cambridge: Cambridge University Press, 1998), 11.27, 486.

29. See Daniel G. König's 'Augustine and Islam' in *The Oxford Guide to the Historical Reception of Augustine*, vol. 1, ed. Karla Pollman (Oxford: Oxford University Press, 2013), 142-150.

30. From Dodds' classic commentary in Proclus, *The Elements of Theology*, trans. E.R. Dodds (Oxford: Clarendon Press, 1963), 300.

31. Marije Martijn, *Proclus On Nature: Philosophy of Nature and its Methods in Proclus' Commentary on Plato's Timaeus* (Leiden: Brill, 2010), 259.

32. Gregory Shaw, 'The Role of *Aesthesis* in Theurgy' in, *Iamblichus and the Foundations of Late Platonism*, ed. Eugene Afonasin, John M. Dillon and John Finamore (Leiden: Brill, 2012), 91-113, including note 42. See also Robbert M. van den Berg, 'Theurgy in the Context of Proclus' Philosophy', in, *All From One: A Guide to Proclus*, ed., Peter D'Hoine and Marije Martijn (Oxford: Oxford University Press, 2017). Proclus' account of truth can, of course, only be fully understood in the larger context of his hierarchical account of reality, for which see our forthcoming monograph on Platonic hierarchy, currently in preparation, and based upon my graduate dissertation at the University of Cambridge, for which my supervisor was the great contemporary Cambridge Platonist, Douglas Hedley.

33. See Miira Tuominen, *The Ancient Commentators on Plato and Aristotle* (Berkeley, CA: University of California Press, 2009), 226.

34. See the useful table of translated works in Cristina D'Ancona, 'Greek into Arabic: Neoplatonism in translation' in *The Cambridge Companion to Arabic Philosophy*, ed. Peter Adamson and Richard C. Taylor (Cambridge: Cambridge University Press, 2005), 22-23.

35. Abū Naṣr al-Farābī, *Kitāb al-Jamʿ Bayn Raʾyay al-Ḥakīmayn*, ed. ʿAlī Bū Malḥam (Beirut: Dār wa Maktabat al-Hilāl, 1996), 72.

36. Avicenna, *al-Shifāʾ*, *al-Ilāhiyāt* I, 48.

37. By 'epistemological', we mean an account of *nafs al-amr* that employs the term to clarify how it is we know a proposition corresponds to objective reality (i.e., by being the conclusion of a sound syllogism), but that does not attempt to answer the question of what objective reality itself *is*, and is thus silent on the ontological and identity question of *nafs al-amr*.

38. Ibid., 50.

39. See Book 9, Chapter 4 of Ibn Sīnā *al-Shifā', al-Ṭabī'iyyāt* 6, *al-Nafs*, ed. Sa'īd Zāyid and George Anawati (Cairo: al-Hay'a al-Miṣriyya al-'Āmma li al-Kitāb, 1395/1975), 208.

40. Ibid., 208.

41. Ibid., 210.

42. Avicenna, *al-Shifā', al-Ilāhiyāt* I, 196.

43. Ibid., 201.

44. It would be outside our focus of attention to treat this fascinating but difficult question here, but it seems clear that when Avicenna speaks of an essence in itself as not having mental existence, he means that it cannot 'exist' in the mind, exactly because it would not then be the essence-*itself* – it would be the essence *in the mind*. What would exist in the mind, in such a case, would be the concept that merely *purports* to be the essence-itself, but that cannot fulfil the impossible conditions required to actually *be* it. In turn, when he says that the essence in itself does not have existence in particularized essences (*al-a'yān*), he means that a given essence in itself (e.g. man in himself) cannot *exist in* its corresponding individual (e.g. an individual man), simply because it would not then be man in-himself – it would be an individuated instance of a man.

45. Ibid., 205

46. Avicenna, *al-Shifā', al-Manṭiq* 1, *al-Madkhal*, ed. George Anawati, Maḥmūd al-Khaḍīrī and Fu'ād al-Ahwānī (Cairo: al-Maṭba' al-Amīriyya, 1952), 69.

47. Averroes, *The Incoherence of the Incoherence*, vol. 1, 192.

48. Ibid., vol. 1, 205

49. Ibid. vol. 1, 208

50. See J. Wolenski, 'Contributions to the History of the Classical Truth-Definition' in *Logic, Methodology and Philosophy of Science IX*, ed. D. Prawitz, B. Skyrms and D. Westerstahl (Amsterdam: Elsevier, 1994), 487-488. Aquinas' celebrated account of 'ontological truth', as involving the disposition of things to be conformed to individual minds is, like so much else that is usually ascribed to Aquinas, directly rooted in Avicenna's explicit teaching, as we intend to demonstrate in a future article 'Avicenna and the Trouble with Thomism.'

51. For aspects of Anselm's doctrine of illumination, see Lydia Schumacher's *Divine Illumination: The History and Future of Augustine's Theory of Knowledge* (Oxford: Wiley-Blackwell, 2011), 66-85 and particularly 74-75.

52. Anselm *Three Philosophical Dialogues*, trans. Thomas Williams (Indianapolis, IN: Hackett Publishing, 2002), 19.

53. Ibid. 30.

54. Etienne Gilson, *The Philosophy of St. Bonaventure*, trans. Dom Illtyd Trethowan and Frank Sheed (Paterson, NJ: St. Anthony Guild Press, 1965), 129.

55. Ibid., 353.

56. Ibid., 385.

57. Thomas Aquinas, *The Summa Theologica of Thomas Aquinas, Complete English Edition in Five Volumes*, trans. Fathers of the English Dominican Province, Notre Dame, vol. 2, (New York, NY: Bezinger Bros., 1948), reprinted by Christian Classics (Notre Dame, IN: Ave Maria Press, 1981), 1a2ae 109.1c., 1124.

58. For a good account of Duns Scotus' critique, see Robert Pasnau, 'Cognition', in *The Cambridge Companion to Duns Scotus*, ed. Thomas Williams (Cambridge: Cambridge University Press, 2003), 285-311.

59. Meyrick H. Carre, *Realists and Nominalists* (Oxford: Oxford University Press, 1946), 118.

60. Ibid., 123. For an exhaustive and brilliant, and soon to be standard account of the transition from Platonic-Aristotelian reason, to a 'modern' reason subordinated to the intuition of the empirical particular as the ultimate standard of knowledge, see Arbogast Schmitt, *Modernity and Plato: Two Paradigms of Rationality*, trans. Vishwa Adluri (Rochester, NY: Camden House, 2012).

61. Robert Pasnau, *Metaphysical Themes 1274-1671* (Oxford: Oxford University Press, 2011), 633.

62. 'It is Kant who forms the great fault line for realism. Although other philosophers had challenged individual tenets of realism, Kant was the first to undermine it radically and offer a coherent, powerful alternative account of reality, subjectivity, and knowledge.' Lee Braver, *A Thing of This World*, (Evanston, IL: Northwestern University Press, 2007), 33. Braver's book is an extended account of the manner in which doctrines of anti-realism in the Analytic and Continental traditions are both ultimately derived from Kant's theory that the mind's ordering of experience precludes its grasping of real extramental essences. Kant's seismic impact on subsequent philosophy is widely recognized: 'It is scarcely an exaggeration to say that the inner drama of analytic philosophy from Frege to Quine and beyond is its century-long love–hate relationship with Kant's theoretical philosophy.' Robert Hanna, *Kant and the Foundations of Analytic Philosophy* (Oxford: Oxford University Press, 2001), 11. 'Recent work in the history of analytic philosophy has shown that it developed largely in reaction to Immanuel Kant's critical philosophy as first expounded in the *Critique of Pure Reason*.' Delbert Reed, *Origins of Analytic Philosophy: Kant and Frege* (London: Continuum, 2007), 2. 'In the beginning there was Kant. In telling the story of philosophy in the nineteenth and twentieth centuries, following Kant, we encounter two narratives. One goes the way of Hegel, Marx, Nietzsche, Schopenhauer, Heidegger, Foucault, and Derrida [continental]; the other travels through Bolzano and Lotze to Frege, and from there to Russell, Carnap, Quine, Davidson, Dummett, and Putnam [analytic].' Anat Biletzki, 'Introduction: Bridging the Analytic-Continental Divide', International Journal of Philosophical Studies, 9, (2001), 291-294. 'Kant, in the positiv-

ists' eyes, had made a lasting contribution to scientific philosophy – particularly in his rejection of the possibility of super-sensible, metaphysical knowledge and his reorientation of theoretical philosophy around the two questions "How is pure mathematics possible?" and "How is pure natural science possible?" In answering these questions Kant developed his famous defence of synthetic a priori knowledge – knowledge independent of sensible experience yet nonetheless substantively applicable to the empirical world.' Michael Friedman, 'Logical Positivism' in *The Routledge Encyclopedia of Philosophy* (London: Routledge, 1998). 'Whether we consider Kant's idea of a self-administered critique of reason, the turn to the 'subject', the concept of the synthetic a priori, the theory of space and time, the transcendental conception of the 'I think', mathematics as the language of natural science, the refutation of all the traditional proofs for the existence of God, or the basic features of a purely autonomous conception of morality, it is quite clear that to study the first Critique is nothing less than to explore the fundamental roots of all subsequent philosophy.' Ottfried Hoffe, *Kant's Critique of Pure Reason: The Foundation of Modern Philosophy* (Tubingen: Springer, 2010), 2. 'For better or worse, almost every philosophical development of significance since 1800 has been a response to Kant.' J. Alberta Coffa, *The Semantic tradition from Kant to Carnap* (Cambridge: Cambridge University Press, 1991), 7.

63. Although the distinction was introduced, as we saw in Chapter 1, by Christian Wolff, and certainly does not describe the deductive structure of the unfolding of traditional science, it nonetheless provides a useful and fairly accurate rubric under which to order the broadest division within metaphysics, that is, broadly speaking, in so far as *general* metaphysics equips us to penetrate into what the inherent structure of an intelligible world tells us about things *in general*, and then employs its results in *special* metaphysics in order to uncover truths about the existence and properties of *particular* nonsensible entities, like God and the soul.

64. Our study is not polemical or even comparative in original intent – indeed, it *intends,* despite the obvious demand and temptation, not to be given to facile parallels with Western philosophy, but instead to provide at least the bare essentials of a complete metaphysical and epistemological view of truth from a deeper, more synthetical traditional of Islamic thought than is usually available. Although the depiction and demonstrative substantiation of such a view on things as they are will lend itself in the fullness of time to the shedding of light upon the flaws of many different systems of Western philosophy, our reason for singling out Kant as an exemplar for this type of application of our study is that, again, his views largely shaped the contours of subsequent discourse on subject-object aporiae, the problems of the putatively subjectivizing human contribution to the form of the world, and on truth more generally. Of course, such a short account

can in no way constitute a comprehensive treatment of Kant's many failings; although we have dealt with the most important fundamentals in this short section, in showing the manner in which his distinctive teaching on the distinction between concept and intuition lies at the root of his subjectivist understanding of appearance and reality, attendant notions like that of the transcendental schemata, the imagination, the derivation of the categories from the classifications of logical judgements, and the distinct faculty of reason have not been dealt with because of considerations of space. For another thing, it is far from clear that it would be desirable to comprehensively 'refute Kant'. For one thing, not every philosophical position Kant maintained is erroneous; moreover, it is much easier, in pointing out his fundamental subjectivizing error, to simply point out, as so many of his most prominent commentators have long held established, that his entire 'critical' project rests on a number of unproven assumptions, many of which attempt futilely to accommodate clear contradictions. Indeed, simply to decline to assume them alongside him would be an act sufficient to entirely frustrate the subjectivizing intentions of his project.

65. For Kant, while it is *conceivable* (hence 'ontological contingency') that we could have been equipped with additional faculties – for example, that of intellectual intuition, for which see below – the cognitive apparatuses that (according to the first Critique) we *do in fact* find ourselves equipped with, represent the necessary conditions (hence, 'epistemological necessity') of human knowledge (for statements making the claim that the *Critique*'s identification of these epistemological conditions is necessary and certain, see for example, the preface to the first edition, xv, and A 46/ B 64; see also B145-146, where Kant claims that 'no further ground' may be offered for his identification of the nature of sensibility and the understanding, in a manner which implies that he believes his identification to be necessary and perhaps even in some sense self-evident; they are, as Lewis White Beck has characterized Kant's non-empirical (and according to Kant's own standards, non-verifiable) principles, 'brutely factual' (Lewis White Beck, 'Toward a Meta-Critique of Pure Reason', in *Essays on Kant and Hume* (New Haven, CT: Yale University Press, 1978).

66. 'Kant claims that the solution immediately proffered by the correspondence theory of truth involves a vicious circle ... to be regarded as true, our knowledge must agree with the object which I can only compare with my knowledge precisely through knowing it. My knowledge must therefore be able to confirm itself, although this contradicts the required agreement with an object that is supposed to be independent of the process of knowing. The theory of correspondence thus initially seems to fail and this impels us to consider other alternatives' (Otfried Hoffe, *Kant's Critique of Pure Reason: The Foundation of Modern Philosophy*, 181). For traditional realism, from the mere fact that *we possess* a *mode* of cognition of the world (in the

broadest sense of the word, proximate to 'awareness of a world of distinct objects'), it in no way follows that that we cannot as a result make the *genuine distinction* between that mode of cognition and an extramental world which that or other modes of cognition may at times succeed, and at others fail to accurately represent; after all, both the intelligibility of the sensible world, and our modes of cognition are two aspects of the same effusion of being. All *conceptions,* as we will see in Chapter 3, correspond to things-as-they-are, because their distinctness implies their subsistence; there is thus no such thing as a false conception, although there are conceptions that *purport* to be conceptions *of* extramental particular objects, yet in fact fail to comprehensively represent them; assents may or may not 'correspond' to reality, and we determine their correspondence or non-correspondence thereto by distinguishing cognitions which succeed in mirroring the distinct essences that extramentality presents to us in terms of conceptual apparatuses that can account for that distinctness and relationality, from those which distort that distinctness with perspectival accretions employed outside of their appropriate domains of reference, or by failing to apprehend the appropriate degree of generality or specificity of a given aspect of an entity; success in this task is largely contingent upon the adoption of a sound general ontological framework, able to uncover, without violating non-contradiction, the intelligible structure in which all things must participate in order to exist. Some important features of this framework will be presented in Chapter 4, where the manner in which the structure of the mind is distinct yet continuous with the inherent intelligible structure of an extramental world, will be outlined.

67. Norman Kemp Smith, *A Commentary to Kant's 'Critique of Pure Reason'* (London: Macmillan & Co. Ltd., 1923), xxxvii.

68. 'Kant defines an intuition as a singular representation that is in immediate relation to its object, while a concept is a general representation that can be related to many objects but is not in immediate relation to any, and for that reason can be related to an object only through an intuition.' Paul Guyer, 'The Rejection of Kantian Dualism', in *The Cambridge Companion to German Idealism* (Cambridge: Cambridge University Press, 2000), 40.

69. Pre-Kantian modern philosophies had broadly subordinated the understanding to sensibility (empiricists) or sensibility to the understanding (rationalists), maintaining a distinction between the two, while acknowledging that they are fundamentally continuous aspects of a single mode of cognition. For these points, see Howard Caygill, *A Kant Dictionary* (Oxford: Blackwell Publishing, 1995), sub 'Sensibility'.

70. For an illuminating discussion, see Guyer, 'The Rejection of Kantian Dualism', 46-49.

71. Braver characterizes this as 'the epoch-making claim that the mind actively processes or organizes experience in constructing knowledge, rather than

passively reflecting an independent reality. To speak metaphorically, the mind is more like a factory than a mirror or soft wax. It is this idea that enabled Kant to incorporate the empiricist dependence on experience into the rationalist ideal of universal and necessary knowledge. At one stroke it both authenticated empirical science as genuine knowledge and placed traditional metaphysics beyond our ken.' Lee Braver, *A Thing of This World*, 3-4.

72. For a good overview, see Helmut Holzhey and Vilem Mudroch, *Historical Dictionary of Kant and Kantianism* (Lanham, MD: The Scarecrow Press, 2005), sub 'Hume, David'.

73. Norman Kemp Smith, *A Commentary to Kant's 'Critique of Pure Reason'*, xxvii.

74. Ibid., xxxi.

75. Ibid., xxxvii.

76. See ibid., xxxv.

77. Ibid., xxxiii, my emphasis.

78. Ibid., xxxiii.

79. Nonetheless, it is significant that prior to his formulation of the radical thesis of the first *Critique* in its fullness, Kant had adhered to a broadly Platonic position maintaining (although with minimal justification) the accessibility of an intelligible world to our concepts, most eminently in his *On the Form and Principles of the Sensible and Intelligible World*, that is, his *Inaugural Dissertation* of 1770. See for example Henry E. Allison, *Kant's Transcendental Deduction: An Analytical-Historical Commentary* (Oxford: Oxford University Press, 2015), 60.

80. Paul Guyer 'The Rejection of Kantian Dualism', 51.

81. Paul Guyer's summary, also in his 'The Rejection of Kantian Dualism', is helpful in shedding light on Kant's rationale for believing that time and space represent a division of cognition distinct from the concepts of the understanding: '[Kant's] two main lines of argument, that the representations of space and time are presupposed by all representations of particular objects and that regions of space and time are represented as parts of something single and all-embracing rather than merely as instances of general concepts, together show that the representations of space and time are intuitions rather than concepts by showing that the two requirements of immediacy and singularity have been fulfilled. "The concept of space is thus a pure intuition, for it is a singular concept, not one which has been compounded from sensations, although it is the fundamental form of all outer sensation" [See Immanuel Kant, *Theoretical Philosophy, 1755–1770*, trans. and ed. David Walford (Cambridge: Cambridge University Press, 1992), 396] Guyer continues: 'What makes the "concept of space" not a concept at all, but a pure intuition – although of course we can form a concept of space on the basis of our pure intuition of it – is both that it is singular

and that its singularity is pre-supposed by the representation of particular objects, which is what makes it immediate' (Paul Guyer, 'The Rejection of Kantian Dualism', 45).

82. Howard Caygill provides useful background to the concept of experience which sheds light on the manner in which it has been redefined by Kant; 'At the end of the *Posterior Analytics*, Aristotle recapitulates the essentials of his account of knowledge, which consists in the movement from sense perception of particulars to universals. Experience plays an important part in his argument, since it is both what emerges from the memory of repeated sense perceptions and 'the source of the universal now stabilized in its entirety within the soul, the one beside the many which is a single identity within them all' (100a, 7-8) ... By experience [John Locke] intends, following Descartes, that derived from either *"external sensible objects"* or *"the internal operations of our minds perceived and reflected on by ourselves"*, namely sensation and reflection. Reflection for Locke was the reflection on sensation, a restriction which leads him to sceptical doubt concerning whether *"our knowledge reaches* much further than our experience."* ... Leibniz, however, in his critical commentary on Locke in the *New Essays on Human Understanding*, shifted the emphasis away from external to internal experience, seeing the "innate truths" of inner experience as prior to, and conditions of, the data and truths of external experience. Kant, who at the end of his career described CPR (*Critique of Pure Reason*) as "the genuine apology for Leibniz" ... attempted to develop a concept of experience ... which [brought] into balance the aspects of inner and outer experience emphasized by Leibniz and Locke ... Kant rejects Locke's view that ideas (in his case, concepts and intuitions) may be derived from outer experience, and inclines to Leibniz's position that they are presupposed by experience.' However, 'Kant agreed with Locke's limitation of knowledge to the bounds of experience, even if his definition of experience was quite distinct. (...) [Kant] defines experience as 'the synthetic connection of appearances (perceptions) in consciousness, so far as this connection is necessary" ... Experience is accordingly synthetic, described as "this product of senses and understanding"' (see Howard Caygill, *A Kant Dictionary*, sub 'Experience').

83. Paul Guyer, 'The Rejection of Kantian Dualism', in *The Cambridge Companion to German Idealism*, 47. He writes further 'Often Kant seems simply to suppose that the fact that we can have a representation of an apparent property or relation of objects without having a representation of the objects themselves, for instance when we represent space or time devoid of any objects in them (see CPuR, A24/B38–9, A31/B46), is enough to prove that what we are representing cannot be any property or relations that the objects have independently of our representing them. But this does not seem obviously true – why couldn't we be created with innate ideas that we

can be aware of without the presence of any external object but that also veridically represent the real character of external objects?' (Ibid., 48).

84. See my forthcoming article, 'The Henology of Nature in Plotinus and Kant'.

85. By 'synthetic', Kant intends that which goes beyond our merely definitional knowledge of a thing, and is learned in an experience; by a priori, he means that which is contributed by the intrinsic character of our cognitive apparatuses, prior to experience.

86. 'The pure a priori forms of intuition, time and space, are "two sources of knowledge from which bodies of a priori synthetic knowledge can be derived" (CPR A 38/B 55). By themselves they cannot yield the conditions of possibility for synthetic a priori judgements; this can only happen when they are aligned with a priori concepts. Nor may pure a priori concepts or categories by themselves provide the necessary conditions for the possibility of synthetic a priori judgements, since "no synthetic proposition can be made from mere Categories" (CPR B 289). For this reason, it is impossible to have "synthetic a priori knowledge of things in general" (A 247/B 303), *against the claims of general ontology*. Synthetic a priori judgements must consequently bring together both intuitive and conceptual elements, with a priori intuitions containing "that which cannot be discovered in the concept but which is certainly found a priori in the intuition corresponding to the concept, and can be connected with it synthetically (B 73)" (Howard Caygill, *A Kant Dictionary* sub 'Synthetic A Priori Judgement').

87. W.H. Walsh, 'Kant's Criticism of Metaphysics: II', *Philosophy* 14, no. 56 (1939), 434–448.

88. W.H. Walsh, *Kant's Criticism of Metaphysics* (Edinburgh: Edinburgh University Press, 1975), 250-251.

89. For a more extended treatment of this question, within the question in Kantian studies that concerns the 'possibility' or 'metacritique' of Kant's critical project, see my forthcoming article (2021), 'The Metacritique of Kant and the Possibility of Metaphysics'.

90. Walsh, *Kant's Criticism of Metaphysics*, 251.

91. Fakhr al-Dīn al-Rāzī, *al-Mabāḥith al-mashriqiyya fī ʿilm al-ilāhiyāt wa al-tabīʿyyāt*, vol. 1, ed. Muḥammad al-Muʿtaṣim Billāh al-Baghdādī (Qom: Intishārāt Dhawī al-Qurbā, 1428/2007), 130-132.

92. The precise meaning of *al-wujūd al-dhihnī* will be discussed very shortly. The passage in question runs as follows: 'Why is it not possible to say "the forms that we intellect or imagine, though they not be present before us (*ḥāḍira ʿindanā*) exist in themselves, either subsistent in themselves as Plato says, or impressed in one of the bodies (*ajrām*) that are invisible to us?" Even if this is far-fetched, compared to maintaining that the impression that obtains during the intellection of the sky in the mind is equivalent to the sky itself … it is easy and not far-fetched at all'. Fakhr al-Dīn al-Rāzī

Sharḥ al-Ishārāt wa al-Tanbīhāt, vol. 2, ed. Ali Rida Najafzada (Tehran: Anjuman-i Asar va Mafakhir-i Farhangi, 1386/1966), 236.

93. Deep reverence of Plato is a very interesting phenomenon that appears in different schools of philosophical thought in the 12th and 13th centuries. The most obvious figure is Suhrawardi (549–587/1154–1191); another is Ibn 'Arabī ('there is nothing of which it is not possible to achieve knowledge by means of unveiling and experience. Being occupied with speculative thought is a veil. Some others deem [unveiling and experience] impossible, though no one amongst the people of the Way of God. Those who deem it impossible are the people of speculative investigation and deduction amongst the scholars of outward appearances, who have not tasted spiritual states. If some of them have tasted spiritual states, like the divine Plato amongst the philosophers, this is rare', *al-Futūḥāt al-Makkiyya*, vol. 2, 523). More surprising is Rāzī's veneration of Plato as evinced in the above quote, and elsewhere in the *Mulakhkhaṣ*, and in *al-Maṭālib al-'Āliya*.

94. Fakhr al-Dīn al-Rāzī, *al-Mulakhkhaṣ*, Ms. Istanbul, Süleymaniye Kütüphanesi, Haci Selim Ağa 723, fols. 76b.

95. We will cite Taftāzānī's formulation of this proof below.

96. If this seems too obvious to be worth constructing a proof for, the subtlety of the issue at hand may have been missed. No one is doubting that abstract objects *obtain* and *become manifest* in the mind – the question is how they can be *knowable* at all if they do not in fact possess an objective, stable existence beyond the specific moment of that obtaining. The Avicennan philosophers, and many of the great *mutakallimīn* after them, were of the opinion that abstract objects do indeed possess stable existence, the locus of which is the mind (on many accounts backed up, as it were, by the 'gold standard' of the intelligibility granted by the Agent Intellect) – and it must be 'the mind' because extramental and mental are opposed to one another – if something exists, it must *fundamentally* do so 'in' one or the other; see for example, 'Alā'uddīn al-Ṭūsī, *Al-Dhakhīra*, released as '*Tahāfut al-falāsifa*', ed. Yaḥyā Murād (Beirut: Dār al-Kutub al-'Ilmiyya, 1425/2004), 132-133. That is, the primary existence of an individual human being is in extramental existence, whereas the primary existence of his universal form, 'man', and of intelligible entities like 'necessity' and 'species' is in the mind (for a useful discussion see Ṭūsī with Iṣfahānī *Tasdīd al-qawā'id*, 317-321). Moreover, the doctrine of mental existence entails that the intelligible form of man is identical to 'man' as existing extramentally, that is, the nature which an individual man instantiates; the mental form is not merely a representation of the extramental reality, it is identical to it, in that the same quiddity has simply become manifest in two different loci (Aquinas' celebrated doctrine of their identity is really a borrowing from Avicenna). Imām Rāzī, as we are in the process of explaining above, disagreed that it was necessary to specify 'the mind'; indeed, much of this study is concerned with the difficulties

involved, in the context of the identification of *nafs al-amr*, of positing that the mind is the ultimate locus of the *distinct* existence of abstract objects.

97. Fakhr al-Dīn al-Rāzī, *al-Mulakhkhaṣ*, fols. 47a.

98. Although earlier *kalām* thinkers were often more reticent to include the latter category in the realm of the subsistent, some prominent later thinkers, such as al-Dawānī and Gelenbevi, firmly embraced the distinct subsistence of fictional entities, as we will discover below.

99. For the context and debates surrounding this central argument, including extended expositions of this particular argument, as well as others for the same position, see, for example, Sayf al-Dīn al-Āmidī, *Abkār al-afkār fī uṣūl al-dīn*, vol. 3, ed. Aḥmad Farīd al-Mazīdī (Beirut: Dār al-Kutub al-ʿIlmiyya, 1424/2003), 387-403; Nāṣir al-Dīn al-Bayḍāwī, *Ṭawāliʿ al-anwār min maṭāliʿ al-anẓār*, ed. ʿAbbās Sulaymān (Cairo: al-Maktaba al-Azhariyya li al-Turāth, 1435/2014), 80-81; Jurjani, *Sharḥ al-Mawāqif*, vol. 1, 189-210, Taftazani *Sharḥ al-Maqāṣid*, vol.1, 79-85. In the less scrupulous of Ashʿarī polemics, the Muʿtazilī position could often be characterized as maintaining the extramental particular existence (*al-wujūd al-khārijī*) of non-existent entities, a characterization that rendered the position starkly contradictory. In fact, this was a 'straw man' allegation; by affirming the *thubūt* of non-existent entities, the *muʿtazila* intended a mode of being, 'subsistence', distinct from extramental particular 'existence', akin in a certain manner to the contemporary distinction amongst certain prominent philosophers between subsistence and existence.

100. See the end of Section 4.1 for an account of how the highly problematic consequences of this early *kalām* view, when maintained in the context of a discussion of the nature of the Divine knowledge, constituted one of the reasons underlying its abandonment by prominent later Ashʿarīs.

101. As we will see throughout this study, the acknowledgement of the distinctness of non-existent entities *in the mind* (*al-tamāyuz fī al-dhihn*) implied by the widespread adoption of doctrines of mental existence by later *kalām* theologians, came to be deemed an insufficient account of their ultimate ontological statuses. Jalāl al-Dawānī, al-Ālūsī and many other major *muḥaqqiqīn* invoked the argument from distinctness to demonstrate the subsistence (rather than extramental existence) of non-existent entities in *nafs al-amr*, as we shall see below.

102. Fakhr al-Dīn al-Rāzī, *al-Mulakhkhaṣ*, fols. 48a.

103. For Rāzī's justification, against Aristotle, of the possibility of an uninstantiated essence, see Section 4.1.

104. See Chapter 4 for the detailed Akbarian context of this doctrine, as well as discussion of the particular doctrine itself.

105. Muḥyī al-Dīn Ibn ʿArabī, *al-Futūḥāt al-Makkiyya*, vol. 3, 456.

106. The term he uses is *al-ʿaql al-kull*. That he is referring to *al-ʿaql al-faʿāl* is clarified below by his student al-Ḥillī.

107. Naṣīr al-Dīn al-Ṭūsī, *Talkhīṣ al-Muḥaṣṣal* (Beirut: Dār al-Aḍwā', 1405/1985), 481. The treatise *Establishing the Existence of the Separate Intellect* is to be found at 479-481.

108. The generality of the *'ulamā'*, stating their standard view that *nafs al-amr* is 'the mind' and *'al-khārij'*.

109. Naṣīr al-Dīn al-Ṭūsī and al-'Allāma al-Ḥillī, *Kashf al-murād fī sharḥ Tajrīd al-I'tiqād* (Beirut: al-Mu'assasat al-A'lamī li al-Maṭbū'āt, 1408/1988), 54. Ḥillī goes on to call the question of *nafs al-amr* 'a distinguished line of inquiry, that cannot be found in [most] books', although he does not go on to venture his own theory.

110. That is, one of the two 'tahāfuts' commissioned by Sultan Mehmet Fatih after the founding of Istanbul. A part of 'Alā'uddīn's illuminating discussion on *nafs al-amr* appears in Section 3.2.

111. Mīr Zāhid in Quṭb al-Dīn al-Rāzī, Ṣadr al-Dīn al-Shirāzī and Mīr Zāhid, *Risālatān fī al-Taṣawwur wa al-Taṣdīq wa yalīhimā Sharḥ al-Risāla al-Ma'mūla fī al-Taṣawwur wa al-Taṣdīq*, ed. Mahdī Sharī'atī (Beirut: Dār al-Kutub al-'Ilmiyya 1425/2004), 266.

112. Dawānī argued that the Agent Intellect need only account for the *intelligibility* of the two terms in a false proposition – it does not however 'think' them or assent to them, but only *preserves* them. See Dawānī in Gelenbevi et al, *Rasā'il al-Imtiḥān* (Istanbul: al-Maṭba'a al-'Āmira, 1262/1846), 168-170.

113. See Section 4.1.

114. That is, by defining *nafs al-amr* in terms of how we *come to* know that a truth-claim corresponds to objective reality or *nafs al-amr*, but leaving unanswered the ontological question, namely what *nafs al-amr* actually *is*.

115. In its deductive and speculative dimension, *kalām* uncovers knowledge through building up ever more nuanced and complex propositions from first principles (thought to be abstracted from extramental particulars), and by applying the rules of logic to deduce various truths on this basis, aided also by sense experience, and as we have already noted, presupposing an immanentist ontology in which essences can only exist as particulars. In so far as it presupposes adherence to a philosophical school, then, *kalām* certainly belongs to the *mashshā'ī* category.

116. Some other examples are i. the identity of the Divine Attributes and the Essence, a position many later *mutakallimūn* preferred to the traditional *kalām* position on the real distinctness of the Divine Attributes and Essence. See e.g. Muḥammad 'Abd al-'Azīz al-Farhārī, *al-Nibrās sharḥ Sharḥ al-'aqā'id* (Istanbul: Asitane , 1430/2009), 278-279, and Ḥāshiyat al-Marjānī in Gelenbevi et al. *Gelenbevī 'alā al-Dawānī 'alā al-'Aqīda al-'aḍudiyya* with the supercommentaries of Marjānī and Khalkhālī (Istanbul, al-Maṭba'a al-'Uthmāniyya, 1318/1900), vol. 1, 295-297; ii. the insufficiency of reason, and necessity of *kashf* or 'mystical unveiling' to discern the truth in certain theological questions. See e.g. *al-Qawl al-faṣl* of Ibn Bahā'uddīn, 79,

174, as well as 'Abd al-Ḥakīm Siyalkoti in his famous supercommentary on Jurjānī's *Sharḥ al-Mawāqif*, passim; iii. the existence of the 'world of im-aginal representations' (*'ālam al-mithāl*). See for example, commentary on Qur'an 12:6 in the famous 'exoteric' exegesis of Abū Su'ūd al-'Imādī, *Irshād al-'aql al-salīm* iv. the (Akbarian interpretation of) the Muḥammadan Reality (Ismail Bursevi states in his commentary on Qur'an 33:46 in *Rūḥ al-bayān*: 'consensus exists amongst exoteric scholars (*ahl al-ẓāhir*) and those of contemplative witnessing (*ahl al-shuhūd*), that God Most High created all things from the Muḥammadan light'. See İsmail Hakkı Bursevi, *Rūḥ al-bayān fī tafsīr al-Qur'ān*, ed. 'Abd al-Laṭīf Ḥasan 'Abd al-Raḥmān (Beirut: Dār al-Kutub al-'Ilmiyya, 1430/2009); v. Gelenbevi's theory of the Divine knowledge and al-Ālūsī's theory of non-existent objects (for both of which see Section 4.4) and many others.

117. See Section 4.4.

118. That is, the occurrence of the full manifestation of the full reality and man-ner of subsistence of a given thing. It is a synonym of *thubūt*, *al-kawn* and *al-wujūd* (see *Kashshāf Iṣṭilāḥāt* sub *taḥaqquq*, Farhārī, *Nibrās*, 65).

119. All references here are to Jurjānī's *risāla* in Gelenbevi et al, *Rasā'il al-Imtiḥān*, 197-198.

120. Because in the usual sense, it is the mind which is *a'amm* with respect to *al-khārij*, since all *khārijī* concepts and propositions exist in the mind, but not all mental concepts and propositions correspond to something in *al-khārij*.

121. As we have already discussed in Chapter 1, an 'extramental particular' is by definition individuated, that is, a 'this', instantiated thing, that admits of being singled out in its particular individuality, in this case, 'your mind' rather than 'my mind'.

122. Because the mind *itself* exists in extramental particulars.

123. Although not necessarily, because on the standard Avicennan and late-*kalām* account, God is the *khārijī* being ('*khārijī*', because He is individu-ated) whence all other beings derive their being, although He transcends time and space.

124. The proposition is true in extramental particulars, because an extramental particular 'colour' can only be one that is physically individuated; however, the proposition cannot be true in *nafs al-amr*, because blackness is always a colour.

125. For example, 'not-animal' as the contradictory of 'animal'.

126. Like 'not-human' as the contradictory of 'human' – there are a wider range of not-humans than there are of not-animals, and so 'not-human' is of wider predicative scope than 'not-animal'.

127. Tahānawī, *Kashshāf Iṣṭilāḥāt al-Funūn wa al-'Ulūm* sub *nafs al-amr*.

128. Put into the most basic terms, the *umūr 'āmma* are properties which tran-scend the Categories, and are directly entailed by 'being', such that noth-

ing that may be called a being may lack them (and that thus come under, *mā yaʿriḍu li al-mawjūd bi mā huwa mawjūd*). In the broad post-Rāzian tradition (notwithstanding some differences in their enumeration), these are essence, individuation, unity, multiplicity, causality, necessity and possibility. Because these properties constitute principles which, applying to all beings, also apply transitively to the objects of all other sciences, such as physics, they constitute one of the most important foundations and warrants of demonstrative science. The present state of general incomprehension, widely suffered in both East and West, of the significance of the vast *umūr ʿāmma* sections of the later *kalām* and broader philosophical traditions is symptomatic of a wider incomprehension of the rigorously demonstrative structure of the post-Rāzian tradition. The translation we have chosen for *al-umūr al-ʿāmma*, the 'transcendentals', links the concept into the wider philosophical tradition, in which the medieval scholastic doctrine is acknowledged to trace its roots to Avicenna, see, for example, Jans Aertsen, *Medieval Philosophy as Transcendental Thought: From Philip the Chancellor to Francisco Suarez* (Leiden: Brill, 2012). Facile charges of anachronism pertaining to this translation, thus, are nullified by the fact that we make no claim that the *umūr ʿāmma* represents the *same* philosophical rubric as the medieval transcendentals, but merely serves to situate the *umūr ʿāmma* within a highly analogous, and recognizable philosophical tradition. Eichner has made some rather cursory remarks, in her wide-ranging but uneven Wittenberg doctoral thesis, *The Post-Avicennian Philosophical Tradition and Islamic Orthodoxy: Philosophical and Theological Summae in Context*, 49, on the shared origins of both Rāzī's account of the *umūr ʿāmma* and the medieval doctrine in the same passage in Avicenna's *Metaphysics* (I, 5). We are currently preparing a study devoted to the transcendentals and their wider metaphysical implications.

129. Taftāzānī, *Sharḥ al-Maqāṣid* vol.1, 102-103.

130. A human being's imitation of sounds is contingent upon and arises from a more fundamental property, namely, rationality, and thus the imitation of sounds cannot be an 'essential' property for 'human being'.

131. Ibid. 103.

132. For explication of this principle, see e.g. Najm al-Dīn al-Kātibī and Mubārakshāh (commentary), *Sharḥ Ḥikmat al-ʿAyn*, 38.

133. See e.g. Najm al-Dīn al-Kātibī and Mubārakshāh (commentary), *Sharḥ Ḥikmat al-ʿAyn*, 43-44.

134. See Naṣir al-Dīn al-Ṭūsī and Shams al-Dīn al-Iṣfahānī (commentary), *Tasdīd al-qawāʿid fī Sharḥ Tajrīd al-ʿAqāʾid*, vol. 1, 406-407.

135. Taftāzānī *Sharh al-Maqāṣid*, vol. 1, 106. Note Taftāzānī's employment of the doctrine of the effusion of forms; instead of the Agent Intellect, however, the *wāhib al-ṣuwar* ('bestower of forms') is God Himself.

136. Jurjānī in Najm al-Dīn al-Kātibī and Mubārakshāh (commentary), *Sharḥ Ḥikmat al-ʿAyn*, with the supercommentary of al-Sayyid al-Sharīf al-Jurjānī, 41. He ascribes this adjustment of al-Kātibī's 'mental differentiation entails differentiation in *al-khārij*' to al-Ḥillī.

137. For a detailed overview, see Ḥasanayn Makhlūf (supercommentary) and Aḥmad al-Sijāʿī (commentary and original text), *al-Ḥāshiya al-Thāniya ʿalā al-Jawāhir al-Muntaẓamāt fī ʿUqūd al-Maqūlāt* (Cairo: Muṣṭafā al-Bābī al-Ḥalabī, 1391/1971). For a more basic, but exceptionally lucid account, see Muḥammad Ramaḍān ʿAbdallāh, *al-Maqūlāt al-ʿAshr Bayn al-Falāsifa wa al-Mutakallimīn* (Istanbul: Haşimi Yayınevi, 2016).

138. Jurjānī, *Sharḥ al-Mawāqif*, vol. 3, 38.

139. See e.g., al-Bayḍāwī, *Ṭawāliʿ al-anwār*, 84, Jurjānī *Sharḥ al-Mawāqif*, vol. 3, 38-39.

140. That is, it does not partake of individuated existence. In other words, it does not exist in 'extramental particulars' (*al-khārij*).

141. Ibid. vol. 3, 39.

142. These are the so-called 'mixed' (*mumtazija*) quiddities, which most clearly illustrate the difficulty of accepting the simple restriction in Tahānawī's definition above, 'not contingent on the perspective of a subject.'

143. Ibid., vol. 3, 39.

144. Najm al-Dīn al-Kātibī and Mubārakshāh (commentary), *Sharḥ Ḥikmat al-ʿAyn*, 48.

145. Al-Bannānī, *Ḥāshiyat al-ʿallāma al-Bannānī ʿalā sharḥ al-Jalāl Shams al-Dīn Muḥammad Ibn Aḥmad al-Maḥallī ʿalā matn Jamʿ al-jawāmiʿ li al-imām Tāj al-Dīn ʿAbd al-Wahhāb Ibn al-Subkī*, vol. 1, 102. Bannānī goes on to explain the two meanings of *khārij* (the first and less common usage being synonymous with *nafs al-amr*, and the second, standard usage denoting extramental, individuated particulars). He then alludes briefly to different theories of *nafs al-amr*: i. a thing as existent and actualized in itself ii. the knowledge of God, iii. the Preserved Tablet. In his supercommentary on Aḥmad al-Sijāʿī's *Naẓm al-Maqūlāt al-ʿAshr*, Ḥasanayn Makhlūf (1277-1355/1861-1936) attributes this distinction between *iʿtibāriyyāt* to al-Sayyid al-Sharīf al-Jurjānī in his *ḥāshiya* on the *Tajrīd*, where *iʿtibāriyyāt* are divided into such as are *iʿtibāriyyāt ḥaqīqiyya* which have subsistence in *nafs al-amr*, and into those which do not, *al-iʿtibāriyyāt al-fardiyya* (*al-Ḥāshiya al-Thāniya ʿalā al-Jawāhir al-Muntaẓamāt fī ʿUqūd al-Maqūlāt*, 15-16). However, Makhlūf goes on to adopt the position that there can be no subsistence in *nafs al-amr* other than subsistence in extramental particulars or in the mind, a position that conflicts with the *taḥqīq* of thinkers like Dawūd al-Qayṣarī, Ibn Bahāʾuddīn, Taşköprüzade, Ibrahim al-Kūrānī, Gelenbevi, Abū Thanāʾ al-Ālūsī and many others – the *taḥqīq* which it is the purpose of this study to elucidate.

146. This would appear to be a result of the decline of the study of the higher books of *kalām*, which, thanks to Rāzī's efforts, would standardly subsume most of the general metaphysics of post-Avicennan philosophy. In North Africa, the relative weakness of a certain type of higher *'aqliyyāt* compared to the situation in the Ottoman lands and Mughal India may be traced to the triumph in the later period of the Sanūsian curriculum, which had already dominated North Africa for hundreds of years by the time of the collapse of the advanced Islamic sciences in the Sunni world at the beginning of the twentieth century (although intellectual giants like 'Abd al-Raḥmān Shirbīnī, Ḥasanayn Makhlūf, and Shams al-Dīn al-Anbābī show that that higher stream of *'aqliyyāt had* continued to exist in Egypt). Mūḥammad Ibn Yūsuf al-Sanūsī (d. 895/1490), popularly revered for his piety and miracles, thought the post-Rāzian philosophical curriculum unsuitable for most students and advocated a didactic, simplified *kalām* that hearkened back to the approach of the early *kalām* theologians. In his commentary on his own *Al-'Aqīda al-Kubrā* (*Sharḥ al-'Aqīda al-Kubrā al-Musammāt 'Aqīdat Ahl al-Tawḥīd*, ed. al-Sayyid Yūsuf Aḥmad, Beirut: Dār al-Kutub al-'Ilmiyya, 1427/2006), 43-44, Sanūsī reveals his somewhat negative outlook on philosophy, lamenting Rāzī's inability to formulate adequate answers to the philosophers, and stating that in some of the positions he had adopted, Rāzī had come close to the philosophers' 'abominable caprices'. He then quotes some anti-Rāzian poetry penned by Ibn Taymiyya, and quotes the latter as having said, 'if I had met Fakhr al-Dīn al-Rāzī, I would have hit him on his head with this stick of mine.' Sanūsī's conservatist concern for the preservation of the Islamic creed was doubtless sincere, and the ascendancy of his *kalām* works in North Africa throughout the last four centuries was in many ways a highly providential phenomenon, not least because of its effect in raising consciousness of the importance of creed amongst the generality of Muslims, the result of Sanūsī's highly commendable insistence on the complete inadequacy of blind following (*taqlīd*) in matters of faith. However, had he had foreknowledge of the tidal wave of the complex, sceptical, atheistic thought that the Islamic world would go on to meet in the twentieth century, one cannot help feeling that Sanūsī might have felt a renewed appreciation for the Rāzian tradition of *kalām*. The Sanūsian approach, which had almost completely removed general metaphysics from its curriculum, proves largely incapable of adequately facing it. This is because the post-Kantian philosophies involve sceptical re-evaluations of concepts such as essence, existence, individuation, causality, mental representation and abstraction, the nature of the most fundamental categories of cognition, and so forth, which are fundamental to their rejection of the validity of traditional conceptions of natural theology. It is only by returning to the *al-umūr al-'āmma* tradition (supplemented, it is our firm conviction,

by a Platonic-Akbarian exemplarism) that traditional realist conceptions of these foundational concepts can be reinforced and defended in our times.

147. This is the danger of reading parts of the higher books of the tradition in isolation from other related (though perhaps physically separate) topics; in most cases, the intelligibility of each is contingent on some degree of comprehension of the whole.

148. Thereby 'actualizing' their form through our contribution of their relational aspect.

149. For they are one of our intrinsically 'universal' modes of *intellection* of the world, that is, concepts that necessarily attend our cognition of extramental particulars, if they are to be intelligible at all. The notion of their independence from the mind is thus simply contradictory, as is the notion that they could become 'individuated' as particulars.

150. In that in order to *be a bed*, the pieces of wood *require* the 'particularized relationality of the perspectival sequence' of the form resultant of their configuration, just as that particularized relationality also *requires* the existence of the pieces of wood to become actualized.

151. Because although that configuration is indeed in its proximate origin 'mental', it nonetheless certainly possesses a form of subsistence in the extramental world, even though the relational makeup of its form cannot, as we have explained above, exist in extramental *particulars*.

152. Although crucially, broad, early and Neo-Ash'arī *kalām* provides no adequate ontology to properly ground this notion, given its denial both of mental existence and of a realm of the 'subsistence' of non-existent entities, or of uninstantiated 'Platonic' Forms. See Chapter 1 for an elucidation of the precise meaning of *wujūd khārijī* vis-a-vis 'the mind' and *nafs al-amr*; a fuller picture of these often subtle distinctions will obtain in the reading of this study in its entirety.

153. It being assumed, for example, that perspectival entities have no independent ontological reality, and are therefore ultimately subjective. In fact, the 'perspectival' aspect of such entities refers to an epistemological phenomenon – the fact that they must obtain in the *perspective* of a knowing subject in order to become actualized. Yet this does not mean that they could not also exist in an uninstantiated form, as in Rāzī's theory. See also Chapter 4.

154. See the accounts of Ījī and Jurjānī, and the relevant supercommentaries of Hasan Çelebi and Siyalkoti in Jurjānī, *Sharḥ al-Mawāqif*, vol. 1, 77 - 84.

155. See ibid.

156. 'The majority' of the *muḥaqqiqīn* according to Gelenbevi in his *Risāla fī Taḥqīq 'ilm Allāh bi al-maʿdūmāt* in Gelenbevi et al. *Rasāʾil al-Imtiḥān*, 187. These (including the likes of Jurjani, Taftazani and many others) would go on to adopt the position that human knowledge (*'ilm*) is from the category of quality (*kayf*), and thereby accepted the reality of 'mental existence'. In

the earlier period, the majority had been of the opinion that knowledge was a relation (*iḍāfa / nisba*), or from the category of affection (*infiʿāl*), both of which are relational and therefore perspectival. Possibly the best philosophical exposition of the whole controversy, which also elucidates the *taḥqīq* position, is Taşköprüzade's *al-Shuhūd al-ʿaynī fī mabāḥith al-wujūd al-dhihnī*, ed. Muḥammad Zāhid Kāmil Gül (Cologne: Manshūrāt al-Jamal, 1430/2009), a work which plays an important role later on in this study.

157. That is, propositions which correspond to *nafs al-amr* rather than specifically to the mind or extramental particulars.

158. Taftāzānī and al-Sanandajī (commentator) *Taqrīb al-marām fī Sharḥ Tahdhīb al-Kalām*, with the *ḥāshiya* of Muḥammad Wasīm al-Kurdistānī (Cairo: Bulaq, 1318/1900), reprinted by Dār al-Baṣāʾir, (Cairo, 2006), 50-51. This is of course a version of a much earlier, Avicennan argument, but it is included here, apart from for its virtues of concision, to demonstrate the manner in which this central argument for mental existence had been naturalized into later *kalām*, in this important textbook, for example.

159. See e.g. Athīr al-Dīn al-Abharī and Maḥmūd Ḥusayn al-Maghnīsī (commentary) *Mughnī al-tullāb Sharḥ Matan Isāghūjī*, ed. ʿIṣām b. al-Muhadhdhab al-Subūʿī (Damascus: Dār al-Bayrūtī, 1430/2009), 76-77.

160. Should we imagine, for example, that the sole existing person be a blind one.

161. This is how how Ṣabrī describes him in *Mawqif al-ʿAql* (vol. 3, 209, note 1). In *Rūḥ al-Maʿānī*, in both his commentary on Qurʾan *Hūd* (11:5) and his commentary on *Al-Anbiyāʾ* (21:17), Al-Ālūsī calls him 'the greatest of the later [scholars].'

162. As testified to by the works of Ibn al-Qarahdāghī (d. 1354/1936) - on his commentary on the *Burhān* of Gelenbevi see Khaled El-Rouayheb, *Relational Syllogisms and the History of Arabic Logic, 900– 1900* (Leiden: Brill, 2010), *passim*, as well as those of his student Shaykh ʿAbd al-Karīm al-Mudarris (1318-1426/1901-2005) and a host of other late logicians and theologians, who employ a mode of classification and treat topics that first appeared in the *Burhān*. Gelenbevi's influence post-1800 in the theological realm was also huge; his *ḥāshiya* on Dawānī's commentary on the *ʿAḍudiyya*, for example, was a major advanced *kalām* text studied in the later Ottoman curriculum. See Muḥammad Zāhid al-Kawtharī, *Maqālāt al-Kawtharī* (Cairo: Dār al-Salām, 1430/2009), 365-366, and Mustafa Sanal, 'Osmanli Devleti'nde Medreselere Ders Programlari'.

163. *Thubūt,* not 'existence' (*wujūd*)

164. That is, not merely potential.

165. Gelenbevi *Risāla fī Taḥqīq ʿIlm Allāh bi al-Maʿdūmāt*, 187.

166. See for example, Bursevi, *Rūḥ al-Bayān* on Qurʾan 33:46.

167. For example, Bursevi, *Rūḥ al-Bayān* on Qurʾan 9:128.

168. George Berkeley, the father of idealism in modern Western philosophy, formulated his *esse est percipi* as a refutation of John Locke's notion of purportedly mind-independently existent substances nonetheless rendered impossible of direct access by Locke's own post-scholastic theory of ideas, which held that those ideas are the sole entities truly epistemologically accessible to us. On this account, the traditional notion of abstraction is retained, but without a tenable justification because of Locke's rejection of the possibility of knowledge of real essences, ensuring that we have no way of knowing whether or not our ideas of substances truly arise from real extramental substances. On one prominent reading of Berkeley, he simply eliminated the inconsistency and tension in Locke's overall theory by doing away with the notion of mind-independent substances altogether. Berkeley moreover grounded his idealism in a rejection of Locke's distinction between primary and secondary substances; the notion of an unperceived version of our idea of quantity (to take one example of a 'primary' quality that unlike secondary qualities supposedly 'resembles' a power in the extramental object) is just as meaningless as that of an unperceived taste (a secondary quality), because in Berkeley's famous dictum 'an idea can be like nothing but an idea'. See M.R. Ayers, 'Berkeley's Immaterialism and Kant's Transcendent Idealism', in *Idealism: Past and Present*, ed. Godfrey Vesey (Cambridge: Cambridge University Press, 1982), 60-61.

CHAPTER 3. ABSTRACT OBJECTS AND METAPHYSICAL NECESSITY

1. See Taşköprüzade, *al-Shaqā'iq al-Nu'māniyya*, 29 for an account of their famous debate, in which Jurjānī was the victor, and directly after which Taftāzānī is supposed to have passed away.

2. Qayṣarī's theory of *nafs al-amr* appeared before that of Taftāzānī, but since the accent of our study is on the conceptual rather than the historical, and we are treating broadly Peripatetic theories before the Akbarian theories that presuppose and transcend them, we will discuss his theory out of strict historical order.

3. Taftāzānī, *Sharḥ al-Maqāṣid*, vol. 1, 94. I am grateful to a dear friend, Mustafa Styer, for pointing out to me the existence of these passages in Taftāzānī's great work, as well as for generously sharing his manuscripts of Rāzī's *Mulakhkhaṣ* and Jurjānī's supercommentary on the *Tajrīd*.

4. A succinct but strong introduction to the issue of the co-extensivity of 'thing' and 'existent' can be found in Robert Wisnovsky, 'Avicenna' in *The Cambridge Companion to Arabic Philosophy*, 105-110, which shows how the notion relates to Avicenna's distinction between essence and existence. For an illuminating discussion by a great later theologian, mystic and exegete able to perceive the nuances in the various positions, see Ālūsī (*Rūḥ al-Ma'ānī*, Qur'an 2:20). In refuting the Ash'arī and broadly Avicennan view,

Ālūsī points out a number of different senses of the word 'thing,' (*shay'*) in the Qur'an, in terms of loci of subsistence, which seems in some sense to confirm the fundamental validity of the ontological taxonomy of *possible extramental particulars existing in the mind (al-mumkin al-khārijī al-mawjūd fī al-dhihn)*, as in Qur'an 18:23-24, *Do not say of something (wa lā taqūlanna li shay'in) 'I will do that tomorrow' except 'if Allah wills', non-existent entities* that subsist in things as they are in themselves (*al-mumkin al-maʿdūm al-thābit fī nafs al-amr*) as in Qur'an 16:40, *When We will a thing, we only say to it 'Be!' and it is (innamā qawlunā li shay'in)* and *actual extramental particulars*, like Qur'an 19:9, *And We created you before, when you were not anything (wa lam taku shay'ā)*. Ālūsī goes on to say, 'every created being is, in beginningless eternity, a "thing", that is, a non-existent that is subsistent in things as they are in themselves' (see also below Section 4.4).

5.   All texts cited in this section are from ibid., vol. 1, 94-96.

6.   Mīr Zāhid in Quṭb al-Dīn al-Rāzī, Ṣadr al-Dīn al-Shīrāzī and Mīr Zāhid, *Risālatān fī al-Taṣawwur wa al-Taṣdīq wa yalīhimā Sharḥ al-Risāla al-Maʿmūla fī al-Taṣawwur wa al-Taṣdīq*, 266.

7.   For a good summary of the views of Rāzī, Bayḍāwī and Abharī on the Platonic Forms, which form much of the background of later discussions that appear in the *Mawāqif* and *Maqāṣid*, see Abū ʿAbdillāh Muḥammad Ibn ʿArafa, *al-Mukhtaṣar al-Kalāmī*, ed. Nizār Hammādī (Kuwait: Dār al-Ḍiyāʾ, 1435/2014), 187-191. For the respective defences of the Forms by Rāzī and Mulla Fenari, see Chapter 4.

8.   Jurjānī, *al-Taʿrīfāt*, sub *nafs al-amr*.

9.   This opinion of Ṭūsī's (universally rejected by *mutakallimūn*, Akbarians, and indeed opposed by Ibn Sīnā's explicitly affirmed doctrine in the *Ishārāt*) is explained in Chapter 4.

10.   This is Arberry's translation, with a slight modification.

11.   See Abū Suʿūd's exegesis on this verse for a useful discussion.

12.   See Fakhr al-Dīn al-Rāzī, *Tafsīr al-kabīr* (Beirut: Dār al-Fikr,1401/1981), as also Abū Thanāʾ Shihāb al-Dīn al-Ālūsī *Rūḥ al-maʿānī* sub Qur'an 6:59.

13.   The Sultan conferred his father Sultan Murad's medrese in Edirne upon al-Ṭūsī, along with a hundred dirhams a day. See Taşköprüzade, *al-Shaqāʾiq al-Nuʿmāniyya*, 61. He gave al-Qūshjī the Aya Sofya medrese, and two hundred dirhams a day. See ibid., 98.

14.   Ibid., 61 and 79.

15.   See ibid., 78.

16.   See ibid., 99 and 84 respectively.

17.   ʿAlāʾuddīn al-Ṭūsī, *Al-Dhakhīra*, 134.

18.   Ibid., 134.

19.   A commonly cited fictional being.

20.   Impossible entities and abstract entities *cannot* become individuated in extramental particulars, in the case of the former because their extramental

instantiation would involve a violation of the principle of non-contradiction (and thus could never happen), and in the case of the latter, because there is no principle of individuation that could act upon their purely intelligible natures. Fictional beings, on the other hand, *could* conceivably exist in extramental particulars, but happen not to.

21. 'Alī al-Qūshjī, *Sharḥ al-Tajrīd*, ed. Muḥammad Ḥusayn al-Zāri'ī al-Riḍāyī, (Qom: Rā'id, 2014), 317.

22. The 'intermediary' here negated is the '*ḥāl*' put forward by the early Mu'tazilī *mutakallimīn*, rejected by Ibn Sīna, and later affirmed again most famously by Imām al-Ḥaramayn al-Juwaynī, a substratum 'between' mental and extramental particular existence designed to account for the apparent inherence of certain types of abstract entities in the extramental particular world. That Qushjī presents the nonreality of the *ḥāl* as an established fact shows the extent to which later *kalām* theologians had achieved consensus in rejecting this notion outright. See Jurjānī, *Sharḥ al-Mawāqif* vol. 3, 2-16 for an overview of the classic arguments employed in the later *kalām* tradition against the *ḥāl*.

23. al-Qūshjī, *Sharḥ al-Tajrīd*, 317.

24. Jalāl al-Dīn al-Dawānī's commentary in *Sharḥā al-Muḥaqqiq al-Dawānī wa Mulla 'Abdullah al-Yazdī 'alā Tahdhīb al-Manṭiq*, ed. 'Abd al-Naṣīr Aḥmad al-Shāfi'ī al-Malībārī (Kuwait: Dār al-Ḍiyā', 1435/2014), 194.

25. 'Isām al-Dīn Abū al-Khayr Aḥmad ibn Muṣliḥ al-Dīn Taşköprüzade, *al-Shuhūd al-'aynī fī mabāḥith al-wujūd al-dhihnī*. He is best known today for his biographical work *al-Shaqā'iq al-Nu'māniyya*. This is rather a sign of our times, as his voluminous oeuvre of twenty-eight philosophical, logical and theological works shows him to be a most able and subtle thinker, and moreover, a very significant synthesist of the way of the *mutakallimīn* and that of Akbarian metaphysical Sufism. His original philosophical works include *al-Shuhūd al-'aynī* under discussion, and *Ajall al-mawāhib fī ma'rifat wujūb al-wājib, al-Ta'rīfāt wa al-i'lām fī ḥall mushkilāt al-ḥadd al-tāmm, Fatḥ al-amr al-mughlaq fī mas'alat al-majhūl al-muṭlaq, Qawā'id al-ḥamliyyāt fī taḥqīq mabāḥith al-kulliyyāt* and *Risāla fī al-qaḍā wa'l qadr*, as well as an influential work in *ādāb al-baḥth wa al-munāẓara*.

26. Taşköprüzade *al-Shuhūd al-'Aynī*, 33.

27. '*Nafs al-amr* is a thing itself, in itself (*nafs al-shay' fī ḥaddi dhātihi*), and the meaning of a thing's existing in itself is that its existence and actualization is not contingent upon someone's perspective or supposition, but rather, were one to ignore all perspectives and suppositions, the thing would still exist ... Now, that existence is either primary existence (*wujūd aṣīl*), or universal existence (*wujūd kullī*), and the realm of things-in themselves thus embraces both the mind and that which is outside of the mind, yet [things-in themselves] is of non-variably wider predicative scope (*a'amm muṭlaqan*) than extramental particulars, for everything that exists in extramental

particulars invariably exists also in the realm of things-in themselves, but not vice versa. This is because there are some mental judgements that do not have referents in extramental particulars, but that nonetheless correspond to things-in themselves. Furthermore, [things-in themselves] is of reciprocally wider predicative scope (*a'amm min wajh*) than 'the mental', due to the possible nature of believing falsehoods, like the evenness of five, which exists in the mind, but not in things as they are in themselves' (ibid., 33).

28. Ibid., 33-37.

29. Rather than 'temporal'. In the Avicennan tradition, the Intellects emanate eternally from God, and His priority is thus essential, not temporal.

30. Ibid., 34.

31. This is the great *Ḥanafī* *uṣūlī* and *mutakallim* 'Ubaydullah Ṣadr al-Sharī'a's (d. 747/1346) *Ta'dīl al-'ulūm*.

32. That is, second intelligibles.

33. Namely, first intelligibles.

34. Taşköprüzade *al-Shuhūd al-'Aynī*, 36-37.

35. Ibid., 38.

36. Ibid., 38.

37. I have used 'not-mental existence' instead of 'nonmental' existence, because Taşköprüzade's use of 'lā' denotes a logical negation, thereby embracing everything that is not 'mental existence', including things which do not exist at all. Otherwise, he might have said '*al-wujūd al-ghayr al-dhihnī*', which would then, on the Avicennan and *kalām* view, be confined to extramental particulars.

38. That is, the relations of productivity that obtain between the various terms and the various premises that constitute a syllogism.

39. The truth of, for example, 'every human is an animal and every animal is a body, therefore every human is a body' applies to extramental particulars but cannot arise from any particular human, animal or body, but rather from the universal relationship between these entities which must precede and give rise to their distinctness in intellection.

40. Ibn Bahā'uddīn does not use the adjective '*al-thābita*' here, sufficing himself with *a'yān*, although he uses the full term al-*a'yān al-thābita* elsewhere in *al-Qawl al-Faṣl* (see for example, 174).

41. Ibn Bahā'uddīn *al-Qawl al-Faṣl*, 190.

42. Taşköprüzade *al-Shaqā'iq al-Nu'māniyya*, 259. He continues 'his treatment of the topics therein is supremely masterful, such that he lifted them up from [mere] knowledge to [direct] witnessing.' Taşköprüzade also records a first-hand experience that he had of Ibn Bahā'uddīn's spiritual abilities (Ibn Bahā'uddīn, apart from his great erudition, was also a well-known Sufi master and guide): 'one of the strange things that transpired between the two of us is that when I was a professor at one of the Eight Courtyards, I

saw in a dream-vision that the Prophet, blessings and peace be upon him, bestowed a crown upon me, that came from Medina the Illuminated; this vision happened in the last third of the night, and when I awoke, I got up and perused the exegesis of al-Baydāwī, which I had been reading during that period. After I had prayed the Dawn Prayer, someone came to me, bearing the greetings of peace of [Ibn Bahā'uddīn], and he said "the Shaykh says that the interpretation of the vision you saw tonight is that you will become a *qāḍī*." No one had visited me after I had seen the vision other than this person who had come bearing the greetings of peace of the Shaykh [Ibn Bahā'uddīn], and I thus knew that what had occurred was the result of his mystical unveiling (*kashf*). I went to visit him a few days later, and I mentioned the vision and his interpretation of it, and he said "Yes, it is thus." I said "I do not seek after [the position of] being a judge," and he said, "Do not seek after it, but if it is conferred upon you without your asking for it, do not refuse it." This was one of the reasons underlying my acceptance of a judicial position.'

43. Both of these concepts will be explained in Chapter 4, in the context of the school of Ibn 'Arabī.

44. Allah's 'withness' in Qur'an *Ḥadīd* (57:4), being explained as His *knowledge* of creation, is an interpretation that goes back to one of the great sages amongst the Prophetic Companions Ibn 'Abbās (3 before *hijra* – 68/619–688) (see, e.g. the commentary on this verse in Ālūsī, *Rūḥ al-Ma'ānī*).

45. Ibn Bahā'uddīn *al-Qawl al-Faṣl*, 39. The notion that God encompasses all things in His knowledge and is 'with' all things through His knowledge necessitates that the ultimate realities of things ('in themselves') constitute their realities in their fullness in His knowledge, not their mere sensible, temporal and limited individual existences; however, as we will see in Chapter 4, the individuated reality can still serve as *nafs al-amr* in accounting for individuated-particular reality *qua* individuated-particular, although it cannot account for the full intelligibility of even the individuated thing; this requires the invocation of underlying degrees of exemplary Form culminating in the Divine knowledge.

46. As do countless other major, mainstream works that are not specifically 'Akbarian' works, but that integrate Akbarian elements very extensively; Abū Thanā' al-Ālūsī's monumental *Rūḥ al-Ma'ānī*, one of the most influential Qur'anic exegeses written in the last two hundred years, is one particularly compelling example, see for example, his commentaries on Qur'an 12:68, 22:74, and 51:60. His exegesis contains tens of discussions of the relative merits of Akbarian and *kalām* approaches, one of which will be treated later in this study. Numerous commentaries on highly orthodox works like Taftāzānī's *Sharḥ al-'Aqā'id*, for example, al-Farhārī's *Nibrās*, refer extensively to Akbarī positions (see note above). Indeed, one of the last great Ottoman philosophers, Izmirli Ismail Hakki (1286-1366/1869-1946), integrated

Akbarī elements extensively into his attempt to renew *kalām, Yeni Kalam*, which was first released in two volumes from 1920-1922, possibly the very last serious Ottoman attempt, before the dismantling of the Sultanate and Caliphate, to counteract the encroachment of Western thought (see Izmirli Ismail Hakki *Yeni Kalam*, for example, vol. 2, 177-188). Of course, many of Ibn Kemal's epistles also contain notable and much earlier exemplars of this synthesis of *kalām* and Akbarian metaphysics (and more often, this might better be characterized as the *subordination* of *kalām* to Akbarian metaphysics) for example, in *Risāla fī Bayān 'Adam Nisbat al-Sharr Ilā Allāh Ta'ālā' in Majmū' Rasā'il al-'Allāma Ibn Kamāl Pāshā*, ed. Ḥamza Bakrī (Istanbul: Dār al-Lubāb, 2018/1439), vol. 5, 390-392.

47.   *Direct* comments on the *Fiqh al-Akbar* amount to little more than five percent of the book, which lends credence to the notion that the commentary tradition in later Islam was often more about *tabarruk*, seeking the blessings of a great *mātin* or writer of a *matn*, than it was about commentary *per se* – many later commentaries and supercommentaries are highly original works that have little to do with the original *matn*; for example, Gelenbevi's supercommentary on Dawānī's commentary on *al-'Aqīda al-'Aḍudiyya*, Khayālī's supercommentary on Taftāzānī's *Sharḥ al-'Aqā'id*, and of course, *Sharḥ al-'Aqā'id* itself. It would be no exaggeration to say that many hundreds of further examples exist.

CHAPTER 4. *NAFS AL-AMR* AND THE EXEMPLARY FORMS OF COGNITION

1.   Proof for this abounds; Dāwūd al-Qayṣarī having been given the task, by Sultan Orhan Gazi, of leading the first *medrese* in Ottoman history, the great Akbarian Mulla Fenari being appointed the first Ottoman *şeyhülislam*, the overtly Akbarian exegesis of Kashani having being placed on one of the few official curricula in Ottoman history. See Shahab Ahmed and Nenad Filipovic, 'The Sultan's Syllabus: A Curriculum for the Ottoman Imperial medreses Prescribed in a ferman of Qanuni I Süleyman, dated 973 AH (1565 CE)', *Studia Islamica*, 98/99 (2004), 183-218). Ak Shams al-Dīn, Sultan Fatih Mehmet's spiritual master, having written a work defending Ibn 'Arabī; Sultan Mehmet himself having commissioned the great Akbari sage 'Abd al-Raḥmān Jāmī to write a work, *al-Durra al-fākhira*, that would adjudicate between the various Islamic investigators of the nature of reality: the *mutakallimūn*, the *ṣūfiyyà* and the *ḥukamā'* (see Taşköprüzade *al-Shaqā'iq al-Nu'māniyya*, 159); Ibn Kemal and Abū Su'ūd's *fatwas* supporting Ibn 'Arabī, and the fact that Mustafa Sabri, himself critical, feels it necessary to concede that the vast majority of the greatest figures in later Islamic theology held broadly Akbarian views on key issues (including, some apparently unlikely figures such as Ismail Gelenbevi) (see his two hundred page critique of the doctrine of *al-wujūd al-muṭlaq* in volume 3 of

his *Mawqif al-'aql*, 85-315. Although the present author respectfully diverges from much in the *şeyhülislam*'s argument, it must be said that the critique is, for the researcher into the *kalām* reception of Ibn 'Arabī, exceptionally and in fact almost peerlessly useful).

2. See Sharḥ al-Maqāṣid vol. 1, 73-75 for his refutation of the Akbarian doctrine of *al-wujūd al-muṭlaq*, and vol. 2, 56-57, where he expresses his wariness about upholding the reality of the world of imaginal representations (*'ālam al-mithāl*). This should not be taken to imply that Taftāzānī opposed 'Sufism'. Quite to the contrary, he acknowledges and details some possible preconditions of mystical unveiling (*kashf*) (see for example, vol. 2, 46-49). Mulla Fenari directly answered Taftāzānī's objections concerning *al-wujūd al-muṭlaq* in *Miṣbāḥ al-uns*, 159-169, and on 420-433 he provides a demonstration, from the perspective of speculative philosophy, of the doctrines of both the world of imaginal representations, and of exemplary Forms, an exposition that should arguably be counted as one of the towering intellectual achievements of the whole Ottoman period of which we are thus far aware (some brief excerpts can be found in Section 4.1). For an explanation of the Akbarian doctrine of *al-wujūd al-muṭlaq*, see also Section 4.1. It is very significant that despite these rebuttals, Mulla Fenari was a leading promoter of the work of Taftāzānī, and greatly facilitated the integration of the latter's works into the early Ottoman curriculum (see Taşköprüzade *al-Shaqā'iq al-Nu'māniyya*, 20). This generosity of spirit was probably partly facilitated by the notion of the subordination of the sciences – that is, while Taftāzānī's work is legitimate on its own terms, as representative of the 'natural theological' method of *kalām*, its results are ultimately subject to correction by 'the science of spiritual realities' (*'ilm al-ḥaqā'iq*), which is 'the supreme science' (see *Miṣbāḥ al-uns*, 27-28).

3. Very shortly after Ibn 'Arabī passed away, Islamic philosophy quite suddenly experienced an efflorescence to rival any other in its history – the appearance of a succession of philosophers who were able to construct a metaphysics-as-universal science that dove into the depths of two poles of natural theology – the Avicennan synthesis and the very rigorous criticism of Imām Fakhr al-Dīn al-Rāzī, (the impact of which was nothing short of revolutionary) – and emerged with enduring formulations that would provide the basis for the triumphant integration of philosophy *qua* philosophy into *kalām*. These philosophers were perhaps most eminently Athīr al-Dīn al-Abharī (d. 663/1265), Naṣīr al-Dīn al-Ṭūsī (597–672/1201–74), Najm al-Dīn al-Kātibī (d. 675/1276), Quṭb al-Din Shīrazī (633–710/1236–1311) and Quṭb al-Dīn al-Rāzī (d. 766/1364), and the great theologians and philosophers, broadly contemporaneous with the latter group, who effected that integration, Nāṣir al-Dīn al-Bayḍāwī (d. 685/1292) 'Aḍud al-Dīn al-Ījī (680–756/1281–1355), Sa'd al-Dīn al-Taftāzānī, al-Sayyid al-Sharīf al-Jurjani, and of course Mulla Fenari the author of *Miṣbāḥ al-uns*.

4. See also Tony Street, 'Kātibī, Taḥtānī and the *Shamsiyya*' in *The Oxford Handbook of Islamic Philosophy*, ed. Khaled El-Rouayheb and Sabine Schmitke (Oxford: Oxford University Press, 2017), 349-351.

5. M. Bayram, 'The Library of Sadr-al-Din Qunavī and its Books,' in *Theoretical Approaches to the Transmission and Edition of Oriental Manuscripts*, ed. J. Pfeiffer and M. Kropp (Beirut: Orient-Institut, 2007), 180.

6. Published as Ṣadr al-Dīn Qūnawī and Naṣīr al-Dīn al-Ṭūsī, *al-Murāsalāt Bayn Ṣadr al-Dīn al-Qūnawī wa Naṣīr al-Dīn al-Ṭūsī*, ed. Gudrun Schubert (Beirut: al-Sharika al-Muttaḥida li al-Tawzīʿ, 1995).

7. See John Walbridge, *The Science of Mystic Lights: Quṭb al-Dīn Shīrāzī and the Illuminationist Tradition in Islamic Philosophy* (Cambridge, MA: Center for Middle East Studies, 1992).

8. See Taşköprüzade, *al-Shaqāʾiq al-Nuʿmāniyya*, 92.

9. Ibid., 15 and 17.

10. M. Bayram, 'The Library of Sadr-al-Din Qunavī and its Books,' 180.

11. Major synthesizers of Akbarianism and *kalām* appearing shortly after the careers of the authors of these works include Shams al-Dīn Muḥammad b. ʿAlī al-Ḥusaynī ('Emir Sultan') (d. 833/1429), Mūḥyī al-Dīn al-Kāfiyajī (d. 879/1474), Muhyī al-Dīn Muhammad b. Qutb al-Dīn al-Izniqī (d. 885/1480), and of course, Ibn Kemal, Taşköprüzade and Ibn Bahāʾuddīn. For more on the reception of Akbarian metaphysical Sufism and its relationship to natural theology and the Islamic sciences amongst the Ottoman ʿulamāʾ, see the present author's *The Mystical Synthesis of Ibn Bahāʾuddīn: An Akbarian Kalām Theologian in 16th century Istanbul* (Tabah Foundation, forthcoming 2021). The late-Ottoman Iraqi Ālūsi provides excellent evidence of the extent of the integration of Akbarianism into mainstream scholarship throughout his *Rūḥ al-maʿānī*, drawing on the works of scholars such as Ibrahim al-Kūrānī, as does the great later Egyptian Azharī scholar al-Bakhīt al-Muṭīʿī (1271–1354/1856–1935) in many of his works (the positive reception of Ibn Arabi in Egypt is of course largely due to the influence of the major names of al-Suyūṭī, Zakariyyā al-Anṣārī and al-Shaʿrānī), as well as the Indian scholar Shaykh ʿAbd al-ʿAliyy Baḥr al-ʿUlūm (1142–1225/1769–1810) (as well as many others in the Farangi Mahalli school) in his extremely philosophically rich commentary, see Abd al-ʿAliyy Baḥr al-ʿUlūm, *Sharḥ Baḥr al-ʿUlūm ʿalā Sullam al-ʿUlūm*, ed. ʿAbd al-Naṣīr Aḥmad al-Shāfiʿī (Kuwait: Dār al-Ḍiyāʾ, 1433/2012) on what is, together with Gelenbevi's *Burhān*, the most widely acclaimed work of advanced logic of the latter centuries – Muḥibullāh al-Bihārī's (d. 1119/1707) *Sullam al-ʿulūm* (see, for example, Baḥr al-ʿUlūm's exposition of Akbarī doctrines on 328-337). The reception of the later Akbari school amongst the putative mainstream of 'normatively' orthodox Sunni ʿulamāʾ is a fascinating subject in need of extensive study.

12. Dāwūd al-Qayṣarī, *Maṭlaʿ khuṣūṣ al-kalim fī maʿānī Fuṣūṣ al-Ḥikam*, ed. Shaykh ʿĀṣim Ibrāhīm al-Kayyālī (Beirut: Dār al-Kutub al-ʿIlmiyya, 1433/2012), 37.

13. See his refutation of the Akbarī notion of *al-wujūd al-muṭlaq*, cited above.

14. Al-Sayyid al-Sharīf al-Jurjānī, *Ḥāshiya ʿalā al-Tajrīd*, Ms. Istanbul Süley-maniye Kütüphanesi, Haci Selim Ağa 723, fols. 14ab.

15. With the accent on 'limitary', that is, graspable in terms of restricted concepts that would seek to reduce God's reality to finitely knowable categories. This does not mean, as some critics of Akbarianism have thought, that God is not *mutaʿayyin*. His *taʿayyun* is identical to His Essence; He is of His very nature Himself, and distinct from all of His creation. See Qayṣarī *Maṭlaʿ khuṣūṣ al-kalim*, 71.

16. Najm al-Dīn al-Kātibī and Mubārakshāh (commentary), *Sharḥ Ḥikmat al-ʿAyn*, with the supercommentary of al-Sayyid al-Sharīf al-Jurjānī, 11.

17. For the detailed version of this line of reasoning see Qayṣarī, *Maṭlaʿ khuṣūṣ al-kalim fī aʿānī Fuṣūṣ al-Ḥikam*, 42-44.

18. The Moroccan Sufi master, Shaykh Muḥammad Ibn al-Ḥabīb (1290-1392/1870-1972), also an important late expositor of Akbarian doctrines in his poetry and litanies, goes so far as to call it metaphorical or 'figurative' (*majāzī*) existence. See Muḥammad Ibn al-Ḥabīb, *The Diwan of Sidi Muhammad Ibn al-Habib,* trans. Abdurrahman Fitzgerald (Granada: Editorial Qasida, 2015), 70.

19. In the sense of being unrestricted by particular individuation.

20. That is, no finite name or description.

21. ʿAbd al-Nabiyy ibn ʿAbd al-Rasūl Aḥmadnagarī, *Dustūr al-ʿulamāʾ* sub *al-wujūd*.

22. Due to the subtlety of this doctrine, and its relying, to be fully understood, on some degree of mystical unveiling (*kashf*), it is often mistaken for an identification of God with creation – and as a representation of the doctrine, this is little short of a travesty. In fact, it is quite the opposite, entailing, rather, the Absolute, unknowable Divine Essence's exclusive possession of true reality. Indeed, despite its abundant potential for causing confusion (largely due to the highly specialized terminology and modes of expression employed by its advocates), the real meaning of the doctrine is unassailable, as it is simply the doctrine of the radical and complete dependence, in every possible sense, of multiplicity upon its Source and Sustainer, God Himself. The doctrine provides the most comprehensive statement of God's utter Transcendence and otherness with respect to His creation, while also explaining the theophanic appearance of the traces of His Names in the creation of the world, thus providing, of all interpretations of the Qurʾanic *There is nothing whatsoever like unto Him, and He is the All-hearing, the All-seeing* (42:11), the closest to adequacy. And 'the scholars of outward appearances named the *appearance* of things [in existence] – that [according

to all] occurs by means of God's [prior] existence – 'originated existence' (*al-wujūd al-ḥādith*), whereas the people of mystical unveiling do not call it [real] existence [at all]. The disagreement is thus [merely] verbal (*fa al-khilāf lafẓiyyun*)'. Muḥammad ibn 'Umar ibn 'Abd al-Jalīl al-Qādirī, *Sharḥ al-Ṣalāt al-Akbariyya*, ed. 'Āṣim Ibrāhīm al-Kayālī (Beirut: Dār al-Kutub al-'Ilmiyya, Beirut, 1430/2009), 39-40.

23. I firmly disagree with William Chittick's (not excessively substantial) reasoning against translating *al-a'yān al-thābita* 'the Immutable Archetypes', or similar, in his *The Sufi Path of Knowledge: Ibn 'Arabī's Metaphysics of Imagination* (Albany NY: State University of New York Press, 1989), 84. The *a'yān* are certainly 'archetypes'. While they indeed contain, in all detail, everything that is subsequently 'unfolded' in the subsequent degrees of manifestation, they also surpass them in 'superessential' (superessential, that is, relative to the subordinate individuation-conditions of the given essence) and superordinate dimensions of the specific essence in question, in which their *only* reality is as images of the Divine Names. The Immutable Archetypes are certainly not the 'same' as their subsequent loci of manifestation in their particularities, because otherwise they would be restricted, simultaneously, in exactly the same manner as all of their subordinate degrees of being, which is absurd.

24. 'Abd al-Razzāq Kāshānī, *Laṭā'if al-i'lām fī ishārāt ahl al-ilhām*, ed. Majīd Hādīzade (Beirut: Manshūrāt al-Jamal, 2011), 424.

25. 'Abd al-Wahhāb al-Sha'rānī, *al-Yawāqīt wa al-jawāhir fī bayān 'Aqā'id al-Akābir*, vol. 1 (Beirut: Dār al-Ṣādir, 2012), 99.

26. Of course, God nonetheless has knowledge of their subsequent self-knowledge, but this only becomes actualized from the *perspectives* of created beings after their existences are 'unfolded' into the first world of creation, that is, the world of spirits (*'ālam al-arwāḥ*).

27. Qayṣarī, *Maṭla' khuṣūṣ al-kalim*, 63-64.

28. Ibid. 64.

29. Qayṣarī, *Maṭla' khuṣūṣ al-kalim*, 83.

30. In order for the background to these points to come into clearer definition, one may wish to consult and compare Taftāzānī's refutation of the Akbarian notion of *al-wujūd al-muṭlaq* with Mulla Fenari's defence, both cited above.

31. As we have alluded to above, in the post-Avicennan *kalām* tradition, the special existence (*al-wujūd al-khāṣṣ*) of each thing is exactly its individuated particularity; the *concept* of existence is then abstracted (*yuntaza'*) from this extramental foundation. An incisive and careful discussion can be found in 'Abd al-Karīm Muḥammad al-Mudarris, *al-Wasīla fī Sharḥ al-Faḍīla*, vol. 1, ed. al-Sayyid Quṣayy Abū al-Si'd and al-Sayyid 'Abd al-Wahhāb Abū al-Si'd (Beirut: Dār Iḥyā' al-Turāth al-'Arabī, 1437/2016), 149. For the larger context, see 145-159 of the same work.

32. See for example, Najm al-Dīn al-Kātibī and Mubārakshāh (commentary),
    Sharḥ Ḥikmat al-ʿAyn, with the supercommentary of al-Sayyid al-Sharīf al-
    Jurjānī, 33, and ʿAbd al-Qādir Sanandajī, *Taqrīb al-Marām fī Sharḥ Tahdhīb
    al-Kalām*, 69-70.

33. See Herbert A. Davidson, *Al-Farabi, Avicenna and Averroes on Intellect*
    (Oxford: Oxford University Press, 1992), 77 and 124 for elucidations, with
    sources, of the *undifferentiated* mode of the existence of forms in the Agent
    Intellect.

34. Qayṣarī, *Maṭlaʿ khuṣūṣ al-kalim*, 43.

35. Effectively although not strictly, because as previously noted, God also ex-
    ists ʿ*fī al-khārij*' according to this immanentist ontology.

36. Hence the difficulty of trying to solve the problem of the guarantor of the
    truth of this proposition by positing that a combination of extramental
    particulars and the mind is *nafs al-amr*; after all, *nafs al-amr* is meant to
    account not merely for any given individual human *cognition* of, for example,
    Zayd standing atop a mountain in a woollen robe (if it *were* the case that
    nafs al-amr is merely the guarantor of the truth of the *appearances* yielded
    by *cognitions*, the combination of extramental particulars and the mind
    would be sufficient); rather *nafs al-amr* is objective reality *itself*, and must
    thus also (and most fundamentally) account for the ontological *grounds* of
    the 'truth' of propositions yielded by human cognition.

37. In this case, the spatiotemporal particulars of the Akbarian *ʿālam al-mulk*.
    That is, as we shortly see, intelligible entities like relations and the *umūr
    ʿāmma* also inform *prior* reality (i.e. prior to the degree of spatiotemporal
    particulars).

38. When we examine Taşköprüzade's synthesis at the end of this chapter, we
    will find that for distinct but related reasons, he also ultimately refuses to
    acknowledge the candidacy of extramental particulars for the status of *nafs
    al-amr*, even for extramental particular propositions.

39. This is a possible objection (namely that an extramental particular propo-
    sition is only *intended* to refer to extramental particular phenomena, and
    nothing more) to the above, which the following clause answers (namely
    that no extramental particular is genuinely intelligible except against the
    background of its exemplary form, such that extramental particulars con-
    sidered in isolation can never constitute the full objective reality even of
    extramental particulars). The extramental particular cannot be fully cog-
    nized in isolation. Moreover, as Mulla Fenari tells us, the exemplary form
    does indeed count all of the individuations and modes of its individuals
    as attributes, but 'not within itself, but rather with respect to that locus of
    manifestation' (*lā fī nafsihi bal min ḥaythu dhālika al-maẓhar*). See *Miṣbāḥ
    al-uns*, 424.

40. Nor, again, can it serve as *nafs al-amr* alongside the mind alone (at risk of
    subjectivism); the invocation of an exemplary 'third realm' is necessary in

order to provide an exhaustive account of any objective truth or reality. Once this is assented to after the requisite demonstrative proof (constituted, it is to be hoped, by the overall argument of this study) *al-khārij* may indeed then be considered an *adjunct* to *nafs al-amr*, in its capacity as one locus of the particularization of aspects of things as they are, and thus as a *branch* of *nafs al-amr*, yet only in terms of that particularity and individuation, but not in terms of the *intelligibility* of its essence (which, as Dawūd al-Qayṣarī has shown above, leads to circularity if attributed to the particular itself), nor the *grounds of the relationality* it bears to any other terms that may be involved alongside it, in true propositions concerning it. That 'the form of "man" has mental existence in this individual mind', for example, is true *in* extramental particulars because the mind exists in extramental particulars, can only be corroborated by a knowing subject that has experienced the mental form of 'man', i.e. by *being* a human being in possession of a mind; clearly, this relationship, between the extramental individuated man, the mind, and the mental form of man, has been defined neither by extramental particulars nor the mind. Again, the invocation of a third realm is necessary, within which the relationship between mentality and extramental particulars is defined.

41.   Fakhr al-Dīn al-Rāzī, *al-Mulakhkhaṣ*, Ms. Istanbul Süleymaniye Kütüphanesi, Haci Selim Ağa 723, fols. 54a.

42.   See Ibn 'Arafa, *al-Mukhtaṣar al-kalāmī*, 190-191 for a discussion.

43.   As we will demonstrate in a long-term study currently in preparation.

44.   Mulla Fenari, *Miṣbāḥ al-uns*, 433.

45.   Both quotes from ibid. 420. Presumably, this is because to deduce the existence of an uninstantiated Form underlying particulars enables one to deduce the existence of the Immutable Archetypes as its prior principle of unity, which on the exemplarist scheme must also themselves possess exemplars (since retaining a degree of multiplicity, they cannot constitute their own principles of unity), of which they are 'images', the Divine Names and Attributes. The only conclusion that can be drawn from demonstrating the rootedness of all natures in Absolute Existence is that those natures are created, perspectival determinations and limitations of that Absolute Existence, which is the ultimate principle of unity of all things, which is in itself utterly non-composite and non-relational and thus requires no principle of unity – hence exemplarism leads directly to the Akbarian notion of Absolute Existence; simultaneously, Mulla Fenari's words strongly suggest that the substance of the Akbarian ontology is a henology. We will expand on this contention somewhat below.

46.   Ibid., 433.

47.   Ibid., 433.

48.   Ibid., 428.

49.   Ibid., 328.

50. For example, the conjunction of "Man' is in Zayd's mind' with "Man' is in 'Amr's mind' etc. Although a single nature is characterized by incompatible predicates, this does not cause any contradiction.

51. Mulla Fenari, *Miṣbāḥ al-uns*, 424.

52. Ibn Bahā'uddīn, *al-Qawl al-faṣl*, 174.

53. Ibid., 175.

54. Qayṣarī *Maṭlaʿ Khuṣūṣ al-Kalim*, 56.

55. *Al-Ishārāt wa al-Tanbīhāt, maʿa Sharḥ Naṣīr al-Dīn al-Ṭūsī*, vol. 1, 279.

56. Avicenna also tells us 'He must know particulars in a sacred manner that is lofty above time – and He must know all things' (*Al-Ishārāt wa al-Tanbīhāt, maʿa Sharḥ Naṣīr al-Dīn al-Ṭūsī*, vol. 3, 296-297). In the midst of possibly the supreme *taḥqīq* treatment of the question of the nature of Divine knowledge (*Gelenbevī ʿalā al-Dawānī ʿalā al-ʿAqīda al-ʿAḍudiyya* vol. 2, 2-76), (along with Gelenbevi's supercommentary), Dawānī, an avowed Ashʿarī (see vol. 1, 38, and 41), tells us he is of the opinion that a real understanding of the position of Avicenna on the Divine knowledge shows him to be undeserving of charges of disbelief (since Avicenna stresses that God knows all things, without exception) although his position that God knows particulars in a universal way is nonetheless not entirely unproblematic (vol. 2, 12 and 18).

57. *Al-Ishārāt wa al-Tanbīhāt maʿa Sharḥ Naṣīr al-Dīn al-Ṭūsī*, vol. 3, 283-285.

58. This is so similar to Taşköprüzade's introduction to his synthesis (see below), that on comparison, it seems inconceivable that his reasoning was not based directly on the work of Qayṣari. For the more general principle of God's knowledge of essences being a necessary precondition of creation, compare also with Rāzī in his *al-Maṭālib al-ʿĀliya* (ed. Muḥammad ʿAbd al-Salām Shāhīn, Beirut: Dār al-Kutub al-ʿIlmiyya, 1420/1999), where he maintains the same principle in the course of enunciating one of his proofs that God knows particulars: 'The world would not be existentiated *ex nihilo* unless the Agent had purposed to existentiate it. Now, it would be impossible for this purpose to obtain unless He had knowledge of its non-existence, such that He then undertake to make it existent. Thus, when it was non-existent, He had knowledge of it as non-existent, and when it became existent, He had knowledge of it as existent. It thus becomes established that were the world existentiated *ex nihilo*, He would have to know particulars' (vol. 4, 93). Against a notion attractive to those wishing to avoid the pre-existent multiplicity that seems to be implied by the assertion of Allah's knowledge of distinct entities, namely that it is sufficient to point to Allah's knowledge of the *temporal* distinctness (*al-imtiyāẓ fī mā lā yazāl*) of entities, in order to preserve the integrity of the comprehensiveness of Allah's knowledge, Rāzī goes on to write that 'the knowledge that [e.g.] the colour black will exist temporally is a judgement concerning the colour black; now, judgements concerning particular quiddities are contingent upon the subject (*al-maḥkūm ʿalayhi*) having been conceived of, for assent is always preceded

by conception. Therefore: the judgement that black will come into existence is preceded by the conception of this quiddity, and [the judgement] only becomes complete after knowledge of the distinctness of this quiddity from that which is other than it [has obtained]. Thus, were the obtainment of this distinctness to be contingent upon that thing's entering into existence, a vicious circle would obtain, which is impossible' (vol. 4, 98).

59.   Qayṣarī *Maṭlaʿ khuṣūṣ al-kalim*, 56.

60.   Ibid., 57.

61.   While an Immutable Archetype comprehends all of its subsequent relationships with other Immutable Archetypes, as well as all of its determinations and limitations with respect to particular knowing subjects in, say, the World of Spirits or the sensible world, it is not *restricted* by any of them.

62.   Qayṣarī, *Maṭlaʿ khuṣūṣ al-kalim*, 62.

63.   In Akbarian terms, this is an allusion to the Muḥammadan Reality in the first degree of its created manifestation in the World of Spirits (see Qayṣarī, *Maṭlaʿ khuṣūṣ al-kalim*, 180-181 for a detailed exposition, as well as Tahānawī *Kashshāf* sub ʿaql). Thus, it does not, as some have presumed, involve an affirmation of the Avicennan doctrine of the First Intellect (readers wanting to confirm this will find, apart from the references just provided, 55-56 of the *Muqaddimāt* especially clear).

64.   Qayṣarī *Maṭlaʿ khuṣūṣ al-kalim*, 57.

65.   Ibid., 59.

66.   Ibid., 45.

67.   That is, an individual the species of which would be represented by the said term, such as an individual 'unity', 'relation', 'existence' or 'possible'. In order to anticipate a common misunderstanding, we must emphasize that the possibility here negated is not that of a unity becoming an 'individual', in so far as it is instantiated within an individual substratum, such as 'this man is a unity', but we are rather pointing out the impossibility of, 'this individual unity is a unity', in which unity and *nothing else* constitutes the species of the individual unity. In the normal, broadly Peripatetic sense of unity, this is impossible, because, if it is not to merely characterize a substratum distinct from itself, as in 'the man is a unity', there is no principle of individuation that could possibly particularize unity in order to distinguish itself, *as a hypothetical individual*, from itself as *a species*.

68.   The intuition of unity challenges us in this way because the other transcendentals are entailed by it, as is also the case with other intelligible principles. For example, determinate 'being' and indeterminate 'non-being' must accompany it; distinct determinations within pure unity (yielding 'essence') require to participate in unity in some way, inasmuch as they must participate in a 'principle of unity' in order to be rendered intelligible as self-identical and distinct; this unification of determinations in turn yields the predicate 'multiplicity'. 'Necessity' characterizes unity, just as 'possibility', the

substratum of which is indeterminacy, characterizes unity's instantiations as the one-many. Since these principles follow on from unity and each is a necessary condition of the instantiation of a *specific* nature as well as its full intelligibility, we not only have as much reason to deduce their reality prior to particulars as we do that of the absolute unity necessarily prior to limited multiplicities *within* unities, but in fact, our natural theological *deduction* of the latter is *contingent* upon this.

69. Fran O'Rourke, *Pseudo-Dionysius and the Metaphysics of Aquinas* (Leiden: E.J. Brill, 1992) contains a useful summary of the meaning of the 'primacy' of being in Aquinas (109-113). O'Rourke also attempts a defence of this priority against some of its detractors, although in the course of this attempt, he somewhat misrepresents the doctrine of 'beyond being' (201-212). Daniel D. De Haan's *Necessary Existence and the Doctrine of Being in Avicenna's Metaphysics of the Healing* (Leiden: Brill, 2020) provides helpful discussions of Avicenna's doctrine of being in the context of Avicenna's celebrated 'primary notions', and he correctly notes that 'Avicenna holds, contrary to Neoplatonism, that henology is subordinated to ontology' (347). However, in our view, he fails to muster an adequately cogent set of philosophical rationales, nor meaningful textual evidence for his conclusion, which is that he has 'proved' that 'necessary' is the *most fundamental* primary notion for Avicenna, 'intensionally prior' even, to being. It is exactly the fact that being construed as 'an accomplished given' is *so*, that yields, in the order of intellection, the further notion 'necessity'; 'necessary', in turn, can only be intelligible if the broadest interpretation of 'existence' is already presupposed – and Avicenna does not, of course, make the distinction between 'being' and 'existence' that De Haan's interpretation would in fact demand. I regard Avicenna as the main inspiration for Aquinas' (nonetheless enormously overrated) doctrine of the *actus essendi*, and I intend to set forth the significant evidence for this in a forthcoming article, particularly in the context of Aquinas' extensive borrowing from Avicenna's theory of truth.

70. This may be construed as the favouring of *aṣālat al-māhiyya* over *aṣālat al-wujūd*, but I consider it, more fundamentally, a statement of *aṣālat al-waḥda*, or in its epistemological manifestation, if you will, *aṣālat al-tawḥīd*.

71. Although in the formulation common to thinkers like Plato, Plotinus, Proclus, Dionysius, (and later, Latin formulations by Meister Eckhart and Nicholas of Cusa), the One is 'beyond being' (*epekeina tēs ousias*), this is because 'being' in this broad scheme is identified with Intellect as one-many, which entails limited, knowably determinate being. The sense of 'beyond being' is thus closely akin to the notion of *al-wujūd al-muṭlaq*, that is *al-muṭlaq ʿan al-qayd*, as we shall see below – the One in itself is not determined by any of the restrictions and limitary qualifications that define the realm of 'being' so defined. As the prominent Platonist scholar Lloyd Gerson affirms, 'beyond being' does not, of course, mean the One does not

exist, but rather that its essence is unlimited and infinite (*Platonism and Naturalism*, 125).

72. Jens Halfwassen 'The Metaphysics of the One', in *The Routledge Handbook of Neoplatonism*, eds. Pauliina Remes and Svetla Slaveva-Griffin (London: Routledge, 2014), 185.

73. Some may deem this a misunderstanding of *mabda' al-āthār*, which refers to the effects directly resultant of a thing's *extramental* individuation; I am, however, questioning the coherence of the very notion, if it is meant to capture something definitive and exclusive about being an 'extramental existent', and this is because some purely mental entities would also seem to be capable of having 'extramental effects'.

74. In order to avoid unnecessarily complicating matters any further, we have refrained at this point from setting forth our own view about the origin of 'fictional' entities–which forms part of a larger theory of art, music and symbolic expression– which is that we arrive at them through a mode of participation of our imaginations in *'ālam al-mithāl*, in which the most symbolically pristine amongst them *exist* prior to their appearances in the creative imagination, whereas others constitute amalgamations and coalescences (of greater and lesser degrees of symbolic resonance) formed by the individual artist.

75. Eric D. Perl, *Thinking Being: Introduction to Metaphysics in the Classical Tradition* (Leiden: Brill, 2014), 116-117.

76. The broadest implication of 'beyond being' is summed up well by Douglas Hedley: 'One of the major tenets of Platonism is the conviction that there is a surplus of ultimate meaning that transcends any attempt to express it: the Good is "beyond being" ... These are those limits of reasoning where, in the occidental tradition, philosophy touches religion: Plato's Good "beyond being"'. Douglas Hedley, 'Platonism, Aesthetics and the Sublime at the Origins of Modernity' in *Platonism at the Origins of Modernity: Studies on Platonism and Early Modern Philosophy*, eds. Douglas Hedley and Sarah Hutton (Dordrech: Springer, 2008), 271.

77. Qayṣarī, *Maṭla' Khuṣūṣ al-Kalim*, 46. Elsewhere (40), Qayṣarī tells us that the essence of 'Pure Being' is not known to anyone but Pure Being itself, which, Qayṣarī is everywhere very clear, is entirely equivalent to saying 'the essence of God is unknown to any but God Himself'. Despite being *valid* as a way of describing the participation of creation (restricted being) in God (pure being), is not the term 'Pure Being' thus rendered entirely unessential? Indeed, as Mulla Fenari notes, 'our saying "He is existence" is only to help with comprehension, not because it is one of His real Names' (*Miṣbāḥ al-uns*, 168).

78. Mulla Fenari, *Miṣbāḥ al-uns*, 302.

79. Attempts to explain the contention that God is Pure Being fail (inevitably, in our view) to be satisfyingly intelligible. Etienne Gilson, for example, makes

such an attempt in his *The Philosophy of St. Thomas Aquinas* (trans. Edward Bullough, Cambridge: W. Heffer & Sons Ltd, 1924) that is especially notable (and surprisingly so, given the indisputable brilliance of Gilson, but such is the danger of strict adherence to doctrine) for the gaping chasms that often intervene between its premises and its conclusions. God is 'nothing but His being' but is yet 'the most universally perfect being.' This follows, Gilson thinks, because 'every kind of perfection reduces itself to the possession of a certain degree of being … to possess wisdom, for man, is to *be* wise. The fact is that, because man, in becoming wise, has achieved a degree of being, he has also achieved a degree of perfection' (83). 'If we, therefore, assume some one thing which possesses total being, this being will also be total perfection, since all perfection is nothing but a certain manner of being' (84). Instead of recognizing that the notion of being in his example arises from the particularized determination of 'wisdom', rather than the other way around, Gilson then leaps from the true fact that a finite being's *possession* of some degree of the perfection of a quality depends upon the *instantiation* of that quality within itself, to the conclusion that despite ostensibly not *instantiating* any qualities (for Gilson, God 'has not even an essence, since His essence is none other than His being, 85) God nonetheless possesses all perfections simply in virtue of the fact that He is Pure Being. Gilson's consistent (and at times alarmingly vehement) enmity towards Platonism is often directed towards its failure to acknowledge that God is 'Pure Being'. See for example, his attempted correction of Dionysius in *The Christian Philosophy of St. Thomas Aquinas*, trans. L.K. Shook (New York, NY: Random House, 1956), 136–141. Likewise, according to Gilson, Augustine's 'Platonism of being leaves him helpless to affirm clearly the act-of-being' (133) 'Here it is as though the proper and direct effect of the creative act was, not the act-of-being, but that condition of the real which justifies the use of the term *being* in speaking of it.' (133). According to Gilson, Augustine was incapable of correctly interpreting Exodus' *I am that I am*, which according to Gilson, must mean that God's innermost nature is Pure Being (Augustine's own interpretation is that it means God is eternal and immutable) because 'dominated by the Platonic ontology of essence', Augustine held that God 'is what He possesses'. He is able to account for creation only as the participation of the mutable in the immutable Divine Ideas, thus, and is thereby forced into an understanding of the Divine as 'eternity' and the world as 'time and space'. This caused Augustine considerable 'embarrassment' (to use Gilson's oft-repeated characterization), when it came to accounting for the possibility of Divine immanence and presence in the world of becoming. 'It is conceivable that time is in eternity' Gilson tells us, 'but how is it conceivable, inversely, that Eternity may be in time?' (135) 'Augustine was far better equipped to establish God's transcendence than to justify His immanence in the soul' (135). Of course,

'Augustine knows better than anyone that everything, even becoming, is the work of the Immutable', but hampered by his Platonism, he was unable to make philosophical sense of this reality, and 'it is precisely at this point that he finds the mystery most obscure' (135). It was only possible to reveal the intelligibility of this mystery 'by moving from God as Eternity to God as Act-of-Being.' (135). Thomas' statement that 'God is his own act-of-being' apparently 'marks clearly the decisive progress attained by his ontology; [it] explains also the ease with which his thought could bind time to eternity, creature to Creator.' To the present author, however, it is difficult to see how Gilson's vague Thomistic notion of the 'act-of-being' can account for God's immanence in the world in a more metaphysically cogent manner than Augustine's *clear* understanding of the participation of the world in the Divine Ideas, which themselves arise from God's knowledge of Himself, and that thus makes profound metaphysical sense of the presence of God in the world in terms of our finite participation, however distant, in His infinite nature.

80. Jens Halfwassen, 'The Metaphysics of the One', 184.

81. Mulla Fenari, *Misbāḥ al-uns*, 584.

82. Ibid., 339.

83. Qayṣarī, *Prolegomena*, 40.

84. Ibid., 230-231.

85. Ibid., 231.

86. This is ongoing, and one of its natural prerequisites must be a comparative investigation, as comprehensive as possible, of the Avicennan primary notions, the post-Rāzian *al-umūr al-'āmma*, the Kantian Categories, the medieval transcendentals, multifarious varieties of Akbarian intelligible principle, the Platonic *megista genē*, especially in terms of the critique of the Aristotelian Categories as expounded in *Enneads* 6.1-3, and so on.

87. See Herbert A. Davidson, *Al-Farabi, Avicenna and Averroes on Intellect*, 245-246 and Thomas Aquinas *Summa Contra Gentiles Book Two: Creation*, trans. James F. Anderson (Notre Dame, IN: University of Notre Dame Press, 1976), II.76.

88. Gelenbevi in *Gelenbevī 'alā al-Dawwānī 'alā al-'Aqīda al-'Aḍudiyya*, vol. 1, 150.

89. Ibid., 151.

90. Ibid., 153-154.

91. One might also translate this 'superficialist.'

92. Dawānī in ibid. vol. 2, 48-49.

93. See Mulla Fenari, *Misbāḥ al-uns*, 423 (4/473) and Qayṣarī, *Maṭla' khuṣūṣ al-kalim*, 58-64 for a more general account of the origin of the Immutable Archetypes in the Divine Essence.

94. That is, the fact that it exists, rather than not, which demands explanation since it is itself possible.

95. That is, that our knowledge exists in the *particular* form that it does.

96. We can however know, because of the ontological guarantor of epistemology that we spoke about above, that our sound everyday knowledge of the world corresponds to things as they are in themselves in the knowledge of God, in so far as that knowledge encompasses all of the different loci of manifestation through which the original essence will proceed, including that of our ordinary experience, all of which are conditioned to trans-world metaprinciples. Taşköprüzade simply makes sound abstraction the condition and guarantor of this correspondence, as we will see shortly.

97. Ṣadr al-Dīn al-Qūnawī, *Ta'wīl al-Sūra al-Mubāraka al-Fātiḥa* (Hyderabad: Maṭbaʿ Dāʾirat al-Maʿārif al-Niẓāmiyya, 1310/1892), 25.

98. Qayṣarī, *Maṭlaʿ khuṣūṣ al-kalim*, 64.

99. Taşköprüzade, *al-Shuhūd al-ʿAynī*, 39.

100. Ibid. 39.

101. Shirbīnī in al-Bannānī, *Ḥāshiyat al-ʿAllāma al-Bannānī ʿalā sharḥ al-Jalāl Shams al-Dīn Muḥammad ibn Aḥmad al-Maḥallī ʿalā matn Jamʿ al-jawāmiʿ lil-Imām Tāj al-Dīn ʿAbd al-Wahhāb Ibn al-Subkī maʿa Taqrīr al-Shirbīnī*, vol. 2, 414.

102. For an excellent summary the reader may consult ibid., 413-415. For a more difficult and detailed account, see Jurjānī, *Sharḥ al-Mawāqif*, vol. 3, 40-53. See also Qayṣarī *Maṭlāʿ Khuṣūṣ al-Kalim*, 61-62.

103. If it be objected that this is a sophistical argument, because before a quiddity has any sort of reality whatsoever, there is no 'it', and therefore no reality to be negated, the point is that intelligible realities are fundamentally timeless, and thus timelessly distinct, and to negate the reality of an intelligible reality because it 'does not yet exist' is to confuse the intelligible reality itself for its instantiations, which *do* come into existence temporally. Furthermore, since creation is contingent on some form of knowledge, negating the *timeless* reality of quiddities entails strictly speaking an absolute negation of their having any form of existence, whereas in fact they do exist, therefore etc. Of course, on the Akbarian account, quiddities are in some sense 'formed' by the Divine Names (in the *fayḍ al-aqdas* or 'Most Holy Effusion') but this is an atemporal phenomenon. Two poles of interpretation of *al-māhiyyāt ghayr majʿūla* exist, one Akbarian and one Avicennan, conveniently exposited by two of these schools of thought's greatest exponents in their correspondence with one another, Ṣadr al-Dīn al-Qūnawī and Naṣīr al-Dīn al-Ṭūsī; for Qūnawī, they are to be identified with the 'images' of the Divine attributes; for al-Ṭūsī, they are merely perspectival entities of a somewhat unclear metaphysical pedigree. See Ṣadr al-Dīn al-Qūnawī and Naṣīr al-Dīn al-Ṭūsī, *al-Murāsalāt Bayn Ṣadr al-Dīn al-Qūnawī wa Naṣīr al-Dīn al-Ṭūsī*, 57-59 for Qūnawī's position, and 103-107 for that of al-Ṭūsī.

104. Taşköprüzade *al-Shuhūd al-ʿAynī*, 39.

105. Aḥmadnagarī, *Dustūr al-'Ulamā'* sub *'al-'ilm al-fi'lī'* defines *al-'ilm al-fi'lī* as 'creative knowledge, that extramental particular existence is derived from, like a conception being formed of a mosque with a particular appearance, and that mosque then being built in accordance with what had obtained in the mind.' Jurjānī, *Ta'rīfāt* sub "*ilm fi'lī*', defines it as simply '[knowledge] that is not derived from another' and that is not therefore 'affective'. God's knowledge of His creatures is *'ilm fi'lī*, because it is 'the cause of the existence of possible beings in extramental particulars,' (*al-Kashshāf* sub *'ilm*) although on the school of thought of the pure Avicennan philosophers, the Divine knowledge is identified with the Divine volition. For Taşköprüzade, who like the Akbarians and *kalām* theologians acknowledges a real distinction between knowledge and volition, the existence of the object of knowledge being made to *preponderate* over its non-existence is contingent on the Divine volition, and the Divine knowledge is thus a necessary, but not a sufficient condition for the existence of an extramental particular. In the sense that volition presupposes knowledge, the Divine knowledge is said to be the 'cause' of the extramental particular; but of course, the relationship between the Divine knowledge and the Divine volition is not temporal.

106. Taşköprüzade, *al-Shuhūd al-'Aynī*, 39.

107. Ibid., 39-40.

108. Ibid., 40. If it be asked why these perspectival modalities, concomitant properties and first and second intelligibles attend essences even in their timeless state pre-creation, it may be relevant to note (if it be proper to 'note' such a profound and fundamental truth) that the notion of essences being truly 'separate' from human beings is a mental supposition, and no more. As Muḥammad Ibn 'Umar al-Qādirī notes in his *Sharḥ Ṣalāt al-Akbariyya*, 'it was from the essence of our Prophet, blessings and peace be upon him, that the [other] essences in the Divine knowledge branched out' (60). The Perfect Man, then, contains the entire world within himself. The necessary *mode* by which essences are perceived by man can thus never be separated from man in any real sense.

109. Ibid. 40.

110. Access via *kashf* to something approaching things as they are in themselves, in their simplicity in the Divine knowledge, is a specialized and exceptional ability that cannot be made the rule, as we have already heard from Qūnawī and Qayṣarī above.

111. In the phrase '*nafs al-amr*'.

112. Ibid., 41.

113. Ibid., 41.

114. Ibrāhīm Kūrānī, 'Maṭla' al-Jūd bi Taḥqīq al-Tanzīh fī Waḥdat al-Wujūd', in *Irshād Dhawī al-'Uqūl Ilā Barā'at al-Ṣūfiyya Min al-Ittiḥād wa al-Ḥulūl*, ed. Aḥmad Farīd al-Mazīdī (Cairo: Dār al-Dhikr, 2007), 287.

115. For a good introduction to these distinctions in English, see Izutsu's arti-
cle 'Basic Problems of Abstract Quiddity' in *Collected Texts and Papers on
Logic and Language*, eds. Mahdī Muḥaqqiq and Toshihiko Izutsu (Tehran:
Mu'assasa-i Muṭālaʿāt-i ʿIlmī-i Dānišgāh-i Makgīl, 1974), 3-25.

116. Ibrāhīm Kūrānī, 'Maṭlaʿ al-Jūwd bi Taḥqīq al-Tanzīh fī Waḥdat al-Wujūd',
in *Irshād Dhawī al-ʿUqūl Ilā Barāʾat al-Ṣūfiyya Min al-Ittiḥād wa al-Ḥulūl*,
287.

117. Ibid. 308-309.

118. Ālūsī, *Rūḥ al-Maʿānī* sub Qur'an 2:20.

119. Given the complex issues that the full passage broaches, issues outside the
already broad subject matter of this study, I will leave al-Ālūsī's profound
words to be discovered in the original Arabic.

120. See Gelenbevi et al., *Rasāʾil al-Imtiḥān*, 166.

121. That is, that God's knowledge 'consists in the Essence's entailment of the
perceptional forms of everything of which a conception can be formed.'

122. These oft-quoted words (usually not verbatim quotes from Rāzī) come from
his commentary on Ibn Sīnā's *Ishārāt*. See Section 2.2.

123. Gelenbevi, *Risāla fī Taḥqīq ʿIlm Allāh al-Mutaʿalliq bi al-Ashyāʾ* in Gelenbevi
et al. *Rasāʾil al-Imtiḥān*, 173-174. The last point concerning the existence in
nafs al-amr even of two contradictories conjunct in the mind, is an allusion to the position of al-Dawānī, who means by this that the components
of the forms of all conceivable objects of knowledge are *preserved* in *nafs
al-amr*, not that the conjunct of two contradictories is *true* in *nafs al-amr*.

124. Ibrāhīm al-Madhārī, *al-Lumʿa fī Taḥqīq Mabāḥith al-Wujūd wa al-Qidam
wa Afʿāl al-ʿIbād*, ed. Muḥammad Zāhid al-Kawtharī (Damascus: al-Sayyid
ʿIzzat al-ʿAṭṭār al-Ḥusaynī al-Dimashqī, n.d)., reprinted (Cairo: Dār al-
Baṣāʾir, 1429/2008), 13.

125. Just as, indeed, via the Muhammadan Reality, all of created reality constitutes a type of branch of exemplary human reality.

126. Said Nursi, *al-Muʿjizāt al-Qurʾāniyya* in *Dhū al-Fiqār*, trans. Lajnat al-Tarjama wa al-Buḥūth al-ʿIlmiyya (Istanbul: Altınbaşak Neşriyat, 1429/2009),
132-134.

127. These Qayṣarī describes as the 'Source-attributes' (*al-Ummuhāt min al-Ṣifāt*),
namely 'Life, Knowledge, Volition, Power, Hearing, Sight and Speech.'

128. Qayṣarī, *Maṭlaʿ Khuṣūs al-Kalim*, 51-52.

129. Mulla Fenari is referring to the *mafātīḥ al-ghayb* of Qur'an 6:59, here interpreted as Divine Names known only to God Himself.

130. Mulla Fenari, *Miṣbāḥ al-uns*, 289-290.

CONCLUSION

1. While we advocate the following of Imām al-Māturīdī or Imām al-Ashʿarī
in creedal doctrine, we also follow the later Ashʿarīs in departing from

Imām al-Ash'arī's position in many areas of general metaphysics, instead affirming the univocity of existence, mental existence, the unformedness of quiddities and so on. Moreover, we contend that after its Ottoman and Mughal marriage to the post-Avicennan philosophy and post-Rāzian *kalām*, the Akbarian school (the fundamental principles of which Imām al-Ash'arī is in agreement with, as Mulla Fenari and other Akbarians tell us) possesses the most powerful and versatile intellectual tools with which to face Western philosophical, scientific and other contemporary challenges, when placed alongside other schools of Islamic thought that impinge on general metaphysics. This has become especially clear in the writings of such luminaries as Dāwūd al-Qayṣarī, Mulla Fenari, Taşköprüzade, Ibn Bahā'uddīn, Ibrāhīm Kūrānī, Ibrāhīm al-Madhārī, Abū Thanā' al-Ālūsī and Baḥr al-'Ulūm, all of whom have appeared in this study.

2.   The emphasis is Cupitt's.

3.   Don Cupitt, 'Anti-Realist Faith' in *Is God Real?*, ed. Joseph Runzo (London: Macmillan, 1993), 48-50. Mercifully, Cupitt is no longer in fashion as a thinker. However, the reader will appreciate how ubiquitous the sentiments he has expressed have become in contemporary thought and society.

Bibliography

'Abdallāh, Muḥammad Ramaḍān. *al-Maqūlāt al-'Ashr Bayn al-Falāsifa wa al-Mutakallimīn*. Istanbul: Haşimi Yayınevi, 2016.

Ahmed, Shahab and Filipovic, Nenad. 'The Sultan's Syllabus: A Curriculum for the Ottoman Imperial Medreses Prescribed in a Ferman of Qanuni I Süleyman, dated 973 AH (1565 CE).' *Studia Islamica* 98/99 (2004): 183-218.

al-Abharī, Athīr al-Dīn and Maybudī, Qāḍī Mīr Ḥusayn (commentator). *Hidāyat al-Ḥikma*. Istanbul: Dār al-Ṭibā'a al-'Āmira, 1262/1846.

Adamson, Peter and Taylor, Richard C., ed. *The Cambridge Companion to Arabic Philosophy*. Cambridge: Cambridge University Press, 2005.

Aertsen, Jans. *Medieval Philosophy as Transcendental Thought: From Philip the Chancellor to Francisco Suarez*. Leiden: Brill, 2012.

Afonasin, Eugene, Dillon, John M and Finamore, John, ed. *Iamblichus and the Foundations of Late Platonism* Leiden: Brill, 2012.

Aḥmadnagarī, 'Abd al-Nabiyy Ibn 'Abd al-Rasūl. *Dustūr al-'Ulamā'*. 4 vols. Beirut: Dār al-Kutub al-'Ilmiyya, 1424/2003.

Anselm *Three Philosophical Dialogues*. Translated by Thomas Williams. Indianapolis, IN: Hackett Publishing, 2002.

al-Āmidī, Sayf al-Dīn. *Abkār al-afkār fī uṣūl al-dīn*. 5 vols. Edited by Aḥmad Farīd al-Mazīdī. Beirut: Dār al-Kutub al-'Ilmiyya, 1424/2003.

Allison, Henry E. *Kant's Transcendental Deduction: An Analytical-Historical Commentary*. Oxford: Oxford University Press, 2015.

Ālūsī, Abū Thanā' Shihāb al-Dīn. *Rūḥ al-Ma'ānī*. 30 vols. Edited by al-Sayyid Muḥammad Sayyid and Sayyid 'Imrān. Cairo: Dār al-Ḥadīth, 1426/2005.

Aquinas, Thomas. *The Summa Theologica of Thomas Aquinas, Complete English Edition in Five Volumes*. 5 vols. Translated by the Fathers of the English Dominican Province, Notre Dame. New York, NY: Bezinger Bros., 1948. Reprinted by Christian Classics (Notre Dame, IN: Ave Maria Press, 1981).

——— *Summa Contra Gentiles Book Two: Creation*. Translated by James F. Anderson. Notre Dame, IN: University of Notre Dame Press, 1976.

Aristotle. *The Complete Works of Aristotle: The Revised Oxford Translation*. Edited by Jonathan Barnes. Princeton, NJ: Princeton University Press, 1984.

Averroes, *The Incoherence of the Incoherence*. Translated by Simon Van Den Bergh. London: Luzak, 1954.

Avicenna. *al-Shifā'*, *al-Ilāhiyyāt* I. Edited by Saʿīd Zāyid and George Anawati. Cairo: al-Hayʾa al-ʿĀmma li Shuʾūn al-Maṭābiʿ al-Amīriyya, 1380/1960.

——— *al-Shifā', al-Ṭabīʿiyyāt* VI, *al-Nafs*. Edited by Saʿīd Zāyid and George Anawati. Cairo: al-Hayʾa al-Miṣriyya al-ʿĀmma li al-Kitāb, 1395/1975.

——— *al-Shifā', al-Manṭiq* I, *al-Madkhal*. Edited by George Anawati, Maḥmūd al-Khaḍīrī and Fuʾād al-Ahwānī Cairo: al-Maṭbaʿ al-Amīriyya, 1952.

——— *al-Ishārāt wa al-Tanbīhāt* with the commentary of Naṣīr al-Dīn al-Ṭūsī. 5 vols. Edited by Sulaymān Dunyā. Cairo: Dār al-Maʿārif, 1983.

Augustine. *Confessions*. Translated by Henry Chadwick. Oxford: Oxford University Press, 1991.

——— *The City of God Against the Pagans*. Translated by R.W. Dyson. Cambridge: Cambridge University Press, 1998.

Baḥr al-ʿUlūm, Abd al-ʿAliyy. *Sharḥ Baḥr al-ʿUlūm ʿalā Sullam al-ʿUlūm*. Edited by ʿAbd al-Naṣīr Aḥmad al-Shāfiʿī. Kuwait: Dār al-Ḍiyā', 1433/2012.

al-Bājūrī, Ibrāhīm Ibn Muḥammad ibn Aḥmad. *Ḥāshiyat Ibn Qāsim*. 3 vols. Edited by Muḥammad Ṣāliḥ Nuwaydir. Amman: Dār al-Nūr al-Mubīn li al-Nashr wa al-Tawzīʿ, 1435/2015.

——— *Ḥāshiya ʿalā Matn al-Sullam* with Shams al-Dīn al-Anbābī's *Taqrīr*. Cairo: Būlāq, 1297/1879.

Baltacı, Cahid. *XV-XVI Yüzyıllarda Osmanli Medreseleri*. Istanbul: Marmara Ilahiyat Fakultesi Vakfi Yayinlari, 2005.

Bannānī, ʿAbd al-Raḥmān Ibn Jād Allāh. *Ḥāshiyat al-ʿallāma al-Bannānī ʿalā sharḥ al-Jalāl Shams al-Dīn Muḥammad ibn Aḥmad al-Maḥallī ʿalā matn Jamʿ al-jawāmiʿ li al-imām Tāj al-Dīn ʿAbd al-Wahhāb ibn al-Subkī*, with ʿAbd al-Raḥmān al-Shirbīnī's *Taqrīr*. 2 vols. Cairo: 1285/1868. Reprinted in Beirut: Dār al-Fikr, 1402/1982.

al-Bayḍāwī, Nāṣir al-Dīn. *Ṭawāliʿ al-anwār min maṭāliʿ al-anẓār*. Edited by ʿAbbās Sulaymān. Cairo: al-Maktaba al-Azhariyya li al-Turāth, 1435/2014.

Beck, Lewis White. *Essays on Kant and Hume*. New Haven, CT: Yale University Press, 1978.

D'Hoine, Peter and Martijn, Marije, ed. *All From One: A Guide to Proclus*. Oxford: Oxford University Press, 2017.

Bertolacci, Amos. *The Reception of Aristotle's Metaphysics in Avicenna's Kitāb al-Shifāʾ : A Milestone of Western Metaphysical Thought*. Leiden: Brill, 2006.

Bein, Amit. *Ottoman Ulema, Turkish Republic: Agents of Change and Guardians of Tradition*. Stanford, CA: Stanford University Press, 2011.

Biletzki, Anat. 'Introduction: Bridging the Analytic-Continental Divide'. *International Journal of Philosophical Studies* 9 (2001): 291-294.

al-Biqāʿī, Burhān al-Dīn Abū-l-Ḥasan Ibrāhīm ibn ʿUmar. *Naẓm al-durar fī tanāsub al-āyāt wal-suwar*. 8 vols. Cairo: Dār al-Kitāb al-Islāmī, n.d.

Braver, Lee. *A Thing of This World*. Evanston, IL: Northwestern University Press, 2007.

Bursevi, İsmail Hakkı. *Rūḥ al-bayān fī tafsīr al-Qurʾān*. 9 vols. Edited by ʿAbd al-Laṭīf Ḥasan ʿAbd al-Raḥmān. Beirut: Dār al-Kutub al-ʿIlmiyya, 1430/2009.

Carre, Meyrick H. *Realists and Nominalists*. Oxford: Oxford University Press, 1946.

Caygill, Howard. *A Kant Dictionary*. Oxford: Blackwell Publishing, 1995.

Chittick, William. *The Sufi Path of Knowledge: Ibn ʿArabī's Metaphysics of Imagination*. Albany NY: State University of New York Press, 1989.

Coffa, J. Alberta. *The Semantic tradition from Kant to Carnap*. Cambridge: Cambridge University Press, 1991.

Craig, Edward, ed. *The Routledge Encyclopedia of Philosophy*. London: Routledge, 1998.

Crivelli, Paolo. *Aristotle On Truth*. Cambridge: Cambridge University Press, 2004.

Davidson, Herbert A. *Al-Farabi, Avicenna and Averroes on Intellect*. Oxford: Oxford University Press, 1992.

al-Dawānī, Jalāl al-Dīn. *Sharḥā al-Muḥaqqiq al-Dawānī wa Mulla ʿAbdullah al-Yazdī ʿalā Tahdhīb al-Manṭiq*. Edited by ʿAbd al-Naṣīr Aḥmad al-Shāfiʿī al-Malībārī. Kuwait: Dār al-Ḍiyāʾ, 1435/2014.

De Haan, Daniel. *Necessary Existence and the Doctrine of Being in Avicenna's Metaphysics of the Healing.* Leiden: Brill, 2020.

Heyworth-Dunne, J. *An Introduction to the History of Education in Modern Egypt.* London: Luzac & Co., 1938.

Dunietz, Alexandra. *The Cosmic Perils of Qadi Ḥusayn Maybudī in Fifteenth-Century Iran.* Leiden: Brill, 2016.

Eichner, Heidrun. *The Post-Avicennian Philosophical Tradition and Islamic Orthodoxy: Philosophical and Theological Summae in Context.* Halle: Habilitationsschrift, 2009.

al-Farābī, Abū Naṣr. *Kitāb al-Jamʿ Bayn Raʾyay al-Ḥakīmayn.* Edited by ʿAlī Bū Malḥam. Beirut: Dār wa Maktabat al-Hilāl, 1996.

Falguera, José L and Martínez-Vidal, Concha. *Abstract Objects: For and Against.* Cham: Springer, 2020.

Fenari, Mulla Shams al-Dīn, *Miftāḥ al-Ghayb wa-sharḥuhu Miṣbāḥ al-uns,* ed. Muḥammad Khawājavi (Tehran: Intisharat-i Mawla, 1415/1995),

——— *al-Fawāʾid al-Fanāriyya.* Edited by Ibrahim al-Hurānī and Muḥammad Diyarbakri. Istanbul: Haşimi Yayinevi, 2012.

Findlay, JN. 'The Three Hypostases of Platonism'. *The Review of Metaphysics* 28, no. 4, (1975): 660–68.

al-Farhārī, Muḥammad ʿAbd al-ʿAzīz. *al-Nibrās sharḥ Sharḥ al-ʿaqāʾid.* Istanbul: Asitane, 1430/2009.

Garrigou-Lagrange, Reginald. *Reality.* Translated by Patrick Cummins. Bradford: Ex Fontibus, 2015.

Gelenbevi, Ismail. *Gelenbevī ʿalā al-Dawānī ʿalā al-ʿAqīda al-ʿaḍudiyya* with the supercommentaries of Marjānī and Khalkhālī. Istanbul: al-Maṭbaʿa al-ʿUthmāniyya, 1318/1900.

——— *Sharḥ Isāghūjī.* Edited by ʿAbdullah Hacdınmız. Istanbul: al-Maktaba al-Hanafiyya, nd.

Gerson, Lloyd. *Platonism and Naturalism: The Possibility of Philosophy.* Ithaca: Cornell University Press, 2020.

Gesink, Indira Falk. *Islamic Reform and Conservatism: Al-Azhar and the Evolution of Modern Sunni Islam.* London: Tauris Academic Studies, 2010.

Al Ghouz, Abdelkader, ed. *Islamic Philosophy from the 12th to the 14th Century.* Göttingen: Bonn University Press, 2018.

Guyer, Paul, ed. *The Cambridge Companion to German Idealism.* Cambridge: Cambridge University Press, 2000.

Gilson, Etienne. *The Philosophy of St. Bonaventure*. Transated by Dom Illtyd Trethowan and Frank Sheed. Paterson, NJ: St. Anthony Guild Press, 1965.

——— *The Unity of Philosophical Experience*. Charles Scribner's Sons, 1937. Reprinted in San Francisco, CA: Ignatius Press, 1999.

——— *The Philosophy of St. Thomas Aquinas*. Translated by Edward Bullough. Cambridge: W. Heffer & Sons Ltd, 1924.

——— *Christian Philosophy of St. Thomas Aquinas*. Translated by L.K. Shook. New York, NY: Random House, 1956.

Hanna, Robert. *Kant and the Foundations of Analytic Philosophy*. Oxford: Oxford University Press, 2001.

Hedley, Douglas and Hutton, Sarah, ed. *Platonism at the Origins of Modernity: Studies on Platonism and Early Modern Philosophy*. Dordrech: Springer, 2008.

al-Ḥillī, Ḥasan Ibn Yūsuf. *Kashf al-murād fī sharḥ Tajrīd al-Iʿtiqād*. Beirut: al-Muʾassasat al-Aʿlamī li al-Maṭbūʿāt, 1408/1988.

Ottfried, Hoffe. *Kant's Critique of Pure Reason: The Foundation of Modern Philosophy*. Tubingen: Springer, 2010.

Hollingdale, J, ed and trans. *A Nietzsche Reader*. London: Penguin Books, 1977.

Holzhey, Helmut and Mudroch, Vilem. *Historical Dictionary of Kant and Kantianism*. Lanham, MD: The Scarecrow Press, 2005.

Ibn ʿArabī, Muhyī al-Dīn. *al-Futūḥāt al-Makkiyya*. 4 vols. Cairo: Dār al-Kutub al-ʿArabiyya al-Kubrā, 1329/1911.

Ibn ʿArafa, Abū ʿAbdillāh Muḥammad. *al-Mukhtaṣar al-Kalāmī*. Edited by Nizār Hammādī. Kuwait: Dār al-Ḍiyāʾ, 1435/2014.

Ibn Bahāʾuddīn. *al-Qawl al-faṣl, Sharḥ al-Fiqh al-Akbar li al-Imām al-Aʿẓam Abī Ḥanīfa*. Edited by Dr. Rafīq al-ʿAjam. Beirut: Dār al-Muntakhab al-ʿArabī, 1998.

Ibn al-Ḥabīb, Muḥammad. *The Diwan of Sidi Muhammad Ibn al-Habib*. Translated by Abdurrahman Fitzgerald. Granada: Editorial Qasida, 2015.

Ibn Kamāl. *Majmūʿ Rasāʾil al-ʿAllāma Ibn Kamāl Pāshā*. 8 vols. Edited by Ḥamza Bakrī. Istanbul: Dār al-Lubāb, 2018/1439.

Ibn Kathīr, *Tafsīr al-Qurʾān al-ʿAẓīm*. Edited by Muṣṭafā al-Sayyid Muḥammad. Giza: Muʾassasat Qurṭuba, 1421/2000.

al-ʿImādī, Abū Suʿūd. *Irshād al-ʿaql al-salīm*. 8 vols. Beirut: Dār Iḥyāʾ al-Turāth al-ʿArabī, 1411/1990.

al-Iṣfahānī, Shams al-Dīn. *Tasdīd al-Qawā'id fī Sharḥ Tajrīd al-'Aqā'id.* 2 vols. Edited by Khālid ibn Hammād al-'Adwānī. Kuwait: Dār al-Ḍiyā', 1433/2012.

Irwin, T.H.. *Aristotle's First Principles.* Oxford: Clarendon Press, 1998.

Izutsu, Toshihiko and Muḥaqqiq, Mahdī, ed. *Collected Texts and Papers on Logic and Language.* Tehran: Mu'assasa-i Muṭāla'āt-i 'Ilmī-i Dānišgāh-i Makgīl, 1974.

Izmirli, Ismail Hakki. *Yeni Ilmi Kalam.* Istanbul: Awqāf Islāmiyya Matbaasi, 1339/1921.

al-Jurjānī, al-Sayyid al-Sharīf. *Sharḥ al-Mawāqif* with the commentaries of Abd al-Ḥakīm Siyalkoti and Ḥasan Çelebi. Edited by al-Sayyid Muḥammad Badr al-Dīn al-Na'sānī. Cairo: Maṭba'at al-Sa'āda, 1325/1907.

———— *Ḥāshiya 'alā al-Tajrīd.* Ms. Istanbul Süleymaniye Kütüphanesi. Haci Selim Ağa 723.

Kant, Immanuel. *Theoretical Philosophy, 1755–1770.* Translated and edited David Walford. Cambridge: Cambridge University Press, 1992.

———— *Critique of Pure Reason.* Translated by Paul Guyer and Allen W. Wood. Cambridge: Cambridge University Press, 1998.

———— *Kant: Philosophical Correspondence 1759-99.* Translated by Arnulf Zweig. Chicago: The University of Chicago Press, 1967.

———— *Prolegomena to Any Future Metaphysics as a Science.* Translated by Peter G. Lucas. Manchester, Manchester University Press, 1953.

al-Kātibī, Najm al-Dīn and Mubārakshāh (commentary). *Sharḥ Ḥikmat al-'Ayn*, with the supercommentary of al-Sayyid al-Sharīf al-Jurjānī. Kazan: Maṭba'at Sharīf Jān wa Ḥasan Jān, 1319/1901.

Pollman, Karla, ed. *The Oxford Guide to the Historical Reception of Augustine.* Oxford: Oxford University Press, 2013.

al-Kāshānī, 'Abd al-Razzāq. *Tafsīr*, published as *Tafsīr Ibn 'Arabī.* Edited by al-Shaykh 'Abd al-Wārith Muḥammad 'Alī. Beirut: Dār al-Kutub al-'Ilmiyya, 1427/2006.

———— *Laṭā'if al-i'lām fī ishārāt ahl al-ilhām.* Edited by Majīd Hādīzade. Beirut: Manshūrāt al-Jamal, 2011.

al-Kawtharī, Muḥammad Zāhid. *Maqālāt al-Kawtharī.* Cairo: Dār al-Salām, 1430/2009.

Kemp Smith, Norman. *A Commentary to Kant's 'Critique of Pure Reason'.* London: Macmillan & Co. Ltd., 1923.

Krämer, Hans Joachim. *Plato and the Foundations of Metaphysics: A Work on the Theory of the Principles and Unwritten Doctrines of Plato With a Collection of the Fundamental Documents*. Edited and and translated by John R. Catan. Albany, NY: State University of New York Press, 1990.

Kretzmann, N and Kenny, A, ed. *The Cambridge History of Later Medieval Philosophy*. Cambridge: Cambridge University Press, 1982.

Kūrānī, Ibrāhīm. *Irshād Dhawī al-ʿUqūl Ilā Barāʾat al-Ṣūfiyya Min al-Ittiḥād wa al-Ḥulūl*. Edited by Aḥmad Farīd al-Mazīdī. Cairo: Dār al-Dhikr, 2007.

Lewis, Frank A. *How Aristotle Gets by in Metaphysics Zeta*. Oxford: Oxford University Press, 2013.

al-Maghnīsī, Maḥmūd Ḥusayn. *Mughnī al-tullāb Sharḥ Matan Isāghūjī*. Edited by ʿIṣām b. al-Muhadhdhab al-Subūʿī. Damascus: Dār al-Bayrūtī, 1430/2009.

al-Madhārī, Ibrāhīm. *al-Lumʿa fī Taḥqīq Mabāḥith al-Wujūd wa al-Qidam wa Afʿāl al-ʿIbād*. Edited by Muḥammad Zāhid al-Kawtharī. Damascus: al-Sayyid ʿIzzat al-ʿAṭṭār al-Ḥusaynī al-Dimashqī, n.d. Reprinted in Cairo: Dār al-Baṣāʾir, 1429/2008.

Martijin, Marije. *Proclus On Nature: Philosophy of Nature and its Methods in Proclus' Commentary on Plato's Timaeus*. Leiden: Brill, 2010.

al-Mudarris, ʿAbd al-Karīm Muḥammad. *al-Wasīla fī Sharḥ al-Faḍīla*. 2. Vols. Edited by al-Sayyid Quṣayy Abū al-Siʿd and al-Sayyid ʿAbd al-Wahhāb Abū al-Siʿd. Beirut: Dār Iḥyāʾ al-Turāth al-ʿArabī, 1437/2016.

Nursi, Said. *al-Muʿjizāt al-Qurʾāniyya* in *Dhū al-Fiqār*. Translated by Lajnat al-Tarjama wa al-Buḥūth al-ʿIlmiyya. Istanbul: Altınbaşak Neşriyat, 1429/2009.

O'Rourke, Fran. *Pseudo-Dionysius and the Metaphysics of Aquinas*. Leiden: E.J. Brill, 1992.

Pasnau, Robert. *Metaphysical Themes 1274-1671*. Oxford: Oxford University Press, 2011.

Proclus. *The Elements of Theology*. Translated with commentary by E.R. Dodds. Oxford: Clarendon Press, 1963.

Perl, Eric D. *Thinking Being: Introduction to Metaphysics in the Classical Tradition*. Leiden: Brill, 2014.

Pfeiffer, J. and Kropp M. ed. *Theoretical Approaches to the Transmission and Edition of Oriental Manuscripts*. Beirut: Orient-Institut, 2007.

Plato. *Complete Works*. Edited by John Cooper. Indianapolis, IN: Hackett Publishing, 1997.

Plotinus. *Ennead IV.8 On the Descent of the Soul into Bodies*. Translated by Barrie Fleet. Las Vegas, NV: Parmenides Publishing, 2012.

al-Qādirī, Muḥammad ibn ʿUmar Ibn ʿAbd al-Jalīl. *Sharḥ al-Ṣalāt al-Akbariyya*. Edited by ʿĀṣim Ibrāhīm al-Kayālī. Beirut: Dār al-Kutub al-ʿIlmiyya, Beirut, 1430/2009.

Qayṣarī, Dāwūd. *Maṭlaʿ Khuṣūṣ al-Kalim fī Maʿānī Fuṣūṣ al-Ḥikam*. Edited by Shaykh ʿĀṣim Ibrāhīm al-Kayyālī. Beirut: Dār al-Kutub al-ʿIlmiyya, 1433/2012.

Quine, W.V. *Theories and Things*. Cambridge, MA: Belknap Press, 1986.

al-Qūshjī, ʿAlī. *Sharḥ al-Tajrīd*. Edited by Muḥammad Ḥusayn al-Zāriʿī al-Riḍāyī. Qom: Rāʾid, 2014.

Qūnawī, Ṣadr al-Dīn and Naṣīr al-Dīn al-Ṭūsī. *al-Murāsalāt Bayn Ṣadr al-Dīn al-Qunawī wa Naṣīr al-Dīn al-Ṭūsī*. Edited by Gudrun Schubert. Beirut: al-Sharika al-Muttaḥida li al-Tawzīʿ, 1995.

———— *Taʾwīl al-Sūra al-Mubāraka al-Fātiḥa* (Hyderabad: Maṭbaʿ Dāʾirat al-Maʿārif al-Niẓāmiyya, 1310/1892

al-Rāzī, Quṭb al-Dīn, al-Shirāzī, Ṣadr al-Dīn, and Zāhid, Mīr. *Risālatān fī al-Taṣawwur wa al-Taṣdīq wa yalīhimā Sharḥ al-Risāla al-Maʿmūla fī al-Taṣawwur wa al-Taṣdīq*. Edited by Mahdī Sharīʿatī. Beirut: Dār al-Kutub al-ʿIlmiyya, 1425/2004.

al-Rāzī, Fakhr al-Dīn. *al-Mabāḥith al-mashriqiyya fī ʿilm al-ilāhiyāt wa al-tabīʿyyāt*, 2 vols. Edited by Muḥammad al-Muʿtaṣim Billāh al-Baghdādī. Qom: Intishārāt Dhawī al-Qurbā, 1428/2007.

———— *Sharḥ al-Ishārāt wa al-Tanbīhāt*, 2 vols. Edited by Ali Rida Najafzada. Tehran: Anjuman-i Asar va Mafakhir-i Farhangi, 1386/1966.

———— *al-Mulakhkhaṣ fī al-manṭiq wa al-ḥikma*. Ms. Istanbul, Süleymaniye Kütüphanesi: Haci Selim Ağa 723.

———— *Tafsīr al-kabīr*. 16 vols. Beirut: Dār al-Fikr,1401/1981.

Reed, Delbert. *Origins of Analytic Philosophy: Kant and Frege*. London: Continuum, 2007.

Remes, Pauliina and Slaveva-Griffin, ed. *The Routledge Handbook of Neoplatonism*. London: Routledge, 2014.

El-Rouayheb, Khaled. *Relational Syllogisms and the History of Arabic Logic, 900– 1900*. Leiden: Brill, 2010.

———— El-Rouayheb, Khaled and Schmitke, Sabine, ed. *The Oxford Handbook of Islamic Philosophy*. Oxford: Oxford University Press, 2017.

Robinson, Francis. *The Ulama of Farangi Mahall and Islamic Culture in South Asia.* London: C Hurst and Co. Publishers, 2001.

Runzo, Joseph. *Is God Real?* London: Macmillan, 1993.

Sabri, Mustafa. *Mawqif al-ʿAql wa al-ʿIlm wa al-ʿĀlam Min Rabb al-ʿĀlamīn wa ʿIbādihi al-Mursalīn.* Beirut: Dār Iḥyāʾ al-Turāth, 1950.

Sanal, Mustafa. ʿOsmanli Devletiʾnde Medreselere Ders Programlari, Öğertim Metodu, Ölçme ve Değerlendirme, Öğretimde Ihtisaslaşma Bakimindan Genel Bir Bakış.ʾ *Sosyal Bilimler Enstitüsü Dergisi Sayı* 14 (2003): 149-168.

al-Sijāʿī, Aḥmad and Makhlūf Ḥasanayn (supercommentary). *al-Ḥāshiya al-Thāniya ʿalā al-Jawāhir al-Muntaẓamāt fī ʿUqūd al-Maqūlāt.* Cairo: Muṣṭafā al-Bābī al-Ḥalabī, 1391/1971.

Sanūsī, Muḥammad Ibn Yūsuf. *Sharḥ al-ʿAqīda al-Kubrā al-Musammāt ʿAqīdat Ahl al-Tawḥīd.* Edited by al-Sayyid Yūsuf Aḥmad. Beirut: Dār al-Kutub al-ʿIlmiyya, 1427/2006.

Scott, Dominic. *Recollection and Experience: Plato's Theory of Learning and its Successors.* Cambridge: Cambridge University Press, 1995.

Schumacher, Lydia. *Divine Illumination: The History and Future of Augustine's Theory of Knowledge.* Oxford: Wiley-Blackwell, 2011.

al-Shaʿrānī, ʿAbd al-Wahhāb. *al-Yawāqīt wa al-jawāhir fī bayān ʿAqāʾid al-Akābir.* Beirut: Dār al-Ṣādir, 2012.

Schmitt, Arbogast. *Modernity and Plato: Two Paradigms of Rationality.* Trans. Vishwa Adluri. Camden House: Rochester, 2012.

Paul Vincent Spade, trans. *Five Texts on the Mediaeval Problem of Universals.* Indianapolis, IN: Hackett, 1994.

Tahānawī. *Kashshāf iṣṭilāḥāt al-funūn wa al-ʿulūm.* Edited by Rafīq ʿAjam and ʿAlī Farīd Daḥrūj. Beirut: Maktabat Lubnan, 1416/1996.

Taftāzānī, Saʿd al-Dīn Masʿūd Ibn ʿUmar. *Sharḥ al-Maqāṣid,* 2 vols. Istanbul: Maṭbaʿat al-Ḥāj Muḥarram Efendi, 1305/1888.

——— *Sharḥ al-Maqāṣid,* 5 vols. Edited by ʿAbd al- Raḥmān ʿUmayra. Beirut: ʿĀlam al-Kutub, 1419/1998.

——— *Tahdhīb al-manṭiq,* with the commentary of ʿUbaydullāh al-Khabīṣī and the supercommentaries of Muḥammad b. ʿArafa al-Dusūqī and Ḥasan al-ʿAṭṭār, ed. Aḥmad Saʿd ʿAlī (Cairo: Matbaʿat Muṣṭafā al-Bābī al-Ḥalabī wa Awlādihi, 1355/1936

——— *Taqrīb al-marām fī Sharḥ Tahdhīb al-Kalām,* with the commentary of al-Sanandajī and the *ḥāshiya* of Muḥammad Wasīm al-Kurdistānī. Cairo: Bulaq, 1318/1900, reprinted in Cairo: Dār al-Baṣāʾir, 2006.

Taşköprüzade. *Miftāḥ al-saʿāda fī mawḍūʿāt al-ʿulūm.* 3 vols. Beirut: Dār al-Kutub al-ʿIlmiyya, 1405/1985.

——— *al-Shuhūd al-ʿaynī fī mabāḥith al-wujūd al-dhihnī.* Edited by Muḥammad Zāhid Kāmil Gül. Cologne: Manshūrāt al-Jamal, 1430/2009.

——— *al-Shaqāʾiq al-Nuʿmāniyya.* Beirut: Dār al-Kutub al-ʿArabī, 1975.

al-Ṭūsī, Naṣīr al-Dīn. *Talkhīṣ al-Muḥaṣṣal.* Beirut: Dār al-Aḍwāʾ, 1405/1985.

Tuominen, Miira. *The Ancient Commentators on Plato and Aristotle.* Berkeley, CA: University of California Press, 2009.

al-Ṭūsī, ʿAlāʾuddīn. *Al-Dhakhīra,* released as *Tahāfut al-falāsifa.* Edited by Yaḥyā Murād. Beirut: Dār al-Kutub al-ʿIlmiyya, 1425/2004.

Vesey, Godrey, ed. *Idealism: Past and Present.* Cambridge: Cambridge University Press, 1982.

Walbridge, John. *The Science of Mystic Lights: Quṭb al-Dīn Shīrāzī and the Illuminationist Tradition in Islamic Philosophy.* Cambridge, MA: Center for Middle East Studies, 1992.

Walsh, W.H. *Kant's Criticism of Metaphysics.* Edinburgh: Edinburgh University Press, 1975.

——— 'Kant's Criticism of Metaphysics: II'. *Philosophy* 14, no. 56 (1939): 434–448.

Williams, Thomas, ed. *The Cambridge Companion to Duns Scotus*. Cambridge: Cambridge University Press, 2003.

Wolenski, J. 'Contributions to the History of the Classical Truth-Definition'. *Logic, Methodology and Philosophy of Science IX* (1994): 487-488.

Zalta, Edward. *Abstract Objects: An Introduction to Axiomatic Metaphysics.* Dordrecht: D. Reidel, 1983.

——— *Intensional Logic and the Metaphysics of Intentionality.* Cambridge, MA: The MIT Press, 1988.